# A Century of Lithuanians in Springfield, IL

## Best of the Blog

### By Sandy Baksys

The story of Lithuanians in Springfield and the surrounding towns of Central Illinois is representative of Lithuanian-American history across the U.S. coal belt. It begins with 2,000-3,000 immigrants who arrived between 1890 and 1914 to mine coal or to marry a coal miner. It includes the children and grandchildren of these first-wave immigrants, as well as a second wave of Lithuanian refugees ("displaced persons") the first-wavers sponsored after World War II.

Whenever freedom in the homeland was extinguished, as after 1940, Lithuanian identity abroad assumed a moral imperative. This climaxed in active support for the successful Lithuanian "Singing Revolution" against the U.S.S.R. in the late 1980s. At other times, assimilation has been the rule, driven by intermarriage and a dearth of new Lithuanian speakers from the homeland.

I believe that the lives and the deferred dreams of Lithuanian-American families of the first wave, who withstood two world wars and the Great Depression, as well as those of the second wave, who suffered the traumas of World War II, hold enduring meaning for our time.

ISBN-10:
1515347729

Library of Congress Control Number: 2015914025
CreateSpace Independent Publishing Platform, North Charleston, SC

*Page design by Dolce Design*
*Cover designs by Melinda McDonald and Dolce Design*

*For my mother Josephine Marie Kohlrus,*
*my father Vincas Vytis Baksys, and my husband Ted Gietl*

*"Tas kas skaita ir rasa, duonas ne prasa."*

"One who reads and writes does not ask
   for bread."

    *--Lithuanian proverb told to Ann Tisckos (Wisnosky) by her father*

On the left: Lithuanian-American coal miner Joseph Pakutinsky (Pakutinskas),
1910s, Herrin, Illinois. *Courtesy of Don Pakey.*

# Acknowledgements

This book, and the blog on which it is based, grew out of a suggestion from writer, reader, marketing pro, and friend Melinda McDonald of Rochester, Ill. In early 2012, I was working with the Illinois State Historical Society on a historical marker to commemorate Lithuanians in Springfield, Ill., and Melinda suggested a blogsite as a marketing vehicle. During some difficult days in my personal life thereafter, working on *"the blog"* became a voyage of discovery. And Melinda became a constant source of inspiration, encouragement and 24/7 technical assistance.

I am also grateful to the "Baby in the Cigar Box," the late Ann Pazemetsky Traeger, who kindly allowed me extended use of several scrapbooks of obituaries and news articles in which she had lovingly preserved milestones in the lives of immigrants who otherwise might have been forgotten.

On the genealogy side, I thank William Cellini, Jr., of Chicago, who embarked on several years of steady research support for my efforts through a single encouraging comment on my blog—and eventually authored several chapters here.

Special thanks, also, to Tom Mann of Springfield for his generous gift of voluminous newspaper and public records research, and to Tim Race of Elmhurst. Tom's discoveries led to some of my favorite chapters in the book.

Last but not least, I am grateful to every individual who shared family photos and stories, commented supportively, or led me deeper into my content, especially Maria (Fry) Race, Elaine Alane, Georgeann Madison and Chuck Tisckos. The people in this book have touched me deeply and become my own extended family.

# Author's Introduction

When I was in high school back in the 1970s, I read the novel *The Jungle* by Upton Sinclair about fictive Lithuanian immigrants to the Chicago stockyards. I gave little thought, at the time, to the fact that in the city where I grew up, I was surrounded by the last survivors and the next-generations of several thousand coal-mining Lithuanian immigrants.

Although the stories in this book are based in and around Springfield, Illinois, I'm sure they are representative of early twentieth-century Lithuanian immigrant families in dozens of other coal-belt cities and towns. These include Scranton and Pittston in the anthracite region of Pennsylvania, Coalton, Okla., the major Westville Lithuanian community south of Danville, Ill., and many smaller enclaves spread across Central and Southern Illinois. Furthermore, the broad socio-economic trends and defining personal and family experiences in this book are also descriptive of other European coal-mining immigrants of the period.

In the early- to mid-1900s, the *Illinois State Journal-Register* reports that Springfield had a patchwork of ethnic neighborhoods based on where European immigrants had settled. While not purely of one group or another, these included a German community around what is now Memorial Medical Center. According to the paper, Italians lived around 10th and Carpenter and east of Grandview. Poles and Lithuanians lived near the Illinois State Fairgrounds.

## Where They Lived

Most specifically, I have tracked Lithuanian immigrants in this book to the Ridgely and Devereaux Heights areas just north, south, and east of the Fairgrounds, from Lithuanian "ground zero" at Peoria Road and North 11th St. all the way east to North 19th Steet at Sangamon Avenue. Other families in this book lived on East Jefferson, Washington, Mason, Carpenter, and especially Reynolds streets, in the area around Pillsbury Mills, and in the southern reaches of 16th Street. There were once so many Lithuanian immigrants in Springfield that in 1908, despite being desperately poor, they managed to build their own Catholic Church, St. Vincent de Paul's, at the corner of Eighth Street and Enos Avenue.

That church was demolished by the Catholic diocese in the mid-1970s. And like so many other European ethnic groups, today our large and vibrant Lithuanian-American community in Springfield is no more. Separated from their immigrant ancestors by as many as four generations, literally thousands of residents of Sangamon County today, without knowing it, are descended from the first wave of poor, rural Lithuanians who immigrated to our local coal-mining communities principally between 1890 and 1914. A second, smaller wave of Lithuanian immigrants after World War II brought my father to Springfield as a "displaced person" under the legal sponsorship of a paternal aunt who had arrived first in Scranton, Penn., and then Springfield during the first wave.

## Where Are We Now?

Based on my educated estimate of 2,000-3,000 first-wave immigrants to our area, upwards of 20,000 Springfield and Sangamon County residents today may have the blood of early twentieth-century Lithuanian immigrants. Yet with the prevalence of ethnic intermarriage after the first American-born generation, that percentage of "Lithuanian-ness" inexorably continues to dwindle. As a result, being Lithuanian in Springfield has become a drastically different experience from what it was 100, 50--or even 20--years ago.

No one could miss the massive changes due to the die-off of first- and second-generation members of our community. Personally, I'll never forget a Lithuanian-American Club dinner-dance I attended with my immigrant father and a visiting group of managers from Lithuania's Azotas Company in the fall of 1990. Several hundred people filled a Springfield union hall and we danced to the music of a small orchestra. By the time I returned to Springfield to live in 1999, dozens of Lithuanian elders were dying every year.

I regret to say that by the time I started blogging in earnest about "Lithuanians in Springfield" in 2012, only a handful of elders—only a few American-born offspring of first-wave immigrants—remained to tell the stories of their lost world. Luckily, I have managed to interview several key survivors. And a few faithful researchers, Tom Mann and Bill Cellini, Jr., have made public genealogy sources and Springfield's newspaper, the *Illinois State Journal-Register,* yield many surprising—even shocking—anecdotes.

As a result, you can count on these collected and edited blog posts to provide some eye-opening facts—potentially a few tears—and an occasional laugh.

## The Story Behind the Genealogy

When contemplating this book, I wondered if twenty-first century individuals and families who had largely lost their European immigrant roots would be willing to read about families not their own. To keep things interesting (both for me and my readers), and to avoid a purely genealogical exercise, I have strived to present facts and photos that, at least in my interpretation, seem to tell a story or shed light on politics and history.

Due to the enormity of the first wave of immigration and my relative unfamiliarity with it, readers may also notice a heavier focus on people and events from 1900 to 1950. That's because *Lithuanians in Springfield* has been nothing if not my personal exploration of unknown, and to a large extent, unknowable, times and events--based on research and certain knowns from my own life as the daughter of an immigrant.

Let me say in advance that I expect differences among families about some of the facts and interpretations presented here. My readers should be aware that all factual information and photos in this book originate from named publications and primary sources—usually a single family member, but sometimes multiple individuals. I, and I'm sure, they, ask your forgiveness in advance for any differences in interpretation or unintentional errors of memory regarding events and people long passed.

## The Responsibility of Memory

History is written by its survivors, and in most of the immigrant families I've written about, the survival of the family story has long rested in the loving hands of a lone, middle-aged or elderly female. In many instances, precious documents and photos have been difficult to locate and identify.

In building my blog, I had hoped to reach widely dispersed readers and family historians who could work together with me to collectively re-create, at least in virtual space, some worthy successor of the lively ethnic community that once existed for our parents, grandparents and great-grandparents. As time went on, I began to conceive of this book as still another vehicle for sharing the love and responsibility of memory.

It is impossible to deny the fact that the more I researched Lithuanian immigrants in the first half of the twentieth century, the more tragic dysfunction I uncovered—largely unexpected by me as a daughter of the second wave, which generally arrived with more education and other advantages. The immigrant road is always a hard one. Still, I found myself and more than a few of my blog readers taken aback by the pervasive alcoholism and more than a little crime, domestic violence, and sexual violence among Lithuanian-Americans of the first wave.

Although my own immigrant father seemed to suffer from post-traumatic stress throughout my childhood, I somehow did not expect to learn that some of Dad's first-wave, American-born cousins (two sons of his paternal aunts) had been jailed for rape and property crime, respectively. Striking the right balance between the good and the bad became a growing dilemma for me, especially when disclosing crimes by individuals with living relatives. And then came the case of my own great aunt, *Teta*, and her older son Benny, born in America, who apparently went astray as a young man, but remarkably seems to have recovered his bearings, I like to think, on the almost supernatural force of an immigrant mother's love.

## Our Best Days

In the end, negative discoveries contributed vastly and unexpectedly to my work. They not only humanized long-dead immigrants, but also drove me to a deeper understanding of the many trials immigrant families faced and the largely invisible, but no less significant heroism they manifested in simple acts of survival, community-building, and family loyalty and love. Ultimately, my balancing act recalls the example of those struggling miners and domestics as they asserted themselves in keepsake photos not as they were, but as they wanted to be—or perhaps, as they were on their very best of days.

Therefore, while this book, for the so-called "big picture," does relate events that no doubt brought shame in their time, such facts are rendered with compassion, from the standpoint of the incredible advantages enjoyed today by we who stand on the shoulders of those far less fortunate.

In the end, I hope readers will find in these pages a balance driven equally by a passion to know and a compassionate understanding of how we would all like to be remembered, if and when we are remembered: on our very best of days.

## For My Native Springfield Readers:

Did you, like me, grow up with furniture from the Lithuanian-American Tisckos Furniture Store? Was your family home, perchance, built by Lithuanian-American builders Bill and Al Klutnick-- financed with a mortgage arranged by Gus Wisnosky of Illinois National Bank, or Walter Rodutskey of Sacred Heart (now Heartland) Credit Union?

Maybe Lithuanian-American attorney Isidor Yacktis once served your family in chancery or probate court. Or someone in your clan got a job with the help of Sangamon County Republican Chairman Don "Doc" Adams (Adomaitis).

You can bet that someone in your family ate Turasky Meats and dined at Gudausky's ("Butch's") Steak House, the Saddle Club or the Fairview restaurant. And that many spent Friday/Saturday night on stools at one of more than a dozen local Lithuanian-American corner taverns (Alby's, White City, Lapinski's,

Bozis's, the Lazy Lou, Cara-Sel Lounge, etc.), followed by Sunday morning in a pew at St. Vincent de Paul (Lithuanian) Catholic Church (or St. Al's or St. Joe's). Wrecked cars were made whole again by the Chepulis Champion Garage. And major life events were photographed by the Bubnis Mercury Studio.

Every one of our immigrant grandfathers and great-grandfathers, uncles and male cousins at some point mined coal, and most were impacted by mine lay-offs and closures and the violent conflict known as the Central Illinois "Mine Wars" (1932-1936). The vast majority of our forebears also consumed home-made alcohol throughout Prohibition, and a good number climbed up and out of dirty, dangerous—and ultimately, dying—coal mines by bootlegging under cover of a corner grocery store or a backyard rabbit "hutch." Bootlegging as a burgeoning cottage industry was not limited to Lithuanian-Americans, of course. Researching my blog, I began to think of Springfield as "the town that illegal alcohol built."

Unfortunately, due to assimilation, the passage of time, and few new Lithuanian immigrants to this area, none of these connections to a common ethnic past is readily apparent today. I never knew about my own family's Tisckos furniture or Klutnick home until I began asking questions for my blog. For almost 50 years, I didn't know there were descendants of another branch of my coal-mining Lith-uanian grandfather's family (the Orbacks) living in Springfield.

The truth is, although I grew up about as close to Lithuanian immigration as you can get, I grew up oblivious to the Lithuanian-American history, families and businesses in close proximity. I grew up oblivious to the role of these people and businesses in shaping modern Springfield.

With this book, based on the "best" of my blog, I aim to answer some of the ques-tions that others also might have neglected to ask, or can no longer ask because that solitary relative who would have known the answer is forever gone.

# Chapter 1
# Historical Background: The First Wave

The vast majority of Springfield-area Lithuanian-Americans are descended from early twentieth century coal-mining immigrants, who, with their families, constituted a community of several thousand by about 1914. In fact, the out-sized immigration from Lithuania to Springfield during this period, compared with the influx from much larger European countries, is quite remarkable, and one of the reasons for this book.

A precise count of first-wave Lithuanians here is impossible because the U.S. Census did not record Lithuanian birth until 1920. Many who had arrived from Lithuania before that date gave "Russia" as their birth country (Lithuania being part of the Russian Empire until it achieved independence after World War I).

However, several sources do provide a broad estimate of Lithuanian numbers in the Springfield area. Several 1920s newspaper articles refer to "a thousand Lithuanian families" in the city. Another source is the census of St. Vincent de Paul (Lithuanian) Catholic Church, which counted over 500 families by 1914, according to the parish's Golden Jubilee book (1956). One thousand and sixty-three infants were baptized at the church just between 1909 and 1919.

Even these figures suggest only a partial count of the community, since a good number of Lithuanian immigrants did not belong to the Lithuanian parish due to socialist political beliefs, or belonged to one of the other Catholic parishes on the city's north side: St. Aloysius, St. Peter and Paul, or St. Joseph's.

Lithuanian labor-socialist radicalism of the kind in Upton Sinclair's novel, *The Jungle*, was based on harsh conditions and injustices suffered in the mines and factories where Lithuanian immigrants worked. Some was also rooted in various anti-czarist movements in the homeland. One thing is clear: political divisions among first-wave immigrants were so passionate that it was difficult in the early 1900s for the community to pull together and build its church. This fact is briefly mentioned on page 10 of St. Vincent de Paul's Golden Jubilee book: "Evidently, the establishment of the Lithuanian (Catholic) parish in Springfield was not an easy or a promising job, for a Lithuanian socialist element was doing much to bring discord in the parish organization."

And Lithuanian immigrants were not alone in their leftist tendencies. Sitting in my Hungarian maternal grandparents' Springfield cellar in the late 1960s, I looked down to find a communist hammer and sickle traced into the cement floor, right next to the first names of my coal-mining immigrant grandfather Joseph and his three brothers, Karl, Anton and Wenzel Kohlrus. It was dated 1912.

By the time first-wave Lithuanian immigrants left their homeland, domination by the Polish nobility of the Polish-Lithuanian Commonwealth (1569-1705), and then repression by the Russian czars (1795-1918), had largely relegated the Lithuanian language and cultural identity to the impoverished country-side for hundreds of years. While Polish, Russian, Yiddish and German were spoken in the towns and cities where economic and political power was con-centrated, Lithuanian survived principally as the language of the hinterland and its poorest of the poor: former feudal serfs who had become landless agricultural workers.

A suppressed revolt again the czar in the early 1860s resulted in heightened Russian oppression--and combined with severe famine in the late 1860s--launched the first significant wave of emigration. Poverty, political and reli-gious repression, and a 20-25-year military draft also were major drivers of late nineteenth-century Lithuanian out-migration.

The mines of Scotland appear to have been the first landing place for dis-placed Lithuanian agricultural workers. By the 1870s or '80s, immigration had expanded to the anthracite region of northeast Pennsylvania (Scranton, Pittston, and Wilkes-Barre). And by 1890, Lithuanian miners and their fami-lies had arrived in Westville, south of Danville, Ill.—a few even making it fur-ther west to the Springfield area, south to Christian County, and even further south to Virden, Herrin, and Benld. It is reported in St. Vincent's Jubilee book that a significant number first reached Springfield via Scotland in the years just after 1900.

My own family story demonstrates this path. My paternal grandfather, Jonas (John) Baksys, born in the 1880s, mined in Scranton, Penn., for about 10 years until he saved enough money to return to Lithuania, buy land and marry. As a result of my grandfather's success working and saving in America, my father Vincas and his eight brothers and sisters were born on their own small farm in Lithuania starting around 1910. However, two of my grandfather's sisters and a brother who had followed him to Pennsylvania all remained in the United States, and all three moved on from Pennsylvania to Illinois--the two married sisters, Mary Yamont and Anna Orback, to Springfield.

Most local Lithuanian immigrants of this period settled near the coal mines on the north and east side of town. Here, as in other communities where they felt secure enough to settle, they signaled their intent to form a community by building their own Roman Catholic church.

# The Immigrant Condition

At the same time that large numbers of Lithuanians were immigrating to Springfield's coal mines, so were Italians, Poles, Slovenians, Slovaks, and Hungarians. Many of these came from a single town or county (Veszprem County, Hungary, like my Kohlrus maternal grandparents). Although Lithuanians, like their counterparts from other countries, often immigrated to join a relative, they appear to have arrived from every part of their homeland, not just one city or county.

It would be a serious understatement to say that nobody who was rich immigrated to the U.S. to mine coal. As a rule, the agrarian immigrants who arrived in Springfield to mine or marry a miner had few other options for staying alive. The vast majority were impoverished not just by the work they were forced to perform and the poor wages they earned--but also by generations of isolation in the remote countryside far from the benefits of higher culture, social progress, and education that were available in the cities and towns where economic and political power were concentrated.

Jonas (John) Baksys, my grandfather, circa 1900.

The extreme deprivation of the pre-immigration lives of the Southern and Eastern Europeans who arrived before WWI is made clear by a May 9, 1920, *Illinois State Journal* article describing outreach to "foreign women" consisting of home visits and lessons in everything from how to "get up in the morning," "make a fire," and "enroll Mary at school," to "preparing breakfast" and "getting Mary ready for school." Since new arrivals were described as not always knowing that items in stores required money, another lesson understandably was called "how to shop at 5 and 10 cents stores." "How to use milk" also crops up repeatedly.

Lessons on name and identification, using U.S. money, sending a money order, and taking care of a sick baby or husband, including how to go to a dispensary, demonstrate what probably was not pertinent, or handled very differently in the old country. Even so, the rudimentary nature of the lesson described as "coat, hat, shoes, shirt" truly gives pause. Are we to assume that modes of dress were completely different in the old country and that immigrants were being coached to adopt local fashions? Or that immigrant women were being exhorted to dress themselves and their families more "completely" and less poorly when they left the house—or both?

The most sympathetic way to read these passages is, as I have already indicated, for clues about how pre-immigration conditions in the homeland differed from the life newly available (and the habits newly expected) in a turn-of-the-century American coal town. For one thing, Italians probably would not have brought with them the custom of drinking cow's milk. Impoverished Lithuanians might not have had access to a milk cow. Regularly having even a little cash to spend in a store—and so many different things to buy—would also have been a revolutionary experience, as well as buying instead of making one's clothes from homespun flax or wool. See *"How They Looked—100 Years Ago"* for more about pre-immigration largely non-cash economies.

## Illiteracy: A Uniquely Lithuanian Affliction

For Lithuanians, in particular, free public education for children was the difference of all differences. Although many European immigrants of the time were illiterate and completely without formal education, the percentage of Lithuanians who could not even write or spell their names dwarfed this percentage among other groups. The reason was simple, although the effects were profound.

In addition to being mostly landless agricultural workers, first-wave Lithuanians originated not from their own nation, but from a "province" of the Russian Empire that had been subjected to a prolonged and brutal program of political, cultural, and religious oppression aimed at extinguishing Lithuanian national identity. Following Lithuanian revolts in 1831 and 1863, and lasting from approximately 1864 to 1905, the use of the Roman (non-Cyrillic) alphabet in Lithuania was forbidden, resulting in a total ban on education and publishing in the Lithuanian language: in effect, a language ban. A companion campaign to forcibly substitute Russian Orthodoxy for Polish-Lithuanian Roman Catholicism resulted in the closing of many church schools that formerly were the only institutions of education in the countryside.

Book-smuggling became a popular occupation, and the iconic Lithuanian rural mother of the time was depicted as teaching her children to read at her spinning wheel. Meanwhile, a Lithuanian national awakening was resurrecting long-dormant national identity and creating new awareness of and pride in Lithuanian language scholarship, literature and music. But this could do little to combat endemic illiteracy in the countryside in the face of the aforementioned language ban and the total absence of public education.

The effects of mass illiteracy were tragic, and endured long after Lithuanian immigrants flocked to the coal mines of Springfield. Hence, the dedication quote for this book, taken from Ann (Tisckos) Wisnosky: *"Tas kas skaita ir rasa, duonas ne prasa* (One who reads and writes does not ask for bread)."*

Illiteracy was an island for many first-wave immigrants that kept them largely locked inside their own community. It severely restricted many from acquiring the English necessary to protect their rights and pursue their interests at work, school and city hall, discouraged U.S. citizenship and raised formidable obstacles to learning anything that might have led to higher social status and pay. And at their worst, Illiteracy, ignorance and superstition exacerbated the underlying degradation and brutality of an almost feudal way of life.

In the following chapters, you will read about the highest and best aspects of the community that formed around St. Vincent de Paul Church, where the immigrants and their children could freely express their aspirations and engage in crucial self-help. You also will read about the alcoholism, despair and crime that was literally a carry-over from the oppressed Lithuanian countryside--reinforced by decades of continued harsh living and working conditions and limited opportunities here on American soil.

## The End of the First Wave

World War I interrupted the massive wave of immigration to the U.S. from Southern and Eastern Europe. The devastation immediately resulting from the war, and from Lithuania's struggle for independence at the end of the war, in which nationalists had to battle/negotiate with Russians, Germans, Poles, French, and the League of Nations, might have resulted in a new wave of immigration from Lithuania to the U.S. However, after 1920, the U.S. slapped drastic restrictions on immigration from European countries that had become major sources not just of unskilled labor, but also of radical labor unionism.

In the 1920s and '30s, coal mine closures and labor strife also eroded the size of the coal mining-based community in Central Illinois, sending many Springfield Lithuanians to Chicago or Detroit to find factory work. Further, the prospect, as well as the reality, of improving conditions under Lithuanian independence compared to increasingly difficult local conditions actually drew some immigrants back to their homeland in the 1920s and '30s.

The Lithuanian exodus from Springfield due to coal mining's sustained decline after 1920 was so pronounced that many in the Catholic diocese speculated that St. Vincent de Paul's, which had been built with so much love and at such great cost to so many poor miners, would not long survive. Fortunately, it survived for 50 more years, and despite declining membership in the late 1960s due to assimilation, would have survived longer if not for a decision by the Catholic diocese to close and demolish it.

The forces of assimilation through intermarriage proved irresistible for Lithuanians in Springfield after the first and second American-born generations, as for every other European ethnic group. However, the history of the Lithuanian community here was, again, unique in that for much of the twentieth century, oppression of the homeland continued to provide a strong moral imperative for preserving Lithuanian identity abroad.

# Chapter 2
# 'An Immigrant Childhood'
## By Ann Tisckos Wisnosky

During the oppressive regime of Russian Czar Nicholas II, my father, Jonas Petras (John Peter) Tisckus, and his parents lived in Kėdainiai and Kaunas. With Father approaching draft age and facing enslavement in the Russian army, Grandfather made arrangements, as did many other parents, to spirit his son out of Lithuania. This was done with the aid of sympathetic Prussian "agents" who lived (in the Konigsberg/Karaliauciaus region) near the Lithuanian border.

Father escaped by ship to live with a cousin in Glasgow, Scotland. There, he met other countrymen who had taken refuge and were working in the coal mines. Father joined their ranks. Although the work was hard, dirty, and dangerous, it posed no language barrier and required no skill. After a year as a miner, Father could afford to continue on to *"Americka."*

In 1906, he arrived in Salem, Mass. Friends helped him obtain work in a hide (tanning) factory, but he could not tolerate the sickening stench that permeated the entire town. In January 1907, he came by train to Springfield to live with a family he had known in Lithuania, in a home east of the city near what is now the (I-55) bypass.

## Springfield's Streets of Mud

The immigrant of those days found a varied scene in Springfield: muddy roads, board sidewalks, gas street lights, outdoor plumbing, and horse-drawn fire engines, trolley cars, carriages and paddy wagons, as well as corner saloons, player pianos, nickelodeons, medicine men, and balloon ascensions. There were also chickens, cows and gardens on city lots, nickel bread and penny ice cream cones. The fashion of the day found ladies in long dresses with "rats" in their hair and plumes in their hats; boys in knickers, girls with braids and ribbons, and men in celluloid collars, striped shirts, and straw or felt hats.

To work and play in this new environment, the immigrant had always to cope with the language barrier. Father, like most men, immediately applied for work in one of the dozen or more coal mines in the area, although Springfield also had over three hundred manufacturing concerns employing several thousand workers. Immigrant women found work as hotel maids or domestics. To supplement its income, nearly every foreign family already established here took in a *"greeneris"* (greenhorn) or a *"boardingerie"* (boarder) or two or three, no matter how crowded the home already was.

## Mother Arrives

My mother, Alexandra (Olse) Urbas, left Aztenu, Lithuania at the age of 17. An older brother living here paid her fare. Sailing to New York as a third-class passenger, she recalled how she had almost died aboard ship from breathing the gas from an extinguished lamp. Crowded conditions and seasickness plagued the passengers; with the latter condition, victims sniffed camphor in an effort to obtain relief.

In April 1908, Mother arrived by train in Springfield to live with a married cousin who had many boarders. Mother earned her keep by cooking and doing housework and laundry, the latter all by hand. She remarked that she had not found America any easier than Lithuania.

Four months after her arrival, Mother married my father in "Old St. Mary's" Catholic Church at Seventh and Monroe Streets. A year later, a son was born—then a daughter (me), followed by three boys in rapid succession. Babies were usually born at home with the help of a midwife who stayed on for several days to assist in the household. After the children arrived, a three-room house on 15th Street near Madison Street was rented. The range and a heating stove supplied warmth, and kerosene lamps supplied light. Hot water was obtained from a nearby railroad roundhouse.

## Mutual Aid in America

Immigrant families felt that owning a home was their greatest security. So, in 1916, my parents made a down payment on a modest home of four rooms on East Reynolds Street in an almost all-Lithuanian community. Most families were buying homes and raising children, chickens, cows, and gardens. With parents and grandparents left behind in Lithuania, neighbors had to rely on each other for help in everyday projects, as well as emergencies. They exchanged tools, seeds, cuttings, recipes, and ideas about life in America. Women helped each other cut out clothes from homemade patterns, and many owned foot-operated Singer sewing machines. *(Unlike in the old country, at least they did not have to make their own homespun fabrics by spinning flax or wool into thread.)*

## From Flour Sack to Embroidered Petticoat

Because most families baked bread, flour was purchased in 50-lb. cotton bags. Empty bags that were not later used for dish towels or bedding were bleached in boiling lye solution, then used for nightgowns and petticoats. Sometimes, the commercial markings were not quite bleached out of the sacks, but even such petticoats boasted hand-crocheted hems of lace made by loving mothers. These were "Sunday best" for many little girls.

Sundays saw most church-going Lithuanians attending a Roman Catholic Church. By 1909, they had built their own, St. Vincent de Paul's, at North Eighth Street and Enos Avenue. It became the center of their religious, cultural and social life, and was a great force in the preservation of their language, songs and customs.

## 'Those Foreign Kids'

Home recreation found children playing with hoops, marbles, home-made stilts, and kites. Some families listened to Victrolas or sang along with player pianos. Occasionally, a nickelodeon movie starring Pearl White or Mary Pickford could be enjoyed. As children, our happy hours of neighborhood play were in contrast to our ambivalent feelings about attending school. When we started Palmer School, we were looked upon as "those foreign kids" and sometimes called names. *(Ann doesn't mention it, but as the daughter of two immigrants, she probably started school without speaking any English. Children like her did not receive instruction in their own languages, but were expected to learn English at school.)*

Other ethnic groups had the same problem. It gave us a deep sense of not belonging in the outside world. Our real world was the family, neighborhood, and church. To add to our educational hurdles, few parents could help with school lessons, for most knew only their native language, manners and customs. Father had learned to read and write by now, but Mother had not. She did learn to write her name and do some reading later through classes held in the homes of immigrants.

The free public school system was an overwhelming joy to Father, compared with the suppression of education he had endured in czarist-ruled Lithuania. As we began school, Father told us, *"Tas kas skaita ir rasa, duonas ne prasa.* (The one who reads and writes does not ask for bread.)" Study was encouraged, and teachers were respected. There were some fine, dedicated and very helpful teachers at Palmer School who understood the problems the frustrated foreign children faced. They encouraged the use of the Lincoln Library, where pupils were introduced to stereoscopes and free books that could be taken home to enjoy. Most immigrants had few, if any, books at home.

## Feathers in My Stockings

On wet days, teachers let children huddle near radiators to dry stockings, while shoes were drying nearby. Many pupils had wool stockings, mittens, hats, scarves, and sweaters–but few owned boots. One freezing winter day, Mother sent me to school with feathers stuffed in my stockings for warmth. Each time a feather stuck out, I bent to pull it free. Finally, the teacher, in a rare moment of exasperation, rapped my knuckles with her ruler. Mother was tearfully told that afternoon that "no other second-grader wore feathers to school."

Home life had its share of other major and minor problems and inconveniences: numerous contagious diseases and indoor pollution from smoke and ashes; the dodging of lines of laundry drying throughout the house during winter; and Saturday night baths in a tub in the kitchen. Economies were achieved by fathers repairing children's shoes with soles cut from large slabs of tough leather. In addition to chores like bringing in coal and wood from outdoor sheds and carrying out ashes, many boys sold papers or had routes. Girls helped with housework, cleaned and filled lamps, and helped with smaller children.

Ann Tisckos and August (Gus) Wisnosky, Sr., September 1927. *Collection of Al Urbanckas, D.D.S.*

In the homes of miners, incomes were far from steady; work was seasonal and strikes frequent. Grocers developed a system of extending summer-long credit "on the book" while mine work was slack. Families lived with uncertainty, and hard work was accepted as a way of life. Uncertainty and disruption had also been the lot of the immigrants in their native Lithuania, but American held the promise of a better living, new opportunities, and certainly, new freedoms. There were milestones along the way—the earning of U.S. citizenship (Father and Mother gained theirs on a happy day in 1918) and subsequent political participation. Eventually, economic gains were realized, and many first-generation American-born Lithuanian-Americans secured advanced education and entered professional and business fields. Certainly, a new diversity had been added to America's talent and character.

*Editor's Post-script:   Long before I started writing about "Lithuanians in Springfield," a very special lady, Ann (Tisckos) Wisnosky (Vysniauskas), wrote the story of her immigrant family under the same title. Ann was the wife of self-made Illinois National Bank executive August, Sr. (Gus), and mother of John, a University of Hawaii art professor, and August, Jr. (Augie), a leading Springfield architect.*

*In addition to being a first-class homemaker who won the Chicago Daily Tribune "Cook of the Month" award for her fruit bread recipe, and a 1948 Tribune recipe contest for her Lithuanian potato kugelis, as well as a Quaker Oats contest, Ann was a talented writer with some touching childhood memories, as you have just read.*

*Her essay was possibly penned around the time of the U.S. Bicentennial in 1976 and adapted for "Historico," a publication of the Sangamon County Historical Society. The piece printed here is taken from Ann's original typed essay as preserved by Ann (Pazemetsky) Traeger, with only minor edits.*

# Chapter 3
# St. Vincent de Paul
# (Lithuanian) Catholic Church

At every stop on their coal mining trail, some Lithuanian immigrants showed their intent to settle by forming a Lithuanian Catholic parish. Here in Springfield, several hundred families and individuals came together in 1906 to form their own. Excavations for the church building began around 1907, with miners digging the basement at night. In 1908, they laid the cornerstone of St. Vincent de Paul (Lithuanian) Catholic Church at Eighth Street and Enos Avenue.

Exterior, St. Vincent de Paul Church. Undated. *Courtesy of Sangamon Valley Collection, Lincoln Library.*

*The church's interior, undated. Jubilee book.*

According to the Illinois State Journal, St. Vincent's was dedicated on May 14, 1911, following a parade and pageant grand marshaled by George Vysniauskas (Wisnosky). The parade was led by a "platoon of police," followed by a marching band from Benld and a squad of Knights of Grand Duke Vytautas (a famous Lithuanian ruler) mounted on horseback *(see photo of the Knights in their uniformed splendor, keeping in mind they were probably all hard-scrabble coal miners).*

## The Grand Procession

At least a thousand Catholics joined in the procession, which began at St. Vincent's and made its way to Sacred Heart Church, then St. Peter & Paul's. At each stop, the procession was joined by marchers from various Catholic societies, finally arriving at St. Vincent's for a dedication by Bishop Ryan of Alton and a solemn high mass celebrated by the Rev. Dean Kranezunas of Chicago, assisted by the Rev. Lawrence Ryan, "master of ceremonies," as well as several other priests and deacons. Homilies were given by the Reverends Skrypko Petraitis and Crosson Clancy of Chicago, according to newspaper articles.

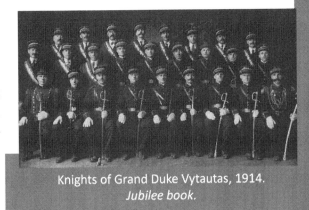
Knights of Grand Duke Vytautas, 1914. *Jubilee book.*

From St. Vincent de Paul's, the St. Vincent's, St. Joseph's, and National Slavonian Society No. 302 marched (not to mention the Knights of Grand Duke Vytautas formerly mentioned). From Sacred Heart, St. Barbara's Croatian Society, St. Boniface Sr. No. 2, W.C.M. and the Sacred Heart Catholic Order of Foresters No. 264 marched.

Participating from Saint Peter and Paul's were the St. Aloysius Young Men's Society, St. Vincent's Society, St. Peter's Court No. 192, Catholic Order of Foresters, and St. Paul's Branch No. 57, Western Catholic Union. A half a dozen languages were reportedly used in the dedication and High Mass. The Rev. John Czuberkis was the pastor of St. Vincent de Paul's on that grand dedication day so long ago.

## 'Our Church Was Everything to Us'

Populated by many clubs and societies, most notably chapters of the Knights of Lithuania and the Roman Catholic Women's Alliance, St. Vincent's proceeded to serve as a culturally and socially rich center of life for Springfield's original Lithuanian immigrants, their children and grandchildren. Many whose circumstances never allowed them to learn fluent English depended on the church community for all their spiritual and social needs.

The church—and the spirit and effort its members poured into it—no doubt were also an elevating force that helped Springfield Lithuanians transcend their harsh lives during the harsh years of the "Mine Wars," the Great Depression, and World War II. Only recently I began to ponder again the significance of the fact that for more than 100 years, St. Vincent's was the only church built in Springfield by immigrants of a single nationality for immigrants of that nationality.

And I came to the conclusion that St. Vincent's significance, though not entirely within our grasp so many decades later, cannot be ignored. In its broadest strokes, the founding of the church must be understood as a declaration of national identity by a people historically denied that identity.

Lithuanians self-exiled and adrift from all they had known were also weighing anchor and asserting themselves in a new land, putting money and labor they could ill afford into the greatest enterprise they could conceive for demonstrating their dignity and higher purpose as human beings. "We may be lost to our parents and homeland," they seemed to be saying, "but we will not be lost to ourselves. We will not be invisible or forgotten. We will have our place on earth."

It seems equally impossible not to consider the church a success in helping its first-wave immigrant founders and their children create a zone of safety, self-actualization and empowerment that, ironically, became less necessary as next generations achieved their own success and entered the American mainstream.

## Death of a Church

When St. Vincent's pastor for 47 years, the Rev. Stanley O. Yunker (Lith. Junkeris), suffered a stroke and retired, the Catholic diocese closed St. Vincent de Paul's on Jan. 1, 1972. Many elderly parishioners were hurt and alienated—some never entered another Catholic church in Springfield for the rest of their lives.

The Rev. Stanley O. Yunker, church pastor for 47 years. Undated. *Jubilee book.*

To try to save their church, a group led by 22-year parish trustee August Wisnosky, Sr., found another Lithuanian priest to lead the parish and appealed all the way up to the Vatican to save their church. But to no avail. St. Vincent de Paul Church was demolished in the mid-1970s, as parishioners carried off the last chairs, pews and candlesticks from the building where they had celebrated the most sacred moments in their lives.

August Wisnosky, Sr., long-time parish trustee. *Jubilee book.*

Before he died, Fr. Yunker established a $100,000 scholarship fund, now held in trust by the Foundation for the People of the Catholic Diocese of Springfield, for Lithuanian-American college students (living and studying anywhere in the U.S.) with a family connection to the church.

The parish's 1956 Jubilee book is preserved in the Sangamon Valley Collection of the Lincoln Public Library. It mentions, with special honor, August Wisnosky, Sr., 25-year trustee Simon (Sam) Lapinsky, 20+ year trustee Anthony Yakst, and 38-year organist and music director Ann (Mosteika) Foster.

Sam Lapinski, Sr., long-time parish trustee. *Jubilee book.*

Ann (Mosteika) Foster, St. Vincent's Music Director 1933-72. Undated. *Jubilee book.*

## Lithuanian-American Priests

In telling the rich history of the parish with photos, St. Vincent's Jubilee book also celebrates the ordination of three young men from the parish in a single day on April 19, 1936: the Reverends Casimir Andruskevitch, Peter Klumbys, and Casimir Toliusis.

The Rev. Charles E. Olshevsky was another Lithuanian-American priest native to Springfield. The son of Wallace and Julia (Shupenas) Olshevsky, Fr. Olshevsky was pastor at Little Flower Parish 1960-64 and St. Cabrini 1986-92, among many other postings in the diocese.

The Rev. John Rodutskey, brother of Sacred Heart Credit Union co-founder Walter Rodutskey, grew up in Springfield with Lithuanian immigrant parents, and seems to have served at St. Vincent de Paul Church. At the time of his mother's death, he was in the O.C.S.O. order in Gethsemane, Kentucky.

Finally, the Rev. James T. Ulak, M.M., the son of Mrs. and Mrs. Ignatius Ulak of Springfield, was ordained to the missionary priesthood at the Maryknoll Seminary near Ossining, N.Y.

# Chapter 4
# What Did They Look Like—
# 100 Years Ago?

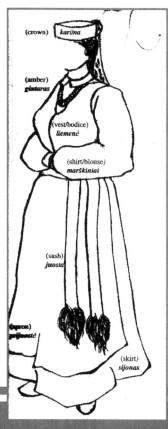

(crown) *karūna*

(amber) *gintaras*

(vest/bodice) *liemenė*

(shirt/blouse) *marškiniai*

(sash) *juosta*

(apron) *prijuostė*

(skirt) *sijonas*

Lithuanian women's homespun holiday garb. Courtesy of "Reflections from a Flaxen Past," *by Kati Reeder Meek.*

In a February 1913 *Illinois State Journal* article located by Tom Mann, columnist Octavia Roberts wrote about a visit to St. Vincent de Paul (Lithuanian) Catholic Church. Roberts' "Through Feminine Eyes" column gives us our best eye witness account today of what first-wave Lithuanian immigrants in their Sunday finest looked like 100 years ago.

The church was packed, with parishioners standing in the aisles and in front of the vestibules, some of them for a full two hours (a longer mass than most of us ever routinely experienced). Men and boys sat on one side of the church, women and girls on the other. It's not surprising to read that, according to Roberts, the "majority had blue or gray eyes," and "were a handsome, sturdy people."

*kykas*

*nuometas*

The netted cap and wimple as above were two types of hair covering used by married women.

Lithuanian married woman's traditional head coverings. Courtesy of "Reflections from a Flaxen Past," *by Kati Reeder Meek.*

The writer makes much, indeed, of the men's thick and wavy hair. Although she doesn't say, I imagine the congregation she observed that day was uniformly young. Elders with balding pates–parents and grandparents–had mostly been left behind in Lithuania. Everyone knew that the light at the end of the immigrant's tunnel back then could only potentially be reached through a lifetime of hard, manual labor—impossible for the old or weak.

"As for the women," Roberts writes, "their pretty hats covered up their faces according to the mode of the year." She goes on to marvel at "how well-dressed" the female Lithuanian immigrant was after invariably arriving in America "in a full skirt with waist of contrasting material worn in her province, with her head tied up in a bright handkerchief and her goods in a great square of cloth, knotted at the corners." Remarkably, she writes, "in an incredibly short time," these immigrant women "would put away the clothes of the old country and be dressed in the latest fashions of America."

## Putting on the New

I like this passage on many levels. Probably the most important meaning is only hinted at: That before coming to America, Lithuanian immigrants knew only traditional homespun clothing in a cash-poor economy where you didn't wear it, use it, or eat it unless you made it or grew and cooked it yourself.

Pattern from traditional Lithuanian weaving, inked by Paul Endzelis. *Courtesy of Barbara Endzelis.*

According to Roberts' article, prior to immigrating, most Lithuanian men were poor, landless agricultural workers (on large estates) earning only about $30 a year. Women no doubt had even less, if any, cash, and it was their job to spin all the family's clothes from flax, a little cotton, and lots of wool. It hardly takes much imagination to conceive of these immigrant women's excitement at being part of a town economy where families had several hundred dollars a year, and retail options for spending it.

St. Vincent de Paul Church choir, 1913. *Jubilee book.*

Since their cash was still far from sufficient, immigrants still made, not bought, much of what they needed, including cultivating most of their own food, just like in the old country. Critical, non-cash subsistence skills still made the difference between success and failure. But the habit of having at least one set of store-bought clothes for Sunday mass, for those who could afford it, was likely a habit carried over from the home country, only to be more fully and finely expressed as post-immigration economics and fashions permitted.

You can also bet that one or two fine and fashionable Sunday outfits would have seemed like a necessary dividing line between the old homespun life and the new: a proclamation that all that had been left behind–given up–was worth it.

As for St. Vincent's well-dressed immigrant ladies the day Roberts visited, once married, none was permitted the public exposure of singing in the church choir. That meant the female choir Roberts observed in early 1913 was composed of the few, small girls too young to marry in a culture where the girls married young.

However, if this photo dated that same year is correct, due to its pastor's efforts (and those of first parish organist Anthony Glemza), St. Vincent's had an adult mixed-voice choir only months later. Perhaps the enlarged choir was composed of unmarried adult women or women with their husbands. (By the 1920s, it was one of the finest church choirs in the city.)

## Homespun to 'Home Clothes'

One of the last things my homespun-wearing, subsistence-farming father did before fleeing the advancing Russians in October 1944 was to bury his store-bought Sunday suit and shoes in a cardboard box– never doubting, of course, that he would return. (Our grandmother's china dishes are also still some-where underground on our lost Baksys land–*musu zeme*.)

Dad's homespun customs, which I never understood growing up, were echoed in our family's pronounced distinction between "home clothes" and school or church attire. Before we were of the age when we could take more control over our appearance, this went beyond formal vs. informal or school vs. play. Until I was seven or eight, Dad wouldn't even let his daughters wear pants in the winter or shorts in the summer: his rule for girls was dresses, no matter what the other kids wore.

I also still remember, as a kindergartener, the shame of being ambushed in my worn and lumpy "home clothes" when a neighbor boy unexpectedly packed his birthday party with our classmates in full party dress. And, I still think, to this day, that our family's "immigrant" difference was most firmly established in my mind by our clothes, and our reaching, as girls, for a normalcy and belonging that was always just out of reach—through clothes that were also always somehow just out of reach.

## Clothed in Dignity

I'm sure others have noticed that poor Lithuanian coal miners and their wives always seemed to take amazingly glamorous "portrait" photos. I puzzled for years over this apparent discrepancy between what I knew about my great aunt, *Teta* (actually Mary Yamont or Marija Jomantiene), and her coal-mining husband, Benedict Yamont (Jomantas), Sr., and their full sartorial splendor in a family portrait dated 1908 or 1909.

The Rev. John Czuberkis, St. Vincent's pastor 1909-1919. *Church Jubilee book.*

It seems improbable that all of our ancestors somehow made and lost millions by the time we met them. And even if real in some cases, great reversals of fortune could hardly explain the pure number of photos wherein glamorous immigrant dress seems to belie a history of poverty. Doubtless these photo portraits aimed to show families not in their informal daily reality, but rather, at their most solemn, dignified and successful.

In true poverty, limited photographic resources would hardly be wasted on papering the world with that era's version of the 1980s goofy Polaroid snapshot—or today's proliferation of digital "selfies." To the contrary, it actually seems logical to me that poverty, itself, and trying to make *bella figura* for the people back home explains the extravagance of early twentieth-century high photographic occasions.

I've even heard that photographers traveled with glamorous wardrobes to entice the poor to become temporary poseurs to wealth. And, what better than a photograph to render wistful permanence to a dead-ended miner or domestic servant's unfulfilled dream of ease and luxury—never to become real in this life?

My great aunt's family: Benedict and Mary (Baksys) Yamont with (from left) sons Benedict, Jr., and Joseph. Circa 1909.

Lithuanian Sunday church, the immigrants' own church that was like a piece of their own home soil, was also a place to dream, and to begin to self-actualize, with the support of community and many social clubs and Lithuanian Catholic lay societies. The Rev. John Czuberkis spoke to columnist Roberts of organizing a large mixed choir, sports and drama clubs. Pastor of St. Vincent's during the parish's peak years for growth and membership (1909-1919), Father C. knew what a different, more fully human identity meant to his parishioners, even if that was achievable only at Sunday church–or on special occasions, for example, when the men donned the full regalia of the "Vytautas, Grand Duke of Lithuania Society."

It's interesting to ponder the role that the individual public statement–and group reinforcement—of Sunday costume likely played for people who had shed so much, and were in the process of clothing themselves anew, in every sense of those words. I'll bet society page writer "Miss" Roberts never knew her visit to St. Vincent's would inspire such a meditation on the social meanings and the elevating power of clothing—100 years later.

# Chapter 5
# Lawyer to Lithuanians

As a lawyer to his fellow Lithuanian immigrants in Springfield, Isidor Yacktis (1883-1953) leveraged his higher education and social status to serve as a mediator between his own people and mainstream Americans to whom the immigrant "hordes" seemed unruly, threatening—and potentially even disloyal. It couldn't have been easy being an ambassador of the higher potential largely invisible within his community of illiterate miners and laborers back around the time of World War I.

Yet it appears that Mr. Yacktis was first publicly called upon—and rose—to this role as soon as he was admitted to the Illinois State Bar. The year was 1915, and the extreme barbarity of World War I in Europe had already become frighteningly apparent. Neutrality-loving Americans were feeling queasy about immigrants here potentially manifesting the national interests and hostilities of their countrymen back home and dragging the U.S. into the Great War.

## Modeling U.S. Citizenship and Patriotism

Expressing those timely concerns, on July 4, 1915, the Illinois governor, lieutenant governor, and other dignitaries held their first large, public meeting to welcome newly naturalized citizens at the arsenal (Illinois Armory) at Second Street and Capitol Avenue, according to the *Illinois State Register*. Somewhere around a thousand people attended and were exhorted by the governor to give up "all former lines of nationality" in hopes "that America might be spared participation in the War."

The "right hand of fellowship" was extended on behalf of the city, and a speech was given on "The Ideal Citizen." Yacktis addressed his own people, and newly-minted U.S. citizens of German, Italian, Scandinavian, English, Scottish and Irish birth did the same, in order to set a public example of "unequivocal allegiance to the stars and stripes." The Declaration of Independence was read, and the state hymn "Illinois" was sung, accompanied by the Capital City Band.

## Flip-flopping U.S. Loyalty Concerns

Eighteen months later, as the U.S. was officially entering World War I, America's loyalty concerns did an about-face, as the U.S. government and public worried that immigrant men would not respond to a military draft. "While nations across the sea are at war, the United States is busy arousing the love of America among her foreign-born citizens," the *Illinois State Register* proclaimed in reference to an "Americanization" rally for immigrants on Jan. 12, 1917 at Palmer Elementary School on Springfield's north side.

Germans, Italians and Lithuanians summoned to the rally were formally addressed by a representative of each of their nationalities, including Yacktis. "The foreigners listened attentively to the admonitions of the representatives of their own governments, who told them they must give unfaltering allegiance to the country of their adoption and be loyal to the American flag and American institutions," the news article declared.

Included on the program were "simple explanations" of American government at the city, state and national levels by a U.S. district court judge. Then a chief examiner for the U.S. Department of Immigration and Naturalization explained the requirements of U.S. citizenship, which soon would include an expedited process for immigrants who became soldiers.

The mass meeting closed with the singing of "America"—and only a few months later, a new military draft that would dispatch young immigrant men to trench warfare in Europe. Many of those probably embarked on their expedited path to naturalization by officially documenting their intent to become U.S. citizens, the first stage of the process. More than a few would achieve citizenship upon their discharge from the military, provided they survived World War I.

## Still Lithuanian at Heart

In 1918, as Lithuania fought for its independence from the crumbling Russian Empire, Yacktis expressed his identity as a Lithuanian by penning an op-ed for the *Illinois State Register* entitled, "Lithuania, a Separate Nation." In it, he argued passionately for the distinct nationality of the Lithuanian people and against Polish designs on parts of post-Russian Lithuania.

Several months earlier, Yacktis leaned a little more to his American side, publishing his name in a display ad in the *Register* supporting the "Committee to Make Springfield Dry." Prohibition was certainly not a sentiment shared by the majority of his immigrant countrymen. However, that may have been precisely why he supported it, as a way to combat pervasive alcoholism and its related social ills.

In 1918, Yacktis appears in an article encouraging community-spirited individuals to join the YMCA and pay for a six-month "Y" membership for two returning soldiers or sailors. Again in his role as an official voice and ambassador for his community, Yacktis lent his name to several additional display ads placed by members of the Illinois Bar on major political and social issues. Still another newspaper report finds Yacktis investing $25,000 in a Flexotile (roofing and wall tile material) manufacturing concern with four other local men, probably lawyers. (I found no further mention of the business, its success or failure.)

## Probate and Family Law

In his general practice legal career, Yacktis seems to have operated from an office at 213 S. Sixth St., where he also rented at least one room for $5 a month in 1946. He also appears in a 1937 newspaper mention for regularly giving food and water to a stray kitten living near the Johnny Orlove Tavern, whose paw had been gnawed off by rats. So our "lawyer to Lithuanians" appears to have been a humane man, as well.

By the end of his career, he had represented the following families in estate matters: Grigisky, Lagunas, Yustus, Kasper, Lukitis/Gedman and Karvelis. He represented the Adeikis and Kaslauckas couples in chancery (divorce) court. He also represented a Max Bracius, who had been struck on his bicycle by a city water truck. These matters happened to be recorded in the newspapers I came across, but I'm sure that in his long career, Mr. Yacktis represented many, many Lithuanians.

# Chapter 6
# From Soldier to U.S. Citizen

*As many as 50,000 Lithuanian immigrants wore the U.S. uniform in World War I. William Cellini, Jr., writes to commemorate all the immigrants who served and to explain how war could unlock the door to U.S. citizenship.*

## Immigrants in War, Citizens in Victory, by William Cellini, Jr.

Foreign-born citizens had served in the U.S. military for over 100 years prior to our country entering World War I. However, the "War to End All Wars" was unique in terms of the number of non-U.S. born men drafted into the military.

On April 6, 1917, Congress declared war on Germany and immediately passed the Selective Service Act requiring all men in the U.S. between the ages of 21 and 31 to register at their community draft boards. Within

Lithuanian immigrant John Joseph Straukas, age 28, of Riverton, American Expeditionary Force, 1918. He received expedited U.S. citizenship as a result of service to our country in World War I. *Courtesy of Joyce Skrobul.*

a few months of the opening of registration, about 10 million men across the country had responded. By the summer of 1918, the age of eligibility was expanded to include men from 18 to 45 years old. Included in this wide net were native, naturalized, and alien men.

As the numbers of immigrant men called up for military service grew, alien draftees were offered an expedited route to full U.S. citizenship regardless of their immigration status. Modifications for soldiers were made to all three key parts of the naturalization process: the Declaration of Intent, the Petition for Citizenship, and the issuance of the Certificate of Naturalization.

Under this modified process, the residency requirement of five years before submitting a Declaration of Intent to become a U.S. citizen was eliminated. In addition, an expedited Petition for Citizenship was granted. Typically, the petition required an oath of allegiance to be taken at the immigrant's local courthouse. As an alternative, immigrant soldiers signed a pledge to the United States called a "written oath" and had two U.S. citizens verify their petition

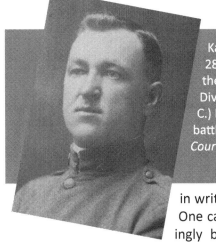

Kansteon Steikunas (Kanstantas Steikūnas), 28, born in Balninkai, Lithuania, served in the Illinois National Guard (later the 33rd Division, U.S. Army, 129th Infantry, Company C.) He was killed by German shelling in the battle of Meuse-Argonne, Oct. 11, 1918. *Courtesy of Arunas Banionis.*

in writing, supplanting the need to go to court. One can imagine written verification quite willingly being given by alien soldiers' U.S.-born commanding officers and comrades-in-arms.

Finally, as an alternative to enduring the waiting period of several years to receive a Naturalization Certificate, once a soldier's petition was filed under the new war-time rules, the certificate was granted immediately upon processing and approval. Conversely, immigrants asking for draft exemption or discharge from service would automatically have their citizenship process cancelled and would be forever disqualified from becoming citizens of the United States.

From May 8 to November 30, 1918, the government counted 155,246 immigrant soldiers among the newest citizens of the United States, not including an undetermined number of alien soldiers granted citizenship while stationed overseas.

Burial of World War I dead from the 33rd Division, U.S. Army, which was largely composed of Illinois National Guardsmen. Undated. Bois de Chaum, France. *U.S. Army Signal Corps.*

The unprecedented number of immigrants culled from a huge and diverse population of non-English speakers and non-native English speakers presented a challenge to their training and consolidation into an integrated fighting force. Seeing the need to address this, the U.S. War Department created a Foreign Speaking Soldier Sub-section (FSS) to assist in the training of immigrants who could not speak English.

Kansteon Steikunas grave, Montfaucon Cemetery, Lorraine, France. *Courtesy of Arunas Banionis.*

Lt. Stanislaw A. Gutowski, a naturalized citizen born in Russian-occupied Poland, led the first step in the training process. Because he could speak Russian and Polish, Gutowski investigated FSS military camps for Slavic-speaking soldiers and witnessed the use of interpreters alongside commanders to instruct non-English speaking inductees.

This method proved ineffective, as inductees were often moved out of combat instruction and placed on kitchen duty. Consequently, Gutowski and his staff developed a plan allowing foreign-born officers to lead ethnic-specific companies "without encouragement of immigrant 'clannishness.'" Such ethnic companies were formed as a contingency so that if called into combat, non-English speaking soldiers would have an officer to communicate with them in the field.

Due in part to the numerous dialects spoken by inductees, the FSS favored using officers who spoke an immigrant language at home with family members over those who had learned a second language through study or travel.

By the spring of 1918, the influx of foreign-born inductees was so large that the U.S. Infantry created "development battalions" of non-English speaking soldiers. At Camp Gordon near Atlanta, an experiment was conducted in the training of several thousand non-English-speaking draftees, who were divided into three groups: a Development Battalion of physically fit men; a Labor Battalion of "disloyal and enemy aliens" and a Non-Combatant Service Group of physically unfit men with proficiency in a trade. At Camp Gordon, the two most populous ethnic companies were Polish-born and Italian-born soldiers. Training in the soldiers' native tongues was supplemented by instruction in English grammar.

By the war's end, one in five inductees in the U.S. military was foreign-born.
*Sources:*

Abbott, G. (1921). *The immigrant and the community*. New York: Century.
Gentile, F. N. (2001). *Americans All!: Foreign-born soldiers in World War I*. College Station: Texas A&M University Press.
Infantry Association. (1919). *Infantry Journal, Vol. 15*. Washington D.C.: United States Infantry Association.

# Chapter 7
# World War I Doughboy:
# John Joseph Straukas

In spring 2014 I met with Debbie, Richard and Nancy Kaylor of Riverton to hear stories and see photos of their deceased Lithuanian immigrant grandfather and proud veteran John Joseph Straukas. Several of the most striking photos of John Joseph, born in 1890 in Plungė, Lithuania, relate to his service in U.S. Army Company F, Fifth Battalion, 22nd Engineers, in World War I.

It's been 100 years since the beginning of that so-called "War to End All Wars," with its mass casualties and horrific trench warfare—not to mention history's most prolific use, ever, of chemical weapons. According to Chris McDonald, Ph.D., an author and political science professor at Lincoln Land Community College, WWI cost the lives of 132 Springfield-area men, 11 percent of the total inducted. (Chris's book is available on *amazon.com*.)

John Joseph Straukas, WWI "doughboy" portrait, 1918.
*Courtesy of Nancy (Kaylor) Betz.*

In 30 percent of those deaths, no cause was ever given. Almost 29 percent of the casualties resulted from the 1918 Spanish flu pandemic that swept the globe like a modern bubonic plague. Healthy, young American soldiers who contracted that flu in their training camps and on troop ships never even made it to the war, as their lungs filled up in just 48-72 hours. Concluding McDonald's numbers: Just over 16.5 percent of local casualties were killed in action, and another 15.5 percent died subsequent to wounds received in battle. Nine percent of casualties were listed as "other," probably non-combat.

A coal miner and skilled carpenter, Straukas had sailed to New York from Liverpool in 1909 on the SS Baltic (reportedly stoking the coal-fired ship's engines along the way, to pay for his passage). At the time of his military induction in 1917, he was living with his aunt Lulu Grigiski (Riverton's most famous moonshiner, according to the Kaylors). John Joseph had left Lithuania with

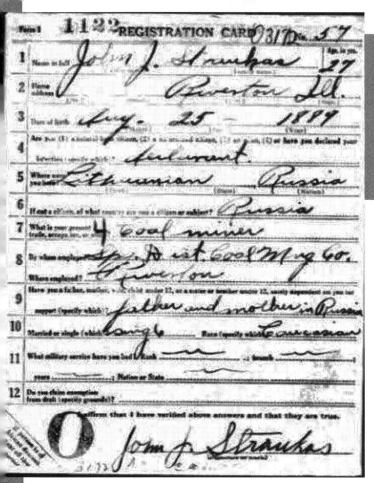

*Straukas draft registration, page 1. Ancestry.com*

his brother when it was part of the Russian Empire to avoid conscription by the Czar. Ironically, just nine years later, he found himself pressed by his adopted homeland into one of history's most lethal wars--only five months before Armistice.

Straukas trained at Ft. Benjamin Harrison, Indiana, and sailed to Europe on September 15, 1918. He saw action in America's high-casualty but successful Meuse-Argonne offensive right at the time of Armistice in November 1918. According to family members, Straukas performed so well that he was offered, and rejected, a promotion to corporal. Under a special expedited program for soldiers, he was granted U.S. citizenship in 1918, and discharged honorably in July 1919 at Camp Grant, Illinois.

**JOHN JOSEPH STRAUKAS**

Private, Company P, Fifth Battalion, 22nd Engineers, U. S. A. Son of John Straukas, Lithuania. Born August 25, 1892, in Lithuania. Address, Riverton, Ill. Entered service June 25, 1918, in Springfield, Ill. Received his training at Ft. Benjamin Harrison, Ind. Sailed overseas September 15, 1918. Was in action in Meuse-Argonne Offensive when the Armistice was signed. Discharged July 7, 1919, at Camp Grant, Ill.

Straukas listing, Sangamon County Honor Roll.

Years later, Straukas, who avoided drink, would huddle at the end of the bar at Butcher Tavern, discussing war experiences with the owner, another WWI veteran. However, Straukas lived a productive and notable life beyond his military service. According to his Kaylor grandchildren, he could fix or build anything. This included his Riverton home, where he employed construction methods ahead of their time, digging his basement by the scoop and shovel method and installing Greenfield wiring. Straukas also made all the cabinets and woodwork in the house himself.

Left: Straukas with Model T on his wedding day in Riverton, 1925.
Right: in leather jacket with 1930s or '40s vehicle. Courtesy of Nancy (Kaylor) Betz.

He proudly kept a "running" car (one that always was in good repair, gassed up and ready to go) in order to take not just himself, but also other miners to and from work in the nearby Denkert Coal Mine. Perhaps the original "designated driver," Straukas also used his car to make sure his buddies who drank got home safely from any and all of Riverton's nine taverns.

Straukas married Esther May Trow (13 years his junior) after a short acquaintance in 1925. The couple had two daughters: Dorothy Jane, who married Richard Dean Kaylor, and Louise, who married James Whitaker. The Kaylor grandchildren, who mostly grew up on the Straukas Riverton farm, are: Deborah, Richard, Denise, Nancy, Sharon, John, and Tammy.

Grandpa Straukas and his wife always kept two gardens: one closer to the house with lettuce, tomatoes, radishes, onions, carrots, and a chicken coop, and a more distant garden with red and sweet potatoes, peas, corn and green beans. After harvest, potatoes were stored in bins in the basement. The Kaylor kids remember eating such ethnic foods as pickled pigs' feet, herring, and "stinky cheese." Chickens were slaughtered outside and cleaned in the basement.

Straukas died of complications of black lung disease in 1973. Today, granddaughter Tammy still lives in the house he built. Nancy's son inherited his great grandfather's advanced carpentry skills.

*Dedicated to the memory of all Sangamon County men who served in World War I.*

# Chapter 8
# 'My Son, Please Come Home'

Letters from 1920s Lithuania: A Call to Come Home
By William Cellini, Jr.

A photo from home: Lithuanian family of immigrant Nancy (Benikas) Pazemetsky, July 15, 1909. *Courtesy of Ann (Pazemetsky) Traeger.*

Among the millions of European emigrants who came to the U.S. in the early twentieth century, Lithuanians stand out due to the precarious situations forcing them to leave their homeland. Most Lithuanian emigrants of the Catholic faith left to escape religious persecution by the Russian Orthodox Church and the Russian czarist regime.

Men also tended to emigrate due to military conscription that began in 1874 under Czar Alexander II.[1] Conscription meant Lithuanian males were obligated to fight for Russia in the disastrous Russo-Japanese War of 1904-05 and in World War I. (Politically, Lithuania was under the Russian Empire and had been since 1795. Therefore, Lithuanian emigres were frequently recorded on ship manifests as having been from Poland or Russia.[2])

Those who left during this period re-made their lives in other parts of Europe and in the Americas, often with no intention of ever returning to their homeland. However, after February 1918 when an independent Lithuanian nation was declared, Lithuanian-Americans had to make a decision about returning, especially when family members wrote letters pleading for them to come home.

Some of these letters contained entreaties from elderly parents wishing to see their children one last time. Other letters conveyed urgency in business matters that had surfaced since the emigrant left. Lithuanian-Americans who did manage to visit, or return for good in the period following World War I, found a Lithuania free from czarist domination and for the most part, free of Polish insurrection.[3]

**Enoch Yakobasky** (perhaps born Ignas Jakubauskas) was a Springfield resident who had emigrated from Lithuania to the U.S. in 1893. He initially worked as a coal miner in Pittston, Pennsylvania, where he was a boarder in the home of a Lithuanian family. By 1915, Yakobasky was living in Springfield, listed in the Springfield city directory as single and a coal miner. He registered for the draft during WWI, but due to his age (birth year listed as 1873), it is doubtful he served in the U.S. military.

Passport photo, Enoch Yakobasky, *Ancestry.com.*

In 1921, Yakobasky received a letter from his parents in Lithuania pleading with him to come back. They wanted nothing more than to "see you while we are alive, you might not find us alive by the next spring." At the time, Yakobasky was 48 years old and unmarried, living at the corner of South 12th and Laurel streets. His lawyer translated into English the letter from his parents, and a part of their message contains reassurances about life in the newly independent Lithuania.

September 4, 1921.

Our Beloved Son Ignac:

We, the old parents of yours, write this letter, beginning it by saying with great respect; Be the Glory to our Lord Jesus Christ, expecting you to answer; For Ever and Ever, Amen. And we say to you our beloved son, Ignac that we still enjoy our health, be the thanks to the God, and state, that we have received two letters, one following the other and we are very pleased for your kind remembrance of us and we hardly know how to express our thanks. It is a great pleasure for us to know, that you are so devoted to us in our old age and extend your assistance to us. Since we received the letter, two weeks has passed, but the money did not come yet. As you ask about the Government of Lithuania, we must reply, stating that the newspapers are stating untruth about it, because the poor people and working people are fully defended, they may go wherever they please, no one beats them or puts them in jail without reason. The master class now is more oppressed than the poor people. The Government penalizes the master class for the sake of the poor peoples; you should not mind the papers and should come back home, as many have already done and no harm is done to them; you were fooling us by your promise one year after another and we are waiting in vain. And we would like to see you while still we are alive, you might not find us alive by the next spring. If you wish so, you may come in the fall, when there is plenty of bread and everything, and the swallow says when it flies away, it leaves the old bins and when it comes back it find them empty. To your inquiry about

Yakobasky letter, translated. *Ancestry.com.*

"As you ask about the Government of Lithuania, we must reply, stating that the newspapers are stating untruth about it, because the poor people and working people are fully defended, they may go wherever they please, no one beats them or puts them in jail without reason."

Other comments carry a different tone: "The master class is now more oppressed than the poor peoples; you should not mind the papers and should come back home, so many have already done and no harm is done to them..."

Such remarks convey a sense of class struggle while providing evidence of just how bad conditions had been for the poor at the time immigrants left. My interpretation of the reference to the reversal of fortune for the "master class" is speculative. However, it may have been tied to events the year prior when Lithuania was embroiled in a war with Poland over control of the regions of Vilnius, Suwałki and Klaipeda.

That war occurred during the same era as the Soviet-Polish War, when the Red Army attempted to use Poland as a conduit for spreading communism into Germany. Lithuania was assisted by the Red Army in re-incorporating the city of Vilnius into the Lithuanian state.[4] (However, Lithuania later lost Vilnius to the Poles, and so Kaunas became Lithuania's provisional capital from 1920 until 1939).

The letter from the elder Yakobaskies indicates that their son previously had promised but failed to visit, and that they are expecting some financial assistance that has not yet arrived. It's not surprising that Lithuanian immigrants would have made remittances to elderly parents when able, in the long tradition of immigrant workers in the U.S.

Whether Enoch made the requested visit, and perhaps even remained with his aging parents, is unknown. He does seem to have left Springfield in the 1920s, as he is not listed or located in Springfield's city directories from 1923 to 1930.

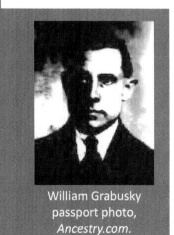

William Grabusky passport photo, *Ancestry.com.*

**William Grabusky** (perhaps Viljamas Grabauskas) was a Lithuanian-American who emigrated to the U.S. in 1906 from the village of Pilviškiai, Marijampolė County. He obtained U.S. citizenship on September 20, 1916 in Springfield, Illinois. Previously, he had resided in Mahanoy City, Penn., where he worked as a coal miner.[5] During WWI, Grabusky and his wife Helen lived on Springfield's north side. On his draft card, he is listed as a '"coal digger" with the "Jones & Adams Mine." Located off Clear Lake Avenue, the mine was an employment hub for many north-end miners.

Grabusky's birth year is listed as 1882.[6] In 1916, he and his wife suffered the death of their infant son, Notbett (Norbert). The funeral was held at St. Vincent de Paul Church, officiated by the Rev. John Czuberkis.[7] In 1921, Grabusky's parents wrote him a letter from Lithuania asking him to visit. From their reply, it seems he had initiated the idea: "Son, as you wanted to come and see us, well if you could come and see us now, because we are old and weak."

Grabusky was 40 years old when he received the letter. His passport paperwork indicates it was the first time he was applying for a travel document. Considering that he had resided in the United States since 1906, his parents must have been very pleased that he was making a visit after a separation of at least 15 years.

Their letter goes on to say, "...Your sisters and brother-in-law would be very glad; as we love to see the sun shine, that's [sic] how we want to see you..."

In a part of his letter to his lawyer, Grabusky indicates there are other letters from his family and they, too, could be used for his passport application: "...I will send you the letters they wrote me, and I have the lines marked for you as evidence, as they say 'we are waiting for you to come home and see us.' " Perhaps evidence was needed to obtain a passport quickly; it seems Grabusky's application was signed December 16, 1921 and his departure date was listed as Jan. 20, 1922.[8]

Per information from the U.S. Census and Springfield city directory, by 1930, Grabusky and his wife were living on North Eighth Street. He was working as a coal miner and she is listed as a "janitress" at the Lincoln Theater downtown. On March 19, 1932, he died of the complications of pneumonia. His body was buried in the abbey vault at Oak Ridge Cemetery.

According to his obituary, he was survived by his wife and by two sisters in Lithuania, Madeline and Agnes,[9] but no parents. Perhaps he had been able to visit them before they died.

**Antanas Senkus** emigrated to the U.S. from Scotland. According to his U.S. passport application, he was born in the village of Raguva, Panevėžys County. After his arrival in the U.S., he initially settled in Pennsylvania, where he became a naturalized citizen in 1914. In 1918, Senkus and his wife Marijona (family name, Rusinaukus/Ružinauskas) were listed in the Springfield city directory living on the city's north end.[10] His recorded occupation is "coal miner" with the "Jones and Adams Company."

Antanas Senkus,
passport photo,
*Ancestry.com.*

By 1920, the couple was listed as having three children. In 1921, Senkus received a letter from his father in Lithuania asking him to come and visit. "[I] am letting you know, son, that I have been sick and in bed since November 1920, so [I] am asking you, dear son, to be so good as to come home as soon as you possibly can as I want to see you, as it is 20 years since I saw you."

His father's letter also contains directions on how to get to their village, "Papilvui" (possibly the village of Papilvis in Kaunas County). The elder Senkus closes his letter saying, "[I] am 66 years old but have no health. Since Christmas, I am not able to walk, only sit down. Please write to me as soon as you receive this letter...Hoping this find [sic] you in good health, we are anxiously waiting."

There is no record, however, of Senkus making the trip overseas to visit his father and family. He died in 1936; his wife in 1954. Both are buried in Oak Ridge Cemetery, Springfield.

## Emigration Is Forever...

Another photo from the old country: Julia Stockus (Wisnosky) relatives, 1920s or 1930s. (The size of the house and dress of the people marks them as relatively successful.)
*Courtesy of Janice Kansy.*

The ease of transatlantic travel in the twenty-first century may obscure the obstacles to even one trip back home by a poor Lithuanian coal miner in the early twentieth century. In reading these letters, it's important to see beyond the emotional appeal of family reunification to understand the many practical obstacles that often made emigration a one-way trip, rendering it impossible for long-separated parents and adult children to see each other even one, last time.

All three of the men mentioned in this piece were coal miners earning meager wages, at times barely enough to support their families. Coal mining in the early twentieth century was not a full-time or even a year-round occupation, and during the summer, miners normally took odd jobs to maintain an income. In short, they could take no break from the struggle to support themselves (20-28 days just for the two-way transatlantic voyage, not to

A Galman (Galminas) family death in Lithuania. Undated. *Courtesy of David Black.*

mention additional time for travel to and from an Eastern U.S. port and then between a European port and the immigrant's Lithuanian destination).

A steamship ticket for a round-trip voyage to Europe, presumably in third-class (steerage), would have cost $80 to $90 in the 1920s.[11] That is about $1,100.00 in today's dollars, and a significant portion of a coal miner's annual wages. Many other tickets and travel costs would also have been required. All of this would have been on top of two months of lost income, accounting for just a few weeks at the old homestead.

Consequently, no matter how much parents and children yearned for a reunion, such a trip involved great personal sacrifice. It could only be afforded at the cost of more basic necessities and the very progress the immigrant had hoped to make by leaving his homeland, and had earned with decades of hard and risky labor and painful sacrifice.

Modern digital communications have changed these harsh facts of early twentieth-century emigration, allowing a new wave of Lithuanian workers scattered across Europe and America today to stay in close touch with their relatives and homeland. First-wave Lithuanian immigrants, however, could rely only on letters (using "scribes" when they were illiterate), and photographs. Photos exaggerating success and status attained in America, and photos of the family home and village in Lithuania, by necessity took the place of in-person visitation and became precious keepsakes of long-lost family members.

Sadly, many immigrants' final "visit" with their long-lost parents took the form of a funeral photograph, with open casket and neighbors and relatives from the village gathered around. In some especially tragic cases, the open-casket photo that crossed the Atlantic was of the unfortunate immigrant who had predeceased his or her elders.

## Sources

[1] Barkan, E. R. (2013). *Immigrants in American history: Arrival, Adaptation, and Integration.* Santa Barbara, California: ABC-CLIO.

[2] Kasekamp, A. (2010). *A History of the Baltic States.* New York: Palgrave Macmillan.

[3] Lithuania's capital Vilnius and its region were under Polish control from 1922 to 1939.

[4] Senn, A. E. (1967). *The Great Powers, Lithuania and the Vilna Question 1920-1928.* Leiden: E.J. Brill.

[5] Ancestry.com.

[6] Ibid.

[7] *Illinois State Journal*, January 1916.

[8] Ancestry.com, *U.S. Passport Applications 1795-1925.*

[9] *Illinois State Journal*, March 1932.

[10] *Jefferson's Directory of the City of Springfield, Illinois.* Springfield, 991: Jefferson's Printing Co., Springfield, IL. 1918.

[11] Jennings, W., & Conley, P. T. (2013). *Aboard the Fabre Line to Providence: Immigration to Rhode Island.*

# Chapter 9
# Entering Illegally by Ship:
# The Story of 'U.S. Mike'

George Rackauskas, late husband of Helen (Sitki) Rackauskas, was quoted in the July 22, 1990 *Catholic Times* about how his father Mike emigrated from Lithuania at the turn of the twentieth century.

After Mike's brother had been forced to work in a Russian slave labor camp for two years, breaking his health, Mike, at age 18, decided to get out of Lithuania before the same--or worse--happened to him.

According to George, his father Mike immigrated first to England. After working in English sugar mills for a few years, the elder Rackauskas earned enough money for passage to America by ship. However, when he arrived at Ellis Island, he had a small growth on his eye, so authorities sent him back to England. After a doctor there certified that the growth wasn't harmful, Rackauskas returned to work to earn enough for a second voyage. And he was determined not to be snared in the same trap again by immigration officials.

## Hidden by Sympathetic Crowd

"(This time) when the ship docked (in New York) and they let down the gangplank, (trying to avoid the health examiners), my father didn't even take his bag with him. He ran down the gangplank and whistles were blowing and everybody was hollering," George told the *Times*.

"There was a group of people down at the end (of the gangplank) waiting for their friends and relatives. My father ran right into the middle of them. They opened, then closed up (around him)." And that is how the elder Rackauskas gave the slip to immigration officials and effectively wrote his own pass into the United States.

Some years later when Rackauskas applied for U.S. citizenship in Springfield, he had to declare that he was here illegally, without papers. But even that obstacle was overcome with signed affidavits testifying to his good character and citizenship.

# First to Buy U.S. Savings Bonds

During World War I, he had proudly become the first in his northside neighborhood to buy U.S. Savings Bonds, picking up the handle, "U.S. Mike." According to daughter-in-law Helen Rackauskas, "After Mike did it, the other miners started buying bonds, too, saying, 'If it's good enough for Mike, it's good enough for us.'"

For many years, Rackauskas mined coal and lived with his Lithuanian immigrant wife Cassie and their children at 1820 N. Eighth St. Although he wanted to get out of mining, no opportunities materialized until he was finally hired by Pillsbury Mills. In the meantime, the family boarded as many as four single miners at a time. Despite the cramped quarters in their home, this was necessary to supplement the family's income as frequent mine closures and strikes left Rackauskas only sporadically employed.

During an interview in July 2012, Helen reported it was her mother-in-law Cassie's job to cook and clean for all the boarders, even washing their backs with hot water from a galvanized

"U.S. Mike" and Cassie Rackauskas with children George and Anne, undated. *Courtesy of MaryAnn Rackauskas.*

steel tub when they returned from their shifts blackened with coal dust.

# Chapter 10
# Lithuanian-American Women
# in Marriage and Divorce

Delores Kavirt grew up in Springfield, the daughter of a miner and bootlegger with an ocean-going background. Delores' father William Bernard Kavirt (Kavish or Kavishia) was born in Lithuania in 1893. In 1932, after nine years of marriage and seven children, he deserted his family, apparently for the freedom to go back to light, wind, and spray–instead of the dark, subterranean world of mining–as his successful bootlegging business was about to expire.

I would also guess that the strains of the Great Depression had their impact on the staying power of this husband and father– even if the impending demise of Prohibition and the illegal alcohol trade in 1933 was probably the straw that broke the camel's back. "My dad left us for reasons unknown and for a destination we never determined when we were all still quite young," Delores recalled. "He wanted to take my brother Willie with him. But my mother made it quite clear that he was not going to do that, throwing a pot of boiling hot water at him to drive home her point."

Delores' mother Bernice (Mazika) Kavirt, circa 1920.

The Kavirt kids, front row, left to right: Delores, Alice and Willie. Back row, left to right: Bernice and Lillian. Late 1930s.

# Women Handicapped in Marriage, Divorce

So far, I have not written about the deleterious impact of the harsh mining life on marital formation and duration among first-wave immigrants and their offspring. The story of Delores ("Dolly") Kavirt's parents demonstrates that marriage was perhaps first and foremost an economic alliance—until it was a liability.

Getting married was many times easier than getting divorced, making desertion a ready alternative for husbands, but leaving wives with many children and little English in harsh economic straits. Such women seem to have had the choice either of going it alone under the conditions of desertion or, if they could locate their AWOL husbands, securing a costly and difficult legal divorce—and afterwards, if they were "lucky"—another marriage.

Anna (Sleveski) Mazika with her granddaughter Lillian Kavirt, circa 1930.

Lithuanian gender relations of the time handicapped women both in marriage and divorce. Men learned at least broken English in the mines. However, girls and women not allowed to stray beyond the cloistered world of home, church and a domestic position in a private home became fiancées, wives and mothers who did not speak or read much English, and who knew little of the ways of men—or the world.

## Seeking Two Divorces at Once

Bernice (Mazika) Kavirt with her daughter Bernice (Kavirt) Manning's children Alice and Glenn, 1955.

A March 1, 1933 article in the *Illinois State Journal* shows Delores' mother Bernice (Mazika) Kavirt making the case that in 1923, when she was an inexperienced and uneducated 19-year-old Lithuanian girl, William Kavirt tricked her into marrying him after her previous marriage (at age 16 or 17?) ended in desertion. In an unusual twist that likely occasioned newspaper coverage, Bernice was making her case not for just one divorce, but two.

Young Bernice (Kavirt) Manning, daughter of Bernice and Willam Kavirt, on porch of Griffiths Ave. home, 1940s.

After Kavirt deserted her in 1932, perhaps it was necessary, in order to receive public relief and food aid for her children, to be a divorced rather than a twice-deserted woman. AWOL fathers could probably still be considered financially responsible even if they could not be found and contributed no support.

It is also true that shedding herself of all marital relationship would have freed Bernice to marry again—legally, this time. However, she does not appear to have re-married until 1947, well after she had struggled through raising five surviving children alone through the Great Depression. The odds of finding a man who would raise another man's children during such hard times were probably so bad that they made public relief the only solution.

Still, it couldn't have been easy to publicly expose her dual-marriage, dual-divorce predicament by going to court. And it had to be particularly difficult after the brutal death of her mother Anna as a pedestrian hit by a car the same year Kavirt deserted the family in 1932. (All this, after infant son Edward died at two months of age in 1931).

By 1933, Bernice (Bertha) was in court in separate suits. One was for $10,000 in damages for her mother's wrongful death. The other was for dual-divorce, after Bernice claimed she suffered a nervous breakdown in 1932 after encountering her missing husband on the street, only to have him thumb his nose at her demand either to resume his family responsibilities or give her a divorce.

The passage below from the March 1, 1933 *Journal* article hints that, in addition to breaking Bernice's nerves, William may also have forced her hand by threatening to publicly expose the fact of her dual marriages if she sued him for divorce.

"Mrs. Kavirt met Kavirt on the street here after his desertion and informed him that she would file a divorce bill if he did not return to their home and their five children at 1025 N. 14th St. Kavirt ridiculed that plan, and revealed that they had never been legally married because her first husband had never secured a divorce."

## Victim of Marital Manipulation?

Bernice (Mazika) Kavirt was born in Hazelton or Minersville, Penn., in 1901 or 1904, the daughter of Michael and Anna (Sleveski) Mazika, both born in Lithuania. Twice married by age 19, was this barely educated young woman the victim of marriage manipulation, as she pleaded in her divorce suit? Or had she known or guessed when she married for the second time, to William Kavirt, that she was not legally severed from her first husband, Alfred Platukas, despite what she described as Kavirt's assurances to the contrary? (These were given, Bernice testified, after Kavirt made a show of traveling to Pennsylvania for several weeks to ascertain her first husband's whereabouts, then returned to report that Platukas had secured a divorce in Detroit.)

We will never know for sure what young Bernice knew or chose to overlook. Even if she had tried to make legal marriage work in her favor, it had not, instead resulting in two desertions, various costly legal knots to untie, seven live births and five surviving children in just nine years, plus sole financial responsibility for her children at age 29. Husbands Platukas and Kavirt, meanwhile, had been able to enter, then abandon marriage when it became too burdensome for them.

Bernice's daughter Delores was the youngest of the five Kavirt siblings who grew up first on North 14th Street, then in a stone bungalow on Griffiths Avenue near Peoria Road. Two other children, including (the aforementioned Edward and) Alice, who was only four when she died, had both perished by the time their father left. Delores recalled: "After Dad left, Momma had to rely on public relief and cleaning homes. I was still too young to be left at home, so she had to take me wherever she needed to go."

## Saved by Jewish Kindness

"Momma used to tell the story of how, growing up in Pennsylvania, she had also tagged along with her Lithuanian immigrant mother Anna, cleaning the homes of well-to-do members of the Pennsylvania Jewish community. Then, as a single mother of five," Delores recalled, "my mother experienced the same consideration by members of the Springfield Jewish community.

"I can remember walking downtown with Momma to the public relief office and then taking our food stamps to Cohen's and other grocery stores. The purchase of candy with food stamps was forbidden, and my mother abided by that. However, quite often, the storekeepers would hand me a small bag of free candy as I exited.

"At about the same time, the authorities wanted to split up our family because they thought our Momma couldn't adequately care for all of us. But with the help of a local attorney named Templeton, whom I think was Jewish, Momma was able to resist that action and keep us all together with her under one roof. For the help of that attorney and those previously mentioned acts of kindness by Jewish homeowners and storekeepers, I hold those of the Jewish faith in high regard," Delores said.

According to Delores' nephew Glenn Manning, Bernice Kavirt also struck a care-giving deal to keep a roof over her children's heads. It was after husband William left that the family moved from North 14th Street to the aforementioned stone house on Griffiths Avenue. The house was owned by John Yuscius. Elderly and infirm, Yuscius let Bernice and her children live under his roof in exchange for the family's care.

## Grandmother Anna Hit by Car

Maternal grandmother Anna Mazika had moved from Pennsylvania to live with her daughter Bernice, and probably, care for the children while husband William was still with the family. But one Saturday in 1932, according to the *Illinois State Journal*, while Anna was walking home from confession at St. Vincent de Paul Church, she was struck and killed as she was crossing Ninth Street at Enos Avenue. The car was driven by a man from Ft. Wayne, Ind., who was reported in one *Journal* article to have been traveling more than 55 mph.

According to Delores, "Anna's spiritual needs were attended on the spot by Fr. (Stanley) Yunker (St. Vincent's pastor)." The newspaper reported that Bernice (Bertha) sued the driver for $10,000, but I could find no follow-up article giving the result of that suit. According to the *Journal,* a coroner's jury created the opening for a civil suit by rendering an "open verdict," neither blaming nor exonerating the driver.

## Bringing up Baby (Hooch)

During Prohibition, which included the entire term of the Mazika-Kavirt marriage, William Kavirt and a brother who lived nearby bootlegged together from the Kavirt home on North 14th. "They were known for producing some very good rye whiskey," Delores said. "My mother Bernice was tasked with transporting the product of their labors from our house to our uncle's house on North Ninth Street, sometimes using a baby stroller as cover – the 'hooch' hidden under a blanket."

In addition, according to Delores' nephew Glenn, "William and Bernice Kavirt used to keep a rabbit hutch out back. Some whiskey customers would bring over their rabbits for breeding as a cover for picking up whiskey." Delores recalled: "Because of this business relationship between Dad and our uncle, as my siblings and I grew into young adults, we turned to our uncle's family for answers about our father. But they always claimed no knowledge of his whereabouts."

## Horses and Houses

Beautiful Delores Kavirt showing a palomino horse named "Pardner," 1940s.

"As a grade-schooler," Delores recalled, "I fell in love with horses. It helped that there was a sale barn only a couple of blocks from our home on Griffiths Avenue. I didn't care as much about extracurricular school functions and dating as I did about caring for and riding horses. I showed horses occasionally but enjoyed simply riding them more. So when my husband and I built our first home in the country in 1969, I had my own horse for a while, 'Amigo.'"

Around the corner from the Griffiths Avenue home, on Peoria Road, Delores recalls a row of stores that included a Piggly Wiggly grocery. Near neighbors were the Malinski and Stankavich families, including five Stankavich sisters: Nellie, Vickie, Fritzi, Eleanor and Martha—and a brother named Stanley.

Delores married Edward (Eddie) Lomprez in 1948 at St. Patrick's Church. He worked in the construction trades most of his life, eventually retiring from the University of Illinois at Springfield. Together, the couple built three and a half homes, not counting the first place they lived: a remodeled chicken coup in Eddie's grandma's large backyard in Clear Lake Village (called the "Dogpatch.")

Delores Kavirt wedding, with Kavirt siblings and mother Bernice with her third husband, Johnny Terasse, late 1940s.

Delores and Eddie's second house was "garage home" that they built on a lot given by Eddie's dad. After Eddie was drafted into the Korean War and returned, Delores recalled, "We caught a lucky break and were able to construct our first, real home as the result of bad luck suffered by my only brother and favorite sibling, Willie."

## Tragedy Befalls 'Wild' Willie

A St. James Trade School football and basketball star, Willie had survived his own service in World War II and returned to working multiple shifts at Pillsbury Mills. Delores had loaned Willie some money so that he could build himself a home. "For reasons we never knew, the home under construction burned to the ground in the spring of 1954. Willie, 27, was uninsured and lost his desire to rebuild. He insisted I take the title to his lot as repayment for my loan. I resisted that and encouraged Willie to rebuild. However, he refused, and I ended up with a nice lot—and a basement full of debris from the fire, which Eddie and I cleared by hand."

Willie Kavirt, St. James Trade School football player, 1940s.

Delores recalled her only brother's wild side. "He liked to stay out late and gamble. I'd bug him from time to time about marrying and settling down. He always said, 'No, my lifestyle now would just make some woman miserable...I'll wait.' By then, several of my nieces and nephews had been born. Willie referred to them all as 'little corned beef and cabbages.'

"Although he seemed to like the little ones and may have ended up a father someday, tragedy struck early one morning, only a few months after the fire that destroyed Willie's home. He and a friend drove their car into the path of a truck and were pronounced dead at the scene. It was such a horrible accident that it was not even possible to determine who had been driving."

The *Illinois State Journal* reported the accident occurred at Route 4 and old U.S. Route 66, at the northwest corner of the Illinois State Fairgrounds. The trailer-truck dragged the auto containing Willie and his friend 150 feet into a ditch, where the cab of the truck shot up, then crashed down on top of the car. The August 25, 1954 *Journal* article reports, "It required nearly two hours for three wreckers to lift the truck from the car and extricate the bodies." Although the truck driver reported the car ran a stop sign, he was cited for speeding.

## Five Acres Near Rochester

Delores (Kavirt) Lomprez is now the last surviving of her siblings: Lillian (husband Joe Trello), Alice (husband Al McKenzie) and Bernice (husband Albert Manning). Lillian lived on North 22nd Street, worked at Sangamo Electric and retired from the cafeteria at St. Aloysius School. She had one child, Phillip. Alice worked at The Springfield Shoe Factory and had one child, Allen Wayne. Bernice worked at Memorial Medical Center and had four children: Alice, Glenn, Elaine and Bryan. Delores worked at Sangamo Electric and retired from the cafeteria at Rochester Public Schools.

"Up until the time my husband died, we enjoyed a large vegetable garden, raising chickens and maintaining five acres at our second rural home. (Nephew Glenn Manning says Delores's rural spread also included a woodworking shop, grape arbor and working windmill.) My husband and I never had children, but we did have the pleasure of many visits, including being summer hosts for our nieces and nephews, mostly on the Lithuanian side of the family.

"Momma (Bernice Mazika Kavirt) lost her eyesight due to diabetes, so later on in life she came to live with my husband and me. She had her own room in our ranch-style house and got along quite well by feel. In our second careers, my husband and I worked opposite shifts, which allowed one of us to be at home with Momma most of the time."

As for the Lithuanian-American twice-deserted wife and mother who struggled to take care of her children alone and prevented them from being adopted out during the Great Depression, Delores says, "To this day, I wear a necklace with a pewter angel to remind me of my dear Momma. She is one of my angels."

*Photos courtesy of Glenn Manning and Elaine (Manning) Kuhn.*

# Chapter 11
# The Mining Life:
# Sporadic Work, Sporadic Wages

*To read more about the actual work of coal-mining and conditions in the mines during the years at the turn of the twentieth century when Sangamon County led the state in coal production, please visit sangamoncountyhistory.org*

*The following excerpt on the sporadic nature of coal mining here and how that affected miners and their families is from the Sangamon County Historical Society's Web page, entitled, "Coal Mining: Boom to Bust:"*

Irregular work in the second decade of the 20th Century meant that miners earned wages only sporadically. In 1914 a research team from the Russell Sage Foundation commissioned to study industrial conditions in the Capital City noted that "irregularity of employment is greater among coal miners in Springfield than in any other important occupation group." The coming of spring each year dropped the demand for coal for home heating to a fraction of its winter-time levels; so severe were these warm-weather slowdowns that many mines simply closed down for the summers.

The industry also was plagued by the existence of many more mines than were necessary to meet demand; the resulting overproduction meant that few mines worked all the time. Finally, just prior to the spring expiration of the biennial wage pacts between the miners and the coal operators, major coal consumers stockpiled coal in anticipation of protracted contract disputes. Accordingly, demand for coal slumped badly after the signing of each new contract as large customers drew upon these fuel reserves to meet their needs.

These factors, aggravated by occasional strikes and shorter layoffs scattered throughout the rest of the year, kept most miners idle for four out of every 10 working days. In the year ending June 10, 1913, Sangamon County mines worked an average of only 181 days out of a possible 300 working days.

## Only Two Days of Work a Week

The economic effects of irregular work on the miners and their families were devastating. The Sage Foundation survey team reported:

Miner after miner told the same story of idle days and uncertain work. A few instances will illustrate. An "entry" man who could make $15 to $20 a week counted on work only half the time. A German miner who could make up to $8 a day usually received only $24 to $30 for two weeks' work. The wife of a

Lithuanian complained that her husband's work was always irregular — only one or two days of work a week. If he could have only three full days of work at $5 a day regularly, she would be perfectly content. An experienced miner forty-four years of age could make $7 a day. Even with three days of work a week his wife declared she could save. She was seen on May 29, and he had had no work since April 1 and there was no prospect of any until September...

A Sangamon County miner in 1914 was paid from 57 cents to $1.27 a ton for coal, depending on the nature of the seam being worked. At these rates, a miner working steadily could bring in $5 a day, and in some cases as much as $7 or $8; his potential yearly income thus would amount to $2,000. In fact, many of Sangamon County's 3,500 miners, their potential incomes slashed by more than a third by forced idleness, earned less than $600 a year.

## Never Out of Debt

"I put in 27 years in the underground coal mines," one miner recalls, "(and) I was never out of debt in those years." Many local miners were forced to seek work elsewhere when the mines were shut down. If they did not, they had to buy their groceries on credit (or "on the book") and let rent and other bills pile up and hope that the pits would reopen before their creditors' patience ran out.

(Chronic underemployment in the mines and the need to make ends meet may have been the genesis of the "corner grocery" operated by so many mining families. Operating a grocery for one's own and surrounding families would have averted the need to be "on the book" to another grocer. Gardening to raise one's own food, and sharing with neighbors, were also common across Springfield at this time. Residential lots resembled small farms, including chickens coops and rabbit hutches.

For those skilled at making alcoholic beverages and willing to break the law, Prohibition provided a supplemental source of income throughout the 1920s, just as numerous mine closures and mass layoffs began to hit local miners hard.)

## 'Wrinkled up in the Gut'

Art Gramlich, another veteran miner (shot nine times, but never fatally, during the 1932-36 "Mine Wars,") remembered what layoffs and strikes meant:

"When (the miners) came out on a strike, when the contract expired, you would get yourself ready for a hell of a long goddam time, because you could strike all summer, because (the operators) didn't need the coal anyhow — at least most of them didn't. They would just wait until November. By that time you was pretty well wrinkled up in the gut. You'd pretty near sign for anything, because the grocery man was hollering and the rent man wanted you to pay some rent because you been there six months and hadn't paid a dime."

Against such forces, the lone miner had no defense. Against these enemies he needed the union. The battle to form unions against the mine owners' opposition, and later factional battles within the union movement itself, formed a violent chapter in central Illinois history. Sangamon County was the scene of some of the worst of the violence during the Illinois "Mine Wars."

*Post-script: Although 1932-36 is the period referred to as the "Mine Wars" in this book, the Sangamon County Historical Society refers to a more extended period starting in the 1920s, when the major forces driving violent conflict began.*

Miners inside the Panther Creek Mine, 11th and Ridgely, 1958. *Courtesy of Gary Lazar.*

Miners collapsing tunnels inside the Panther Creek Mine, 11th and Ridgely, 1958. *Courtesy of Gary Lazar.*

# Chapter 12
# Honoring Central Illinois Mine Casualties

Coal mining was extremely hazardous work during the early years of the twentieth century, when labor was plentiful and cheap, and workplace protections few. After "shot-firers" worked at night to blast the coal seams apart (or take down the walls of coal), men on the day shift loaded "trips" of cars full of coal. "Clod men" cleaned the rooms and passageways of fallen slate. Timbermen timbered ceilings to create supposedly stable passageways and work "rooms," but as you'll see from the casualties below, slate (roof) falls were extremely common causes of death and injury.

In the early days, mules were used to haul trips of cars to the surface. Men got to go home after their shifts. Mules spent their entire lives in cramped and dark underground stables, frequently perishing in fires. Unfortunately, men and mules were generally alike in the eyes of the mine owners and bosses, except, as one mine boss was famously quoted as saying, "I have to pay to replace a mule." (From Carl Oblinger's book, *Divided Kingdom: Work, Community, and the Mining Wars in the Central Illinois Coal Fields During the Great Depression*.)

## Blaming the Victim

In fact, human casualties were so common that some historical records log only accidents in which two or more miners died. Public blame usually fell on victims, despite routinely dangerous working conditions that would never pass muster today (mainly improperly buttressed walls and ceilings, explosive coal dust and a lethal cocktail of gases known as "afterdamp.") Oblinger's book provides good detail of what could go wrong underground, as well as management—and sometimes, even union—practices that compromised safety.

The local Lithuanian-American casualties listed alphabetically below, almost all of them immigrants, form part of a much larger number of Lithuanian miners who were crippled or maimed in mine accidents or lost years of health and life due to the complications of black lung. (I personally remember the 1990s Springfield funeral of Lithuanian-born miner Tadas Rizutis, a friend of my father's, who was crippled in a coal mine accident in the 1960s.)

Most of the deaths recorded below are from Sangamon County, although a few are from Christian and Macoupin counties, and several from the catastrophic Centralia Mine Disaster. We have this listing thanks to the meticulous research of newspaper articles and genealogy websites by retired Springfield police officer **Tom Mann.** Among the sources he combed were archives of the *Illinois State Journal-Register* and the Sangamon County Coal Mine Fatalities web pages from "Wayne's World of History and Genealogy." When in doubt, the ethnicity of the deceased miner was verified by newspaper or U.S. Census records. (Unfortunately, birth towns and cities were almost never recorded by either of these sources.) Please see *http://hinton-gen.com/coal/sangamonfatal.html*

## Lithuanian-American Mining Deaths

**John Adamitis**, age 32, 16th Street and Sangamon Avenue, married with four children. Reportedly stuck his pick into a keg of powder to open it to prepare a "shot" to blast coal from the wall of his "room." The powder was ignited and exploded. He died about a week later from his burns. Illinois Midland Coal Co., Springfield, Sept. 28, 1907.

**John Adamates (Jonas Adomaitis)**, 31, of Springfield or Sherman (buried in Gillespie). A trip rider, he was killed when he fell in front of a trip of cars and was run over. Peabody Coal Co. No. 6, Sherman, Nov. 19, 1920.

**Anthony J. Augustine (Antanas Augustitis)**, age 66, 2332 Peoria Rd., survived by wife Marcella, daughter Bernice Povse, brother Frank and sister Antoinette Rafalowece. Died two days after being crushed by a slate (roof) fall—and two days before his 67th birthday. Peabody Coal Co. No. 59, Springfield, Aug. 15, 1945.

**Joe Bendick**, age 24, single, of Divernon. A laborer employed to clean away slate taken down by the day shift, he was killed at 1 a.m. by falling slate about three feet thick, 10 feet long and three feet wide. Madison Coal Corp.'s No. 6 mine, Divernon, March 5, 1914.

**Joseph Benneky (Juozas Benikas)**, 36, of 1023 N. 15th St., member of the St. Vincent's Society and UMWA No. 317, leaving a wife. Buried under 16 tons of slate that fell on him when he was walking along the main entryway to his "room." Peabody Coal Co. No. 8, Tovey, Sept. 3, 1907.

**Anton Brazinsky (Antanas Brazinskas?)**, age unknown, presumed of Springfield. Died of pulmonary embolism in St. John's Hospital after surgery to treat injuries sustained in a roof cave-in five days earlier. Sangamon Coal Company No. 2, March 5, 1926.

**John Budwites (Jonas Budwitis)**, age 35, 1127 Percy Ave., survived by his wife and three sons. Died from the explosion of a "windy shot" while working as a substitute shot-firer 2.5 miles from the mine pit. Springfield Cooperative Coal Co. mine, Springfield, Jan. 10, 1923.

**Frank Embrolitus (Aubrutis)**, age 50, single, of Gillespie, World War I veteran, member of the Progressive Miners of America (PMA). Survived by his aged mother Eva, brothers Peter and Tony, sisters Marcella of Lithuania, Mrs. Tony Krakakusky, and Mrs. John Moleski, with whom Frank lived. Buried under a rock fall at the entrance of the mine. Liberty Mine, Macoupin County, Nov. 25, 1941.

**Peter Gerchey**, age 55, single, of Auburn. Killed instantly by a crushing rock (roof) fall. Springfield District Coal Mining Co.'s No. 54 mine, Auburn, Sept. 15, 1919.

**John Gudesky or Guduskus (Jonas Gudauskas)**, 32, single, of Kincaid. Crushed by a slate fall, Peabody Coal Co. No. 7 mine, Kincaid, June 12, 1919.

**Kazimier (Kazimieras) Gedudis**, 40, 1418 S. Pasfield St., with a wife and three children. A naturalized citizen, and "a man of perfect physical mold, sinewy, big-boned and of a strength almost phenomenal...worked with an industry that was most admirable." While he was working alone in his room, a slate (roof) fall crashed down. "The first fall battered in the back of his head, and the following avalanche of rock struck him on the left breast as he lay prostrated. It broke the ribs of the left side and crushed through to his heart." – "Death in the Shaft: Giant in Build Meets Tragic End Alone," *Illinois State Register*. Springfield Coal Mining Co.'s Black Diamond Mine, Aug. 16 1904.

**Andrew Janesky**, 17, of Auburn, single. Killed by a rock fall, Chicago-Virden Coal Co. No. 2 mine, Auburn, Jan. 21, 1902.

**Stanley (Yasukinas) Jasukenas**, age 49, single, Auburn. Crushed in a rock fall, Peabody Coal Co.'s No. 8 mine, Tovey, Aug. 18, 1944.

**Joseph Kasulis (Juozas Kisielius?)**, 35, 1629 E. Washington St., with a wife three children, member of St. Joseph's Lithuanian Society and the UMWA. A shot-firer, he was killed in the explosion of a black powder keg near him in his room. Alternate explanations are that he pinched off an end of fuse, tossed it away, and it fell through a hole in the top of the keg—or that he bent over to examine a faulty fuse, and a spark from his oil headlamp fell into an open powder keg. Sangamon Coal Co. No. 2, Riverton, Dec. 10, 1907.

**Tony Malkowski**, age unknown, of Auburn, leaving a wife. Killed by a cave-in estimated at 50 tons of slate when a trip of empty coal cars jumped the tracks, and was driven forward by the motor as the cars knocked out supporting roof timbers. The *State Journal-Register* article described the two Lithuanian victims as "shapeless masses," except for their faces. Solomon Mine, Feb. 26, 1916.

**Alexander Malisky**, age unknown, 1716 E. Adams St., miner's asthma by ruling of a coroner's jury. March 5, 1915.

**Frank Markunas**, 54, of Springfield, with a wife and three adult children. Killed by a rock fall, Peerless Coal Co. mine, Oct. 13, 1920.

**Frank Meszeika (Meszeikis)**, age unknown, 1815 N. Ninth St., leaving a wife, Magdelena, two adult daughters, two adult stepsons, and seven grandchildren. A resident of Springfield for 45 years and member of the Progressive Miners of America Local 63. Crushed by a roof fall, Panther Creek No. 5, Dec. 23, 1947.

**William Mickalites (Mykolaitis)**, 57, of Benld, survived by a wife, a son, a daughter, step-son and step-daughter. Born in Jurbarkus, Lithuania. Died in an accident at the Superior Coal Co. No. 1 at Eagerville in Macoupin County Nov. 12, 1943.

**William Muckakitas**, age unknown, Auburn, unmarried mine carpenter. Crushed by a ceiling cave-in estimated at 50 tons when a trip of empty coal cars jumped the tracks, and was driven forward by the motor as the cars knocked out supporting roof timbers. The *State Journal-Register* article described the two Lithuanian victims as "shapeless masses," except for their faces. Solomon Mine, Feb. 26, 1916.

**John Pauliski**, about 60, of Moweaqua, widower with many grown children. Died in a roof fall in the Moweaqua coal mine July 8, 1900.

**Stanley Payauys (Pajaujis)**, 57, of 1904 Peoria Rd., UMWA and Lithuanian Alliance of America member, married with a grown son, two daughters and one grand-daughter. Died in a roof fall while loading cars in a room three miles northeast of the shaft entrance. Peerless Mine No. 59, three miles east of Springfield on Sangamon Avenue, April 19, 1939.

**Charles Pittcavich (also Pattecabbage)**, 55, of Auburn, married with five children. Killed in a roof fall in Springfield District Coal Co. No. 4 two miles south of Auburn, Dec. 8, 1916.

**Anton Skrobul (Antanas Skrabulis)**, 53, of Beckemeyer, survived by a wife and eight children. Killed with 110 other miners in the infamous Centralia Mine Disaster, when a blown-out "shot" ignited a profusion of dry coal dust in Centralia Coal Co. No. 5, March 25, 1947. At the time of the explosion most of the 142 men in the mine were at the entryways of their "man trips," waiting for the shot firers to complete their work knocking down the coal. Sixty-five miners were killed by the blast and burns, and 45 by afterdamp (lethal gases). There were Congressional investigations, and Woody Guthrie later memorialized the notes miners left for their families in a song called, "Dying Miner."

From the list of the dead, I surmise that victims **Frank Paulauskis, Anthony and Stanley Tickus, and Joe Zinkus** were also Lithuanian-American. For more information, please see *http://www.chs68.com/minedisaster/* and *http://kbbgenblog.blogspot.com*

**William Strunk**, age unknown, of Springfield, widower with a step-daughter, UMWA member. Died in a roof fall, Springfield Coal Co. mine, Taylorville, Oct. 30, 1914.

**Tony Tutorites (Totoraitis?)**, 48, Wilsonville, Macoupin County. Killed in a slate (roof) fall, Superior Coal Co. No. 4, Litchfield, Sept. 12, 1930.

**Paul Widowski**, 34, of Divernon, unmarried, survived by two sisters, a veteran of World War I and a member of the American Legion and UMWA. Killed while investigating why a "shot" hadn't fired, when it suddenly exploded. Madison Coal Corp. No. 6, Divernon, Oct. 22, 1923. (As a veteran's benefit, the U.S. government furnished a simple headstone free of charge.)

**John Wisnoski**, 46, of 1430 E. Carpenter St., survived by a wife, a son, two daughters, one brother, four sisters, and parents Mr. and Mrs. Peter Wisnosky. His brother Clements, with whom he was working in the same "room," suffered a fractured leg, and John died on route to the hospital after being crushed in a roof fall in Sangamon Coal Co.'s No. 2 mine at 2300 E. Phillips St., Nov. 26, 1928.

**Joe Yanushitis (Janusitis)**, 22, of Taylorville, survived by a wife and one child. Had fired a shot on the left side of his room and was buried by a sudden avalanche of coal while loading his car. Christian County Mine No. 58, Dec. 15, 1904.

**Ike Yaris (Jaris?)**, 54, of 1928 N. 14th St., immigrated in 1902, survived by a wife and three sons. Died of an apparent heart attack while drilling and loading coal into a car in Sangamon Coal Co. No. 2, Springfield, Nov. 23, 1935. As he fell, his carbide headlamp ignited his clothing and the smoke attracted help.

**Stanley Yasukinas (Jasukinas)**, 55, Auburn, survived by a nephew. Member of the Lithuanian Alliance of America #27. Killed in an undescribed mine accident in Tovey, August 19, 1944.

**Michael Zilkus**, 35, of Pawnee, survived by a wife and two small children. Killed by a coal cutting machine, Peabody No. 7, Kincaid, March 9, 1914.

**Peter Zubles**, 42, single, boarded with Joe McKinnis of Bulpitt. Fell between the cars of a "trip" and was run over, Peabody No. 8, Tovey, July 8, 1925.

**John Zwingles (Zvingilas?)**, 43, 218 W. Scarritt St., survived by a wife. Crushed after the loaded coal car he was pushing along a shaft alley was hit by another car that had become detached from another "trip" and careened down a slope. Panther Creek Coal Co. No. 1, Auburn, March 16, 1920.

# Chapter 13
# The Mine Wars

*From 1932 to 1936, Central Illinois was ground zero for one of the most important labor conflicts of the Great Depression. Three eloquent sources on the Central Illinois "Mine Wars" and the Progressive Miners of America (PMA), which included large numbers of immigrant Italian, Lithuanian, Hungarian, Polish, Slovenian, and Slovak miners and their descendants, are minewar. org, sangamoncountyhistory.org, and hinton-gen.com.*

Immigrant miners in Illinois were soft-coal, deep-shaft miners who cut and loaded their daily quotas (as much as five tons) by hand. By the late 1890s, the Central Illinois coal mines had been organized by the United Mine Workers of America. District 12 of the UMWA (state of Illinois) had a strong democratic rank-and-file tradition, according to Carl Oblinger's book, *Divided Kingdom: Work, Community, and the Mining Wars in the Central Illinois Coal Fields During the Great Depression.* Local wildcat strikes protesting harsh working conditions, operator shut-downs that threw miners out of work, and increasing mechaniza-

Oblinger book.

tion that cost miners' jobs, were supported by the UMWA leadership prior to World War I.

(Early twentieth-century mine work in Central Illinois was seasonal, at best, due to slowdowns or strikes almost every April as annual contracts expired, and mines regularly being closed for the summer due to a lack of demand for coal. Many Lithuanian miners excavated basements by shovel or hand-scythed grass in local cemeteries during the summer, in addition to tending gardens and livestock to keep their families fed.)

## UMWA in Collusion with Operators?

During the 1920s, under the leadership of John L. Lewis of Springfield, according to Oblinger's book, the UMWA began collaborating with local coal companies–against Illinois locals and their rank-and-file tradition–in order to strengthen and centralize the UMWA's authority. This included undermining job-sharing and other "time-honored" labor-friendly contract provisions, and even expelling 24 locals whose membership challenged centralized UMWA authority.

The struggle came to a head 1932-36, when the UMWA attempted to force upon Central Illinois miners already on strike an already rejected contract that cut wages by 20 percent and ignored their concerns about mechanization and resulting mass layoffs during the deepest trough of the Great Depression. In accordance with their unionist and immigrant communal traditions, Oblinger writes that most of the local miners wanted to negotiate a slower pace of mechanization, along with job-sharing, so that no miner worked overtime while another miner was unemployed. Mutual aid in the tight-knit ethnic mining communities could compensate for the sporadic unemployment that was typical of the industry—and a certain pace of job loss—but not the draconian wage and job cuts planned by the industry and the UMWA.

According to Oblinger's book, Lewis and the UMWA also joined with operators to cut wages and jobs and bring in mechanical cutters, loaders and conveyor belts to "save" the Illinois coal industry, which by 1930 was in crisis because coal was more expensive to mine here than in other parts of the country. The result was a confrontation that put Central Illinois at the center of one of the most important—and violent—struggles for U.S. labor rights in the 1930s.

## Rift Starts in Christian County's Midland Tract

Most of the unprecedented violence of the 1932-36 "Mine Wars" occurred south of Springfield in the so-called Midland Tract of Christian County from Taylorville west to Kincaid and Pawnee. While Lithuanians nearly equaled Italians in the mines of Sangamon County, in Christian County they had a significant presence only in Taylorville (and in Bulpitt, where they were as much as 90 percent of the population), according to Oblinger's book. Italians were the dominant immigrant group through the rest of the Tract, where Peabody had sunk several new coal mines—even building the company town of Kincaid—and planned to invest heavily in mechanizing its new mines.

In the spring of 1932, when operators wouldn't negotiate on major wage and workforce cuts, miners in the Tract saw no alternative but to reject the proposed contract and strike to save their jobs, families and communities. Instead of trying to negotiate better contract terms for its local members, the UMWA took the operators' side and issued an emergency order for the strikers to return to work under the discredited contract. When strikers organized mass protests and pickets, the UMWA brought in members from other areas to break the strike. That's when the Progressive Miners of America (PMA) formed to pursue a life-and-death struggle against both the operators and what was once their own union.

Founding convention, Progressive Miners of America, Gillespie, Ill., 1932.
*Courtesy of John Fritsche via minewars.org and Wayne's World of History
& Genealogy.*

Hoping to avoid violence and prevail by their numbers and organization, in the summer of 1932, the PMA organized a peaceful mass march to Mulkeytown, Ill. After the unarmed, peaceful marchers were brutally attacked, the writing was on the wall. For details of just how bad the violence got, including in Springfield, please see *http://sangamoncountyhistory.org/wp/?p=3316*

Following is an excerpt:

*Art Gramlich (1904-73), a PMA miner who was shot nine times in various confrontations with union opponents, later described the environment during the worst of the intramural violence. The following is from a 1972 oral history interview.*

*"We had quite a few scrimmages, no doubt about it. There was a lot of street fights and gun fights. Several times I came out on top, more than I didn't (laughter) but I'm still here.*

*We tackled them on the streets or around taverns at night. At out-of-the-way taverns, you know, you would walk in where they was at and right away you could smell them and you let them know that they had a certain odor about them and, goddamn, the hell would start. Sometimes you got the s— knocked out of you and sometimes you didn't (laughter).*

*It was common—well you thought half of the goddamn miners in Springfield were Jesse James or cowboys, they all packed their goddamn gun in their belt. The police wouldn't do anything too much to you.*

*It was to survive, that's all. It was survival of the fittest because it was pro and con, you see. I don't want to sit here and brag, but I survived nine bullets of which I still carry two. So you can see how easy it would be for a guy to get shot because there's plenty more around here just like I am and there's plenty more around here just deader than hell, too. They just didn't have a chance."*

"In two and a half years when the violence was at a peak, an estimated 40 men died as miners of both factions were beaten, shot at, and bombed in the streets, alleys, and coal mines of central Illinois," James Krohe Jr. reported in his *Midnight at Noon* (Sangamon County Historical Society, 1975). "The number of wounded ran into the hundreds."

## Springfield and Lithuanian Victims

Shooting victim Edris Mabie (inset) and the scene at Sixth and Washington streets following the fatal confrontation on Easter Sunday 1935. *Sangamon County Historical Society and State Journal-Register.*

One of the most famous incidents in the "Mine Wars," the Easter Sunday riot of 1935, in which PMA member Edris Mabie was killed, occurred at Sixth and Washington streets in Springfield. (Only this year I realized that my great aunt, Mary Yamont, who sponsored my father's immigration from Lithuania after World War II, is buried not more than 50 feet from this most famous of the Progressive martyrs in Oak Ridge Cemetery. Since both of *Teta's* sons were coal miners, I have to believe this is not mere accident, and that my relative's gravesites were probably bought in a group purchase through the PMA. My Hungarian coal-mining maternal grandfather Joseph Kohlrus and his wife Theresa are buried 20 feet from Art Gramlich in Springfield's Calvary Cemetery.)

Thomas Urban, 36, a Lithuanian-born timberman who lived in Divernon at the home of Tony and Barbara Budreski, was shot and killed at the Peerless Mine on Sangamon Avenue in 1933. That same year, according to newspaper reports, Mrs. Andrew Blazis, wife of a Progressive miner in Springfield, was injured by a bomb placed in the corner grocery in front of the Blazis apartment at 431 E. Iles Ave. There were also bombings or bomb materials found at the Cornell Street railroad crossing and the Hazel Dell railroad underpass in Springfield.

## Organizing Immigrants, Women

Through its stated opposition to the anti-foreign sentiment that had character-
ized the United Mine Workers, the PMA enlisted many local second-generation
immigrant miners who had not previously belonged to the UMWA. According
to Oblinger's book, thousands of women also participated in the new union's
Auxiliary and encouraged their husbands to break with the UMWA, join the
PMA and organize strikes and picket lines. Women collected and distributed
food and other aid, and participated on the picket lines in the most dangerous
direct confrontations with replacement workers (called scabs), armed company
enforcers, and the state militia. Ten thousand white-hatted women from the
PMA Auxiliary marched on the State Capitol in Springfield in 1933 to protest
violence against strikers and violations of their civil rights by hired thugs and
local law enforcement. See *http://www.minewar.org/?p=1273*

## Early PMA Successes Undone by Brute Force

Early in "Mine Wars," 20,000 PMA strikers succeeded in closing all mines
in Randolph, St. Clair, Christian, Madison, Washington, Sangamon and Ful-
ton Counties, and in re-opening some smaller mines under their own contract. However, according to pages 24-25 of Oblinger's book, "Peabody Coal,
the largest and most advanced of the coal companies in Illinois, opposed
re-opening under the PMA contract, (reopened their mines under the UMWA
contract) and made extraordinary efforts to defeat the new union and the
striking miners...They hired large numbers of strikebreakers from southern
Illinois; imported gun-toting 'enforcers' from the same southern Illinois coal
fields; and organized an extensive campaign of sabotage aimed at (framing
and thereby) discrediting the striking miners." This sabotage largely took the
shape of bombings, especially a concerted campaign of bombings against the
Illinois Central Railroad, for which PMA strikers were blamed by law enforcement and the public.

See this link for the names and timeline of the killings of 22 PMA miners/fam-
ily members *http://www.minewar.org/?page_id=67* (There is one victim from
Springfield on this list: Fred Gramlich, Sr., a tavern owner killed on May 23,
1936, perhaps mistaken for his son, Art.) Mass arrests and beatings of PMA
strikers and picketers were also common. However, as Art Gramlich's oral
history demonstrates, once UMWA, operator, and government forces combined to attack picket lines and break their strike, PMA miners also engaged
in shoot-outs and fist-fights with the other side. This included ambushes and
sniper fire.

Peabody also used its production powers to break the PMA's strike. The company concentrated production at its more efficient, more mechanized mines in Christian County while closing or interrupting operations at older/smaller mines. This created irregular employment at Peabody's Springfield mines, where coincidentally, many Lithuanian-Americans worked. At the same time, Peabody channeled full employment to its mines in the Midland Tract largely worked by replacement miners the UMWA had sent in from Southern Illinois.

Illinois State Militia at Peabody #7, Kincaid, Ill., 1932. Law enforcement and the powers of government were overwhelmingly arrayed against the PMA. *minewars.org.*

Facing a total siege in which state and local authorities sided with the United Mine Workers and mine operators, the PMA strikers had no choice but to begin trickling back to the UMWA and the mines they had struck as initially successful communal relief efforts like PMA commissaries flagged over time and eventually ended. Those who trickled back sooner were more likely not to permanently lose their positions to replacement workers. However, many strikers were shut out of their jobs permanently.

## Convicted in Federal Mass Trial

On page 35, Oblinger writes: "The non-competitive nature of the PMA mines and the advantage mechanization gave to Peabody Coal were decisive factors in the demise of the PMA and the capitulation of the striking miners. But the most chilling factor was the 1936 indictment of 41 PMA strikers and strike leaders for bombing the Chicago and Illinois Midland Railroad tracks near Taylorville." According to MineWars.org, "41 federal indictments were issued in connection with 23 railroad bombings, six attempted bombings, and one railroad bridge burning that occurred between Dec. 17, 1932 and August 8, 1935. This was the first time in U.S. history that indictments were returned on the federal anti-racketeering act against a labor union."

Thirty-six of the accused PMA miners were convicted of interfering with interstate commerce and obstructing the mails in a federal district court jury trial in Springfield in 1937 and ultimately received sentences of two years and fines of $10,000 each. One of the convicted was 27-year-old Lithuanian-American Anthony Chunes. Another was a relative of PMA martyr Fred Gramlich, Sr. (According to newspaper reports, Lithuanian-American UMWA member Fred Markunas was famously shot and killed in Taylorville by Springfield District PMA board member Ray Tombazzi in 1934, three years before Tombazzi was convicted in the mass trial for railroad sabotage.)

The Mother Jones monument at Mt. Olive, Ill., where many PMA victims of the 1932-36 "Mine Wars" and the 1898 Virden Mine Massacre are buried. Labor organizer Mother Jones died in 1930, just before the outbreak of the famous conflict between the UMWA and Peabody Coal vs. the PMA. *Courtesy of Joe Williams.*

Newspaper reports at the time said the evidence in the mass trial was "circumstantial." But a non-immigrant, non-mining jury voted to convict. Most of the men appealed, but ended up serving out their two-year sentences in Joliet and Leavenworth prisons. In 1942, President Franklin Roosevelt commuted the $10,000 fines for each convicted miner by Executive Order. However, Oblinger's book concludes that the mass trial, "many...believed, broke the spirit of the strikers and strengthened the hand of the UMWA. After that episode, peace existed in the Christian County coal fields for the first time since 1932."

*See this post about the responsibility of Peabody for inciting violence when the Progressives began as a peaceful movement–and the responsibility of Peabody to pay reparations today: http://www.minewar.org/?p=1428*

# Chapter 14
# The Baby in the Cigar Box

While chronicling coal-mining immigrants to Springfield in the early 1900s, how could I overlook the Lithuanian immigrant women they married, whose lives were equally, if not more difficult? In November 2013, I heard the remarkable story of Lithuanian immigrant and super-mom Nancy (Anastazija Benikas) Pazemetsky, who did the impossible: keep alive, at home, in 1927, a premature twin baby girl who weighed only 1.5 pounds at birth. That baby, the late Ann (Pazemetsky) Traeger, not only survived infancy, but lived to be more than 87 years old.

Ann told me that when her mother first arrived as an unmarried young woman, she worked at the downtown Leland Hotel, where she received room and board and $8 a month for labor that included hotel laundry and scrubbing the sidewalk outside the hotel on her hands and knees.

Nancy (Benikas) and Adam Pazemetsky with baby Helen. Circa 1920.

Once a woman was fortunate enough to marry, it was her job to keep the home and garden and children, often with little money and a husband who was idled by the mines a good part of year. Many wives also had to board single male miners and clean homes to supplement the family's income. Some had to compete with the corner tavern for their husband's wages. And almost all, it seems, faced the heartbreaking loss of newborns, infants, or children.

## Loss of Infants

According to Ann, by the time she was born, mother Nancy had already lost an infant son. Then, when Nancy went into labor two months prematurely with fraternal twins, her boy-twin was killed by a puncture wound to his skull during an attempt at forceps delivery. When girl-twin Ann was born, the doctor, possibly to minimize his heartbreaking error, predicted that she, too, would soon die. Nancy reportedly replied in broken English, but with great anguish and determination, "No, this baby is going to live!"

Baby Ann was placed in a cloth-lined wooden cigar box warmed day and night with hot water bottles. Some sources in the community report that the box was kept in a warm oven, but Ann mentioned only bottles to me. She said she was so small that she might have been fed with a dropper and diapered with handkerchiefs. But to mother Nancy's everlasting credit, baby Ann disproved the doctor's prediction, though a friend reported she did struggle with life-long respiratory problems.

Tall and stately Ann went on to graduate from Fleishman's High School, marry Al Traeger, a federal highway engineer, work at Pillsbury Mills for many years--and sing in the renowned choir at St. Vincent de Paul (Lithuanian) Catholic Church. Ann was a devoted former St. Vincent's parishioner who served the church in many roles, and was a founder in 1988 of our local Lithuanian-American Club.

Adam Pazemetsky and Nancy Benikas wedding, circa 1915.

Nancy Benikas's father, mother, and brother Juozas in Lithuania. Undated.

Ann always minimized her own story to focus on her immigrant mother Nancy's, particularly how hard Nancy worked all her life. She also often thought about the courage it took for her mother to sail alone to America when she was just 18. Nancy's Lithuanian family had intended to send one of their daughters to live near Ann Mazrim, a maternal aunt in Springfield. However, Nancy was chosen after her sister became ill at the last moment. Then the first ship she was to take sank in the harbor before the passengers were supposed to board. Fate smiled on Nancy, though, when she was the only passenger not to get seasick during her subsequent transatlantic voyage.

Adam Pazemetsky's mother (left, seated) and sister (standing) with unknown female, in Lithuania. Undated.

After arriving in Springfield, Nancy married Panevezys, Lithuania-born coal miner Adam Pazemetsky (Adomas

Pazimtsius or Pazimskas) 1884-1946. The couple struggled for years to make the family's living, particularly when the mines closed for the summer. Adam dug basements for $1 a day and scythed cemetery grass. Nancy cleaned homes for $1 a day. Later, possibly as a result of the "Mine Wars," Adam worked at Pillsbury Mills. According to daughter Ann, he couldn't leave mining soon enough, and often went outside in the evenings to cry in secret, where his daughters would not see him, over the bitterness of his fate.

## Should Have Been Priest, Musician

Ann's uncle, Adam's brother, was able to express his religious devotion in the new Republic of Lithuania (1918-1940) by becoming a priest, which is probably the course Adam would have liked to take, had he the opportunity. This is my guess due to the devotion Adam showed by always carrying a pocket-size Lithuanian-language prayer book printed in 1863, even into the darkest corners of the mines.

Adam's brother Siminojas, who went on to become a priest. The family's home near Panevezys, Lithuania. Undated.

Ann also remembered that even though the family lived at 17th and East Adams streets, almost two miles from St. Vincent's, her father always insisted that his daughters walk to and from church every Sunday. That may not sound so tough, except when you consider that on Christmas and Easter, when the High Mass was at 5 a.m., this meant the children being up and out of the house around 4:30 in the morning.

Adam Pazemetsky's musical talents with the clarinet and the concertina, which he frequently played as part of a trio at Lithuanian weddings, suggest another reason for the deep spiritual distress he suffered as a coal miner. What if he were meant to be a musician? For an immigrant struggling to survive in those days, real avocation and natural talent, unfortunately, did not matter.

Ann reported that her father often played a special wedding song he had composed, himself, as newlyweds would arrive at the bride's home for their reception and a sweet, hot swig of whiskey-based *krupnikas* or *viritos*. This photo of the musical trio makes me think they were likely the same three who played at the September 1927 "Three-Day Lithuanian Wedding," of Eva Kasawich and Victor Alane, also in this book.

Left photo: Adam Pazemetsky with clarinet, Mr. Karalitis with fiddle, and Mr. Petrovitch (seated) with concertina, 1920s. Right photo: Pazemetsky with concertina, 1930s.

I came into contact with Ann through many Lithuanian-American events, but especially when I began researching material for my blog. Through scrapbooks collecting obituaries and articles of note about scores of local Lithuanian-Americans over many decades, she served as the community's historian and laid the groundwork for my blog and book.

As for brave mother Nancy, who saved the life of her 1.5 pound infant girl-twin after her boy-twin was killed at birth, she was cared for in her old age in the home of that devoted daughter, forever known as the "baby in the cigar box."

L to r:
Nancy Pazemetsky, friend Bernice Kurila, Ann (Pazemetsky) Traeger, circa 1980.

*Dedicated to the memory of Ann (Pazemetsky) Traeger (1927-2015), a beautiful lady, a beautiful spirit, and my help and friend.*

# Chapter 15
# A Miner with a Heart of Song, the Family that He Left Behind

The Leonard Naumovich (Lith. Naumovicius?) family is one of the largest Lithuanian-American families in Springfield, thanks to Len and wife Jean's 10 children and their children. Like many great families, it grew from modest roots and weathered real adversity. Len and brother Joe's mother Josephine was the daughter of Lithuanian immigrant coal miner Benedict Deresker. Josephine Deresker married twice, and lost two successive Lithuanian immigrant husbands to the mines, including Len and Joe's father Leonard Naumovich, Sr.

Len, Sr., died in 1934 when his two boys were just seven and five years old, leaving Josephine (Deresker) Naumovich with no husband (again), and a total of five children to support through the Great Depression, including three from her deceased first husband.

It seems to me that some women just know how to pull their family together to survive extreme conditions. They just keep on working and doing the right thing day by day. Josephine was such a woman. After being widowed for the second time in the midst of the Great Depression, she supported her family as long-time housekeeper for the Cathedral of the Immaculate Conception downtown for $30 a month.

Leonard Naumovich, Jr., in full altar boy regalia, circa 1932. *Courtesy of Tom Mann.*

The cost of taking the bus to and from work ate into even that small sum.

Yet somehow, despite everything, Josephine found the time and energy to remain active in St. Vincent de Paul (Lithuanian) Catholic Church. Joe and Len can still see in their minds the carefully cleaned bathtub at the family home at

Leonard Naumovich, Sr., with mandolin, undated. *Courtesy of Tom Mann.*

1127 Percy Ave. filled with the ingredients for the stuffed kielbasa their mother always hand-mixed for the church's annual bazaar. Josephine also served as an officer in the church's women's sodality. A 1936 newspaper article (two years after second husband Len, Sr., died) also lists Josephine on the refreshments committee of the Lithuanian Republican Club of Springfield.

## Death by Mining

Josephine's youngest sons Joe and Len were no slouches, themselves, holding down newspaper delivery routes while going to school and helping around the house. They can still remember their dad's 1934 wake, held at home, according to the custom of the day. Len Naumovich, Sr., had died suddenly of pneumonia after an accident at the mine at 11th and Ridgely forced the miners to use a distant exit (well north of the Illinois State Fairgrounds) and walk home in the middle of winter without their coats. A base layer of black lung disease, the universal miner's scourge, no doubt contributed to the onset and severity of Len's lethal pneumonia.

John Budwitis (or Budwites), Josephine's first husband, had died in 1923 at age 33 in an explosion in the same mine, where he was a "shot firer" igniting gunpowder to create controlled explosions to break up seams of coal. One newspaper account actually says he was a last-minute "substitute" in that most dangerous of jobs, which could explain the so-called "windy shot" accident that took his life.

## Laid Out in the Living Room

Len and Joe's dad was laid out in the living room of the same two-bedroom home where the visitation for Budwitis probably had been held 11 years earlier. Mourners who came and went from the house all night were fed ham and sausage from the kitchen, which also held a keg of beer. A huge flower bouquet on the front porch marked theirs as a home in mourning. After a 24-hour wake, including an all-night vigil, their father's body was taken to St. Vincent de Paul's, where the open casket was photographed on the steps of the church surrounded by mourners. (This custom made it possible to give relatives in distant places, including those left behind in Lithuania, a last look at a loved one they might not have seen in decades.)

Immigrant miner Len Naumovich, Sr., had been a sacristan at St. Vincent's. His collection of musical instruments found in the attic, after he died, included a mandolin, violin, trumpet, and baritone horn. A hand-inked music book he left behind is probably now more than 100 years old.

Once translated, Len, Sr.,'s music book revealed that he was not only literate and educated, but a fan of Jonas Mačiulis, a.k.a., "Maironis" (1862-1932), the leading poet of Lithuania's national revival after hundreds of years of Polish, then Russian domination. This determined late-nineteenth century renaissance of the marginalized Lithuanian language and the re-awakening of Lithuanian national consciousness, while the country was still under the rule of the Russian czar, coincided with Len Naumovich, Sr.,'s own life and times.

Did Len, Sr., write the words and music to Lithuania's most famous songs after he came to the U.S.? Or was his personal music book a precious piece of home that he carried into exile?

Although Len left behind no written record of the dreams he once had for his life, his fragile, 100-year-old music book is a pretty powerful clue that his dream was NOT coal mining. Luckily, his book still survives today as a precious family keepsake and a testament to the spirit of music and poetry that lived in the heart of a poor immigrant coal miner with no opportunity for the life he would have chosen.

Front cover of Leonard Naumovich, Sr.'s, hand-inked music book. The quality of his handwriting suggests he was literate before he arrived in the U.S. to mine coal. Note the Polonized "Naumovicz" that resulted in today's "Naumovich" spelling.

# The Lithuanian Songs That Len Loved

The poetry of Maironis was famous for uniting lyrical visions of the Lithuanian countryside with Lithuanian folk music. The mysterious words *"Kur bėga Šešupė"* that Len, Sr., wrote on the bottom front cover of his book turn out to be the opening of the most famous Maironis poem of all: "Where the Šešupė River Flows:

*"Kur bėga Šešupė, kur Nemunas teka*: Where the Šešupė River runs, where the Nemunas River flows;

*Tai mūsų tėvynė, graži Lietuva:* That's our fatherland, Lithuania the beautiful..."

According to *Wikipedia*, "Almost every Lithuanian can recite these words by heart. The poem is so well-known that it is treated as an unofficial national anthem."

Inside Len, Sr.'s, book are also the words and music to another Maironis poem: *"Jojau Diena"* or "Riding Day." The poem in translation begins: "Although I rode all day and I rode all night, I arrived at nothing; Then suddenly, I came upon a beautiful lake..."

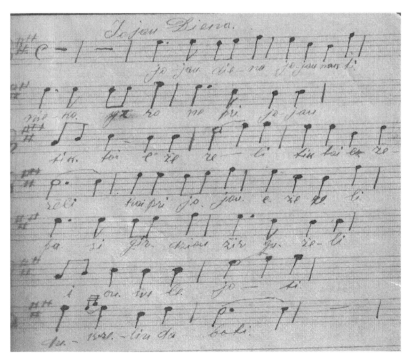

A page from Len, Sr.'s, personal music book. *"Jojau Diena"* words and music in his own hand. Being able to write Lithuanian was rare for an immigrant of the time due to the Russian czar's language ban. Len, Sr., also obviously had some music education before he was forced to make his living as a miner.

## Growing Up Fatherless

Not being able to grow up with their father couldn't have been easy for the late Leonard Naumovich's young sons Len, Jr., and Joe. But life for the two boys did go on, closely charting the ups and downs of the Lithuanian-American experience in Springfield.

As a teenager, one of the boys briefly worked for Jake Cohen at the Cohens' Peoria Road grocery store for a nickel an hour—until he left to work at a nearby grocery for 10 cents an hour. During Advent every year, St. Vincent's pastor, Fr. Stanley Yunker, made his round of home visits to collect the annual parish dues of $8 per family. Len and Joe remember wooden kegs of herring for Advent and *Kucios*, the Lithuanian Christmas Eve observance, that were sold by Wally Mouske's grocery on Peoria Road south of Griffiths Avenue.

Len and Joe also remember voters being coaxed to the polls with the reward of a small bottle of liquor, each. And the night "Shorty" Casper's illegal still near the Peoria Road railroad tracks exploded, burning down the alleged canning shed that hid it, to Shorty's exclamations that it must have been his tomatoes that blew up. Ethnic Lithuanian picnics at the Wedgewood Pavilion north of the Fairgrounds were well-attended—and frequently punctuated by brawls.

## Poverty, 'Mine Wars,' Corruption

During the outbreak of violence known as the "Mine Wars" (1932-36), miners from the opposing unions, not to mention hired thugs, were accustomed to walking around with loaded guns in their waistbands. Len and Joe remember state militia men lining Sangamon Avenue on both sides, from the 11th Street mine entrance east to St. Aloysius parish, to create a corridor of safety for children to walk home from school.

Endemic corruption in Springfield and Sangamon County included suspected police collusion in prostitution and the punchboard business, a widespread form of gambling, until Greek-American state's attorney George Coutrakon arrived to "clean things up" in the late 1940s and '50s. The popularity of gaming through the Great Depression and afterwards was understandable, given the grinding and ubiquitous poverty of daily life, the lack of modern forms of entertainment, and the fact that those who worked manual jobs and/or went to war found life, itself, a game of chance.

I imagine the public problem with gambling on every corner and in every business establishment was twofold: expenditures by fathers and husbands whose families routinely suffered, and the generation of prodigious profits that could be used to buy-off police and government officials for any number of corrupt purposes.

Gambling was illegal within city limits, but legal in the surrounding county until Sangamon County Sheriff Harry Eielson singlehandedly announced a ban in January 1939, according to newspaper reports. Nevertheless, gaming continued somewhat in the open until Eilson became Springfield's mayor in 1947, and Coutrakon arrived in 1948, which might not have been a coincidence.

One Lithuanian-American I know was connected to Springfield's vice- and corruption-busting campaign. Ann (Tisckos) Wisnosky worked as a secretary to the state's attorney's office in the Old Illinois State Capitol/Sangamon County Courthouse for several decades, starting with George Coutrakon, according to her son Augie. (How ironic that in 2013 and 2014, Springfield brought back video gaming in a big way, with government officially sharing the profits.)

## The Passage from Poverty

Joe Naumovich still passionately remembers the grinding poverty of the Great Depression. He reports that the lack of jobs and money continued, despite President Roosevelt's New Deal, all the way until World War II, when weapons production finally re-opened idled factories.

Both brothers mentioned the helpful role of August ("Gus") Wisnosky, Sr., a banker who helped many of his fellow Lithuanian-Americans in the 1940s and '50s by extending credit and loans from Illinois National Bank. In exchange, the Lithuanian-American community generally took its banking business to INB.

Many long decades of Lithuanian-American poverty finally ended after World War II, with the dynamic growth of the U.S.'s post-war economy and the increased availability of jobs and credit. Today Joe can look back on a long and successful career at the Internal Revenue Service. Len, Jr., worked at Sangamo Electric and later City Water Light & Power as a building and stores supervisor. Both graduated from Cathedral Boys High School, the predecessor of Griffin High School.

# Chapter 16
# Bankers to Lithuanians

For decades after their arrival in Springfield, the amount of wealth Lithuanian immigrants could accumulate was limited by low wages, minimal credit, un- and under-employment, and the lingering effects of mine closures and the Great Depression. However, after World War II, two sons of Lithuanian immigrants, August P. (Gus) Wisnosky, Sr., and Walter Rodutskey, began to help put more money in their countrymen's pockets as "bankers to Lithuanians."

## Gus Wisnosky & Illinois National Bank

Gus Wisnosky, St. Vincent de Paul Jubilee book, 1956.

August "Gus" was born in 1906, the son of Lithuanian immigrants George and Anna (Prapuolenis) Wisnosky (Vysniauskas). A graduate of Ridgely Grade School and Springfield High School, where he took general business courses, including typing, Wisnosky joined Illinois National Bank (INB) when he was 18 years old in 1924. It took 15 years, but around 1940, he was appointed assistant teller. By 1945 he was head teller, and in 1952, he became a loan officer. Wisnosky was promoted to assistant vice president in 1957. He retired from the bank in 1970 after a career of 46 years.

It hardly seems a coincidence that the bank where Wisnosky rose up the ranks, INB, was the only one that took seriously the application for a $100,000 loan from uneducated Lithuanian immigrant John (Makarauskas) Mack and made the loan that in 1957 launched the Mack fast-food empire. In gratitude, the Mack McDonald's franchise, which went on to include all eight of Springfield's first McDonald's restaurants, did all its subsequent banking with INB.

Wisnosky's bank also went on to garner a large share of the Lithuanian-American community's banking business, reportedly based on an openness to Lithuanian-American borrowers who might have been discriminated against or not treated as positively elsewhere. Don't get me wrong—it's likely that Gus

Wisnosky extended the same fairness, human insight and business savvy to all his customers. Otherwise, one can't imagine him being promoted to the C-suite. Nevertheless, it's clear that Lithuanian-Americans in Springfield knew Gus would help them get a fair hearing and a fair deal, and so they became loyal account-holders and recommended INB to their friends and relatives.

## Belonging to the City and Its Lithuanian-Americans

Along the way, just like Lithuanian immigrant attorney Isidor Yacktis, Wisnosky became a shining representative of his ethnic community within much larger, city-wide organizations, such as the Community Chest, Elks Club, Knights of Columbus (K of C), and ultimately, the Sangamon County Board of Supervisors (1957-65). He also participated in such civic organizations as the Springfield Art Association, Illinois State Museum Society, and Abraham Lincoln Association.

At the same time that he participated in multi-ethnic organizations (for instance, the K of C's Major League Bowlers and its annual Lake Springfield Festival at Villa Maria), Wisnosky remained true to his roots: a pillar of his own ethnic community.

Following in the footsteps of his father George, who in 1911 was grand marshal of the pageant/parade celebrating the opening of St. Vincent de Paul (Lithuanian) Catholic Church, in 1971 when St. Vincent's was slated by the diocese for closure and demotion, Gus led a committee of parishioners striving to save their church. Gus had been a lifelong parishioner, violinist, choir member, and 22-year trustee of the church until its final days. Tragically, his death in February 1972 at age 66 followed by only one month St. Vincent's closing, so that his funeral mass had to be held elsewhere.

Young Gus Wisnosky and his wife-to-be Ann Tisckos in this photo of the September 1927 Alane-Kasawich wedding party. *Courtesy of Elaine Alane.*

Gus and wife Ann's son John went on to become an art professor at the University of Hawaii. Son August (Augie), Jr., is a distinguished local architect, now retired. Augie was resident architect from 1966-68 at the site of the most ambitious historical renovation ever undertaken in Springfield: the stone-by-stone deconstruction and rebuilding of the Old Illinois State Capitol where Abraham Lincoln delivered his "House Divided" speech. The Old State Capitol later served as the backdrop for the presidential and vice-presidential announcements of Barack Obama, 44th President of the United States.

Gus and Ann's son Augie Wisnosky at the 40-year tribute to the historic Old State Capitol reconstruction project, March 25, 2008. *Courtesy of same.*

## Walter Rodutskey & Sacred Heart (Heartland) Credit Union

By coincidence, both Gus Wisnosky and Walter Rodutskey got into their positions to loan money to Lithuanian-Americans at the start of the post-World War II economic expansion that finally made real prosperity possible—if not for the immigrants who had come to Springfield 50 years earlier, at least for their children and grandchildren.

The Shenandoah, Pennsylvania-born son of immigrants Kazimieras and Frances (Matulaitis) Rodutskey, Walter was a bonafide working man: a machinist at Allis Chalmers for 25 years. In 1946 he joined with famous "labor priest" Fr. John Brockmeier of Sacred Heart Church to become an organizing director of what was first known as Sacred Heart Parish Credit Union.

Fr. Brockmeier's philosophy drove him to combine labor organizing and arbitrating labor disputes with founding banks, credit unions and chambers of commerce in a civic, Christian spirit that encouraged working people to work together through a variety of organizations in addition to their parish church.

In the Rev. Brockmeier's words: "There is a tie-in between labor unions and credit unions. Both tend to improve the standard of living for the working class."

The new credit union was founded by pooling initial deposits into the modest sum of just $102.74. As Catholics, Brockmeier, Rodutskey and the other founders put Sacred Heart parish at the center of this new effort at financial self-help by locating the credit union inside the parish office. In the beginning, the credit union cost just 25 cents to join, was open to any family with one Catholic spouse, and made loans ranging from $10-$300.

By 1950, it had assets of $53,518.48 and 276 members. Office hours were Monday evenings at Sacred Heart parish, "7 p.m. to close," according to historical documents graciously provided by today's Heartland Credit Union (Sacred Heart's successor). By 1996, the credit union had main offices at South Grand and Glenwood Ave. and an administrative branch on West White Oaks Drive. Membership had climbed to 7,700, deposits to $13.2 million, and loan amounts accordingly.

Walter Rodutskey, who retired from the credit union in 1984 after 30 straight years of board service, played an important role in this non-profit banking institution, often as the board's secretary. He was so committed to the credit union movement that he also served as an officer of the Springfield Chapter of a statewide league of credit unions, which included representatives of most of the city's largest employers, including Pillsbury Mills, Sangamo Electric, and Bell Telephone, as well as the local teachers' and firefighters' unions.

Rodutskey died at age 88 just three days after the death of Margaret, his wife of 40 years, in January 1991. The credit union that he helped found was led into the new millennium by another Springfield Lithuanian-American: Ed Gvazdinskas (also a *State Journal-Register* Sports Hall of Fame honoree).

# Chapter 17
# 'Knights' of Music, Baseball, Politics

Back in the 1920s, music was at the core of almost every Springfield Lithuanian gathering. There were elaborate musical programs at Sunday High Mass on Easter and Christmas. Operas and operettas were performed by Lithuanian voices and musicians for the general public at the Springfield High School Auditorium and the Knights of Columbus Hall. And Lithuanian folk songs were sung by 60-100 voices at summer picnics that also featured extremely competitive men's fast-pitch baseball and women's softball.

The Lithuanian-language operetta, *"L'Tevyne"* ("The Homeland"), composed and staged here in August 1923 by St. Vincent de Paul's famous music director Alexandras J. Aleksis, dramatized the "uplifting power" of music to regenerate a badly degraded Lithuanian nation—if not in the homeland, then on U.S. soil. No one knew the harsh lives of their fellow immigrants—and the poverty, ignorance, alcoholism and crime that afflicted them—better than more-educated Lithuanian elites and those who somehow managed to rise above these conditions spiritually and become the guiding lights and social conscience of their community.

Crucially, in the late 1910s and early 1920s, such individuals decided to seize the cultural, political and artistic freedoms available to every American– even while economic progress remained elusive–to elevate themselves and their Lithuanian countrymen. The banner under which they chose to organize, perhaps to counter similar organizing by Lithuanian leftist labor groups, belonged to the Knights of Lithuania, with local branch 48 sometimes being called the K of L of St. Vincent de Paul Church.

To amplify the impact of their spiritual and cultural enrichment campaign, the talented and dedicated activists who poured their hearts into the Knights also decided to model Lithuanian cultural elevation to both the Lithuanian-American masses and the American public at large. The Knights' famous choir and its frequent exhibitions of musical virtuosity successfully projected a more refined image of Lithuanian immigrants both to Lithuanians, themselves, and mainstream Springfield. This desired image appeared in the August 1923 *Illinois State Journal-Register*, which declared: "An intense love for music is a national characteristic of the Lithuanian people."

It's true that music had remained part of the Lithuanian character even when stripped for generations to its most primitive core. Even when denied the spelling of their own names, Lithuanians never lost the music and words of their folk songs or *dainos* for work, birth, weddings and funerals. Maybe that's why Professor Aleksis, the most famous Lithuanian "music man" ever to grace Springfield, so perfectly embodied the campaign for progress through cultural and spiritual enrichment. Certainly no Lithuanian I've discovered in Springfield wielded the power of music for ethnic self-help with more missionary zeal.

## Aleksis and the Knights of Lithuania

Born in Lithuania in 1886 and a graduate of the Warsaw Conservatory, Aleksis appears to have arrived from Detroit on July 1, 1921 to work as organist and music director for St. Vincent de Paul (Lithuanian) Catholic Church. Within two weeks, he was elected president of the pre-existing (and expressly Roman Catholic) Knights of Lithuania branch affiliated with the church, and became director of the Knights' 60-voice choir that performed in national costume.

Composer Is Taking Prominent Part In Convention In City

In one *Illinois State Journal* article, Aleksis was identified as the first president of the Knights of Lithuania national organization (founded in 1916) and composer of the Knights' national anthem. The Knights' current website identifies Aleksis as having been named a "Member of Great Honor" just three years after the organization's founding, while he was organist at Chicago's Providence of God Church.

Professor Alexandras Aleksis, *Illinois State Journal*, August 22, 1923.

No doubt Aleksis played a major role in securing a great honor for Springfield's Lithuanian community when in August 1923, the 800,000-member K of L held its national convention here. That three-day event (August 22-24) in the hall of the Illinois House of Representatives was attended by 200 delegates from 14 states. "Prominent men of the Lithuanian race in the U.S. were among the delegates participating in what is probably the most unusual and unique convention ever held in Springfield," the *Journal* declared.

The ambassador to the U.S. from the newly recognized Republic of Lithuania made a point of giving a eulogy of Abraham Lincoln at Lincoln's Tomb. Aleksis's operetta *"L'Tevyne"* (book by Edward Silelio) was presented by the best local and Chicago Lithuanian-American voices at the Springfield High School Auditorium. The operetta dramatized how drinking, carousing Lithuanian immigrant men could be civilized and elevated by the uplifting influences of democracy, education, music and art in America. In the rousing grand finale, singers filled the stage triumphantly waving American flags. This echoed the business side of the K of L convention, which was conducted completely in

English, according to newspaper reports, and was capped by a resolution that all prospective members henceforth would first have to attain U.S. citizenship. The convention also re-elected Aleksis its national president.

## It Takes a Choir

So many Lithuanian immigrants and their children lent their voices to the local Knights of Lithuania choir (renowned as one of the best in the city) to enrich and uplift their fellow immigrants—and so many great local Lithuanian-American singers and musicians served as leaders of the national K of L organization and its local chapter.

Perhaps the biggest local Lithuanian activists, ever, Anthony and Catherine (Gillette) Cooper (Kuperis) were K of L national delegates and sang in the group's choir and concerts, including Anthony's turn as a memorable bad guy in *"L'Tevyne"* (he was also president of the local K of C chapter when Aleksis arrived from Detroit). Albinas Kuprevicius was elected the local Knights' financial secretary in 1921, the same year that Aleksis was made president, Joe Miller vice-president, Helen Beveridge secretary, and Julia Gedman (Lukitis) treasurer. Catherine Cooper also was a leader of the Lithuanian Roman Catholic Women's Alliance Chapter 56.

Julia Gedman, a talented dancer, singer and piano soloist for many of the group's programs, was re-elected treasurer of the local Knights and a national K of L trustee in 1923. Also in 1923, Josephine Sugent, a soprano who soloed in many of the choir's programs, was elected second vice president of the K of L's national athletic division, which was headed by Joe Miller of Springfield. Anna Gudauskas (Gudausky), elected a local K of L trustee with Peter Stirbis in 1921, that same year became the only woman from Springfield elected a K of L national officer (second secretary).

Not only did the K of L appear to give women a chance to play very active leadership roles; in the group's Springfield leadership, we again see an almost evangelical confluence of music with social activism. Much like the K of L female leaders, most or all of the K of L male leaders were also members of its choir: Joe Miller, Peter and Alex Stirbis, Anthony Cooper, Charles Ruplankas, Anthony Zelvis and later, John Adomaitis (Adams).

Other female voices were Anna, Mary, Helen and Petronella Marciulionis and Anna Mosteika (mother of Ann (Mosteika) Foster, who would serve as St. Vincent de Paul's longest-term organist and choir director from 1933 until the church closed on Dec. 31, 1971). Helen Beveridge also sang--along with Estella and soloist Helen Brazaitis, described by the newspaper as a "well-known Springfield soprano."

Faces of the St. Vincent de Paul "Knights of Lithuania" chapter, circa 1924. Jubilee book.

The 10-piece Grigas orchestra accompanied the Knights of Lithuania choir when it performed at St. Vincent's and other venues. Stanley Grigas played the violin and Charles the clarinet and saxophone (they also operated the Grigas Bros. grocery on North Ninth Street). "Banker to Lithuanians" August "Gus" Wisnosky, his immigrant father George (Vysniauskas) Wisnosky, and my father's own first cousin Benedict Yamont, Jr., played in the violin section. Bertha and Gertrude Miller (Milleris) played piano at a 1924 benefit for the Lithuanians of Vilnius commemorating the tragic Polish takeover of Lithuania's historic capital in 1922. Also active in that musical observance, according to newspaper accounts, were: John Grustas, P. Burcikas, and A. Kazlauskas, chairman of the event.

Eighty new K of L members were initiated at a meeting on April 18, 1922. Joseph Loda and Anthony Cooper were credited with bringing in the most new members. (The Knight's local "junior" chapter was led by Adolphina Stanslovas).

Professor Aleksis, who staged/conducted many of his own compositions, like "Shed No Tears," "Going There," and "Love," also put on the Russian opera "Nastute" (sung in English) only months after his arrival in Springfield. In 1922, through his connections with the Rev. F.M. Kemesis,, a member of the Lithuanian Legation in Washington, D.C., Aleksis also organized the Lithuanian Roman Catholic Alliance of Labor, Branch 101. In January 1923, the local chapter, headed by A. Kazlauskas, organized a presentation by Rev. Kemesis in Springfield entitled, "The Catholic Church and Labor."

## Baseball, Picnics, Politics

Many Knights' activities allowed local Lithuanians both to have fun and to express an enduring connection to their Lithuanian identity and homeland. Picnics and baseball at Lincoln Park and Camp Lincoln seem to have been frequent summertime events.

The Knights also organized a formidable men's baseball team, which played against a K of L women's team without keeping score as the main event of the K of L's annual picnic July 25, 1921 at the Nokes dairy farm east of Springfield. The picnic, like anything else Lithuanians did back then, also included 100 voices singing Lithuanian folk songs, according to newspaper reports. Another Knights' picnic was held on July 31, 1921 as a benefit for the Lithuanian National Relief Fund Chapter 69. It featured a "fast amateur baseball game" between the Knights and Chicago-Springfield Coal Co., with Joe Miller as pitcher and "V. Allenis" (probably Victor Alane) as catcher. An Aug. 21, 1921 K of L picnic was billed as featuring a "girls' game."

The Knights' annual picnic must have been quite a standout affair to be described in a 1922 newspaper article as "one of the big events of the outdoor season in this city." Certainly, the group poured much effort into organizing recreational activities that the Knights hoped would win new members.

## Something to Prove Through Baseball

Although men's vs. women's games might not have been about keeping score, competitive passions ran high during the K of L men's regular weekly fast-pitch baseball games against teams organized by other K of L chapters in Chicago and Waukegan, and against local business, church and municipal teams in Springfield, Rochester, Chatham, Jacksonville, Loami, Pawnee, Dawson, Havana, Kincaid, and Waverly. Home games were often at Watches Field. The "Virden Slovaks" seem to have been a particular nemesis for the Knights, who carpooled to many "away" games.

On April 17, 1922, the Myers Brothers team claimed an official municipal league win for what K of L captain Joe Miller said was only a practice game granted by the Knights when Myers was looking for a field to play on. The dispute continued to be played out on the baseball diamond and in the newspaper when Myers' coach subsequently moved to deny official status to his team's defeat by the Knights

Knights of Lithuania youth basketball team with unknown sponsor. John Zibutis back row, left edge. Undated. *Courtesy of Al Urbanckas, D.D.S.*

in their regularly scheduled game July 22, 1922.

Newspaper accounts also describe a much anticipated Knights' game against a "colored" men's team called George Neal's Union Giants. The Giants had their own east-side ballpark, which the Knights were said to be contemplating "taking over" in August 1922. Due to the success of Springfield adult amateur baseball, a "Kidsville" league was also established with Myers Brothers, the Knights and others sponsoring their own junior teams. In 1924, the Knights' junior team, managed by saloon-keeper Simonas (Sam) Lapinski, won the city-wide Kidsville title.

One of the Knights' earliest men's baseball teams organized by Joe Miller and noted for its dominance on the diamond seems to have had few Lithuanian players. This led to a brouhaha that included Knights members not attending that team's only home game in May or June 1921–followed by a directive that henceforth, the team would include only Lithuanian players. Defending the promotional value to the organization of his winning Knights' team, however constituted, Miller aired the spat in local newspapers. He then took his team outside the Knights for a short period while he barnstormed to become the K of L's national athletic director. Once Miller achieved that position, he returned to the field with a new Lithuanian K of L team that featured J., W, and T. Grigiskis, and other players by the names of Koski, Laskaudis, Oleseskis, Kutskill, Ballon, Laukitis and Chestnut. Still other Knights baseball players of the 1920s were surnamed Diksonas, Lukitis, Denkevicius, Keturaki, Marcinkus, Tamoliunas, Repaitis, and Bokainis.

## Passing the Baton

Perhaps the Knights were negatively impacted in their recruiting by the requirement, after August 1923, of U.S. citizenship for new members, at a time when increasing mine mechanization and layoffs began driving an exodus of immigrant coal-mining families from Springfield. It is clear that a choir/corps of Knights musical activists held concert after carnival after party after picnic in the early- to mid-1920s to raise the group's profile among their countrymen and in the community. Joe Miller, who seems to have been quite a promoter, did the same through baseball. But by the 1930s, the group appeared somewhat smaller on the public stage.

And by 1926, Professor Aleksis had already moved on—perhaps because of his restless artistic spirit and the inherently small pond that Springfield represented. (It also seems likely that St. Vincent's small organist salary could only have been in decline as the mine family exodus reduced the parish census.) I would also not discount politics and possible friction in the ranks of the Knights, who were becoming divided between St. Vincent's and the new St. Aloysius parish and between labor unionism/socialism and conservative Roman Catholic values. Labor-related political divisions could only have become more inflamed during the lead-up to the convulsion of violence known as the Central Illinois "Mine Wars" (1932-36), which pitted Lithuanian vs. Lithuanian.

By 1925, newspaper reports describe an operetta, "Sylvia," directed by St. Vincent's new organist Anthony Kvedaras (Kwedar?) in English at the Knights of Columbus Auditorium to benefit the church. (Anna Mosteika, Anna Gudausky and Vera Lanauskas were among the singers.)

Mrs. Julia Casper (Swinkunas) — — — — — — Inglewood, California
Mrs. Marge Ehringer (Casper) — — — — — — East Lansing, Michigan
Mrs. Anna Frisch (Gudausky) — — — — — — — New York, New York
Mrs. Della Gerke (Wayne) — — — — — — — — — Chicago, Illinois
Mrs. Josephine Thompkins (Sugent) — — — — — Calumet City, Illinois
Mrs. Julia Lukitis (Gedman) — — — — — — — — Springfield, Illinois
Mrs. Bertha Adams (Yates) — — — — — — — — Springfield, Illinois

One female core cadre of St. Vincent de Paul's K of L chapter, 1920s, with married and maiden names. *1956 Jubilee book.*

The K of L Chapter 48 officers that year were: Spiritual Advisor the Rev. Stanley O. Yunker (Junkeris), who had become St. Vincent's pastor in 1923; President John Adomaitis (Adams), Vice-President Victor Alaunis (Alane), Financial Secretary Catherine Cooper, Secretary Anna Gudausky; Trustees Helen Shupenas and John Thomas (Tomasunas); Treasurer August Vysniauskas (Gus Wisnosky); and Marshals Anthony Gridzuis and A. Kuperis.

Josephine Sugent, Anna Gudausky, Catherine Cooper and Julia Svinkonif (Swinkunas?) did the "hostess" heavy-lifting for the officers' installation meeting that also discussed the need for an "extensive membership drive," according to the newspaper. I should mention that a core group of female friends (including Gedman-Lukitis, Gudausky, and Sugent) appears to have kept the Knights and other Lithuanian Catholic organizations, including the Lithuanian Roman Catholic Women's Alliance, going for at least 20 years.

One hundred K of L members reportedly attended the group's 20th anniversary banquet and dance in the roof garden of the Elks Club in 1936. Fr. Yunker gave the invocation and keynoted a speech about the Knights' history and principles, while Miss Bernice Brazaitis presided as president of the club and "toastmistress."

## Lithuanian Song Festival

Professor Aleksis, called one of the "outstanding Lithuanian musicians, composers, and teachers of music in the United States" by the Aug. 10, 1942 *Journal*, went on to organize the Lithuanian League of Choirs in Chicago. Later, he conducted four choirs and gave studio lessons in his then-home with wife Marcella in Watertown, Conn. (Marcella was named a Knights "Member of Great Honor" in 1968.) The professor died at age 97 in 1983 in Connecticut.

But before that, he played another important role in the musical history of Lithuanian America. As a Chicago member of the American-Lithuanian Roman Catholic Organists Alliance, Professor Aleksis helped organize the repertoire of the first national Lithuanian Song Festival that was held in 1956. The festival featured performances in the Chicago Coliseum by 34 choirs and about 1,200 singers and raised $22,000 for Lithuanian causes. (For more about the song festival, please go to: *https://www.dainusvente.org/en/more/history*)

According to the *dainusvente* website, music critic Vladas Jakubėnas wrote about that first Lithuanian Song Festival in the journal *Aidas*:

"The repertoire was not just sung by the unified choir − some songs were sung only by women, some only by men, and some by select choirs. On the day of the festival, a cool summer suddenly turned hot, with temperatures reaching 100 degrees. The Coliseum had no air conditioning, and the heat was almost unbearable in the sold-out arena. In the end, however, a moral victory had been achieved. With the success of the first Lithuanian Song Festival, American and Canadian Lithuanians achieved self-respect and encouragement for future cultural projects."

Apparently, ethnic uplift and self-help through cultural enterprise (specifically, music) wasn't just for Springfield or just for the 1920s, but rather, a major and ongoing tradition in Lithuanian-American life.

*In memory and honor of Professor Alexandras Aleksis and the other full-time St. Vincent de Paul organists/music directors, including Ann (Mosteika) Foster, Anthony Kvedaras, Stanley Zylius, Joseph Karecka, and part-time organists Roman Hodalski and the Rev. J. Cullen O'Brien—and every member of their dedicated choirs.*

ST. VINCENT DE PAUL CHURCH CHOIR

Left to right—First row—Wm. Blazis, Margaret Rodutsky, Bernice Kurila, Anne Foster. Minnie Lapinski, Romulda Sidlauskas, Kostas Lelys.

Second row—Rema Paulionis, Berniece Stevens, Adele Bishop, Ann Wisnosky, Mary Ann Foster, Ann Urbankas, Patricia Urbankas, Julia Petreikis, Marilyn Urbankas, Angele Abramikas.

Third row—Charles Foster, Catherine Turasky, August Wisnosky, Leon Kelert, Peter Urbankas, Alfred Urbankas, George Wisnosky, Betty Buguveski, Adolph Kelert, Walter Rodutsky.

Not present—Carl Uzgiris and Vyt Uzgiris.

The choir has always been outstanding throughout the years. From 1924 to 1932 there was a succession of full time organists: Anthony Kvederas, Stanley Zylius, and Joseph Karecka. Mr. Karecka left on account of illness and, because of the difficult depression times, the parish could not afford to employ another full time organist. Mr. Roman Hodalski of Springfield Junior College and Rev. J. Cullen O'Brien, then a student, were generous in helping out as part-time organists. On occasions, Rev. George Windsor assisted the parish with his musical talent. Finally in 1933 Mrs. Ann Foster was prevailed upon to accept the position of organist and choir director which she is filling capably and successfully to this very day. The choir as a whole, has been at all times, a most helpful group to parish and pastor. So, on this Golden Jubilee Day, to the choir and to the organist: "Ad Multos Annos".

A sad note must be added to this chapter—on July 29, 1955, God chose to call out of this life Mrs. Connie Kelert. Connie Kelert's voice, her grace and her charm had endeared her to the entire parish. For over 20 years she was engaged in every parish activity. She was one of the organizers and past presidents of the Altar and Rosary Society, active in the Confraternity of Christian Doctrine and for many years did much of the parish secretarial work.

The church choir with names. *1956 Jubilee book.*

# Chapter 18
# Up from Mining and Bootlegging: The Political Rise of the Adomaitis and Yacubasky Families

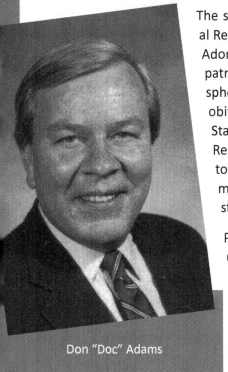

Don "Doc" Adams

The story goes that for decades, state and national Republican Party leader Don "Doc" Adams (Lith. Adomaitis) of Springfield exercised significant patronage power in both the public and private spheres. When "Doc" died in 2011 at age 75, his obituary listed leadership roles with the Illinois State Republican Central Committee, the Illinois Republican State Convention, the Illinois Electoral College, and the Republican National Committee. These roles put him at the heart of city, state and national politics for decades.

Pretty impressive for the grandson of a Lithuanian immigrant killed in our local mines. But maybe not surprising to those who knew "Doc" as the product of the union of two families, the Adams-Adamitises and Yates-Yacubaskies. These two families had been working together since at least the early 1930s, and separately from the 1920s, to climb up from the mines–through bootlegging and the grocery/tavern business–to the ultimate prize of patronage-rich politics.

## Death in the Mines

On the Adams side, the story begins with "Doc's" grandfather, immigrant coal miner John Adamites (Adomaitis), who died in 1907 as a result of an accident at Springfield's Illinois Midland Coal Co. mine, leaving behind a widow and four children. One of those children was "Doc's" father John Joseph Adamitis/Adamites, who was born in 1899 and served in World War I.

In 1924, a "Mr. and Mrs. John Adamites" were issued federal "liquor writs," along with 11 other central Illinois individuals and couples, enjoining them from using their soft drink business in Pawnee to sell "intoxicating liquor." Since Adomaitis is a fairly common Lithuanian name, perhaps this was a different John and wife.

However, in 1927, an *Illinois State Journal-Register* article reports that brothers John Joseph and William Adamitis of North 17th Street in Springfield were arrested after a police raid of rooms above their grocery at 1530 Sangamon Ave. Captured in the raid were a 20-gallon copper still, "some home brew mush, 120 bottles of home brew, nine gallons of alcohol, and a quantity of alleged whiskey." (All this before John Joseph's recorded marriage to Bertha Yacubasky in 1932 and "Doc's" birth in 1935.)

In the early 1920s, newspaper reports also say that a John Adomaitis sang in the locally renowned Knights of Lithuania (K of L) Branch 48 choir. In 1925, he was elected president of the Knights' local chapter following the departure of charismatic leader and composer Alexandras Aleksis.

## From Knights of Lithuania to City-Wide Politics

In 1931, according to newspaper reports, Adomaitis began to build his "bridge" from St. Vincent's/Knights of Lithuania politics into traditional county-wide partisan politics. He did this by working with his wife-to-be Bertha Yacubasky and her two brothers, Joseph and William (as well as other Lithuanian-American friends and neighbors from St. Vincent's and the K of L), to found the Lithuanian Social and Political Club of Sangamon County.

In the classic story of ethnic politics, Adomaitis got his feet wet in the smaller pond of his own group before moving on to deeper waters. I imagine he and other Lithuanian-Americans who organized their new social and political club shared a vision of finally taking their place at the city's multi-ethnic table of power by uniting a strong and reliable Lithuanian base.

The benefits of a seat of power had probably become obvious back in the 1920s to every Lithuanian-American involved in the illegal alcohol trade, when it would have been highly useful to have political protection from police raids, fines, and the specter of going to jail for a little moonshine.

## Political Club Goes Republican

Perhaps under the influence of the Yacubasky-Yates, who already by 1931 had been involved in Republican precinct organizing, the new Lithuanian political club that first met in 1931 at the Labor Temple at Sixth and Washington streets, by 1936 had been renamed the Lithuanian Republican Social Club. And that same year, the Lithuanian Republicans met at the Arion hall to hear an address criticizing President Franklin Delano Roosevelt and The New Deal.

John Joseph Adomaitis was chairman of the Arion program, supported by committee chairpersons Mrs. Joe Welch (Wilcauskas), William Yates (Yacubasky), William Stankavich, and Mrs. Wallace (Julia) Olshefsky. Subsequent meetings, according to the newspaper, were held at Republican headquarters on the west side of the Old State Capitol square. There were also many picnics and other social events to gather and galvanize the Lithuanian-American Republican faithful, including food, musical performances, and games and activities for children.

At the same time, a full spectrum of ethnic Lithuanian beneficial and political organizations proliferated through the 1940s, in some cases serving as stepping stones for their leaders into community-wide politics. An *Illinois State Journal* article from 1943 mentions no fewer than seven local "Lithuanian societies" as sponsors of a 25-year celebration of Lithuanian independence that year at the Centennial Building next to the Illinois State Capitol.

Among these were: the Lithuanian Roman Catholic Alliance of America Branches 275 and 158 and the Federation of Lithuanian Workers Branch 29 (a communist-leaning successor of the Lithuanian Roman Catholic Alliance of Labor. The Catholic Alliance of Labor may have also been the forebear of the Lithuanian Socialist Federation, which was later named the Lithuanian Association of Workers branch 29 or the "Lithuanian Lodge."). Also represented at the 25th anniversary of Lithuanian independence celebration were the Lithuanian Roman Catholic Women's Alliance Branch 56; the Lithuanian Democratic Social Club; the Lithuanian Cultural Society; and the L.D.L.D.A.(?)

## The Yates & The Blue Danube

Here our story backtracks to "Doc's" maternal line, the Yacubasky-Yates family. Tony (Antanas) Yacubasky immigrated to the U.S. in 1890. His first stop was the Shenandoah, Penn., coal fields, where he married Mary Lesko and daughter Bertha was born. In 1906, the family moved to 1501 Pennsylvania Ave., (a few doors down and across the street from the yellow stucco bungalow at #1504 where my German-Hungarian mother Josephine Kohlrus grew up). Sons Joseph and William Yacubasky and two more daughters were born.

The Yates family were co-founders in 1931 of the aforementioned Lithuanian Social and Political Club. After serving as a Republican precinct committeeman for several years, 25-year-old William was selected the Republican candidate for county auditor in 1932. After his election defeat, William was appointed deputy probate clerk. In 1933, as Tony Yacubasky and sons Joseph and William prepared to advance their family even more ambitiously in business and politics, they decided to become more explicitly Americanized and filed in circuit court to change the Yacubasky surname to Yates.

Also in 1933, which saw the end of Prohibition, the Yates family built a large tavern/dinner club called The Blue Danube next to their grocery on Keys Avenue. The tavern was managed by Joseph Yates, as his brother William was already working for the county. The Blue Danube had a kitchen, a dance floor that was "well sanded and waxed," and an ample area for tables and booths.

But its claim to fame was its "magic bar." One *Journal-Register* writer described it as "electrically charged in such a way that when specially-treated glasses are placed on it, they are illuminated in many colors. This gives the appearance of nothing short of magic, and has proven a very popular source of entertainment."

The Blue Danube's advertised motto was, "where courtesy prevails." It featured festive New Year's parties and Sunday dinners of either roast young duck, fried milk-fed spring chicken, T-bone steak, frog legs, breaded veal cutlet, or roast loin of pork with many different sides, including "Chinese" celery salad and lime and grapefruit salad, plus a full spread of desserts—all for just 65 cents. Also on the menu were "fancy mixed drinks, the finest of wines, liquors and beer, good music and dancing."

## Liquor License Wars & World War II

However, as early as December 1934, The Blue Danube was caught in a liquor license dispute between Springfield Mayor John Kapp and the city's liquor board. The Yates family claimed that they had paid the city clerk for their license, which was never issued, and that they were operating under a personal pledge from Republican Mayor Kapp.

The licensing board cited The Blue Danube not just for the failure to have a license to sell alcohol, but also for hosting dancing without a permit and serving alcohol after 1 a.m. The establishment's windows were also cited because they did not provide a good view into the club from the street—thereby making it easier to serve alcohol after hours without detection.

In 1935, at age 68, immigrant Tony (Antanas) Yacubasky died. Perhaps as a result of this loss and ongoing "political" troubles, in 1938, The Blue Danube was sold to Kenneth Goby and Harold Cusick—reportedly, so that Joseph Yates could devote all his time to the grocery side of the family business.

By 1942, Joseph's brother William was chairman of the central committee of the Sangamon County Republican Party. Joseph had closed the Keys Avenue grocery and enlisted to serve in World War II. He is reported by the newspaper to have rushed home to his ill mother's bedside, with the aid of the Red Cross, just before shipping off to military service. The brothers later operated Y-B Market at First and North Grand Avenue, as well as the nearby Ann Rutledge Pancake House--in my childhood opinion, the most wonderful restaurant in Springfield--as they continued in Republican politics.

## 'Doc' Picks up the Mantle

I would guess that when it was his turn to carry on—and build upon—his father's and uncles' political legacy starting in the 1960s, "Doc" Adams got a nice leg-up from the Republican contacts and organization his three elders had formed. However, although "Doc" no doubt wore their mantle as he entered politics, it's a testament to his own hard work and political skills that he managed to eclipse the wildest dreams of his immigrant/ethnic forebears by serving and being a leader in the Republican Party both locally and nationally for more than 30 years.

# Chapter 19
# Leftist Lithuanians

From the 1930s through the late 1950s, Springfield seems to have been home to the "Lithuanian Lodge," a.k.a, the local lodge of the leftist fraternal benefit society known as the Association of Lithuanian Workers (ALW). In October 1949, the *Illinois State Journal* ran an announcement of a lodge picnic at the Pakutinsky (or Pakey) farm on Mechanicsburg Road about seven miles east of the city.

*Wikipedia* says the ALW was established in June 1930 as a communist-leaning splinter of the Lithuanian Alliance of America. I quickly get lost in the alphabet soup of twentieth-century American leftist organizations with Lithuanian-language branches, let alone exclusively Lithuanian left-wing groups.

Joseph Pakutinsky on left, Herrin, Ill., 1910s.

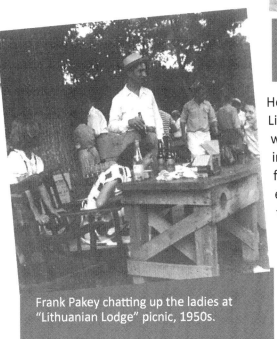

Frank Pakey chatting up the ladies at "Lithuanian Lodge" picnic, 1950s.

However, two facts about leftist Lithuanian immigrants of the first wave seem interesting: According to some sources, Lithuanians frequently constituted the largest foreign language group on the early American left. Second, although illiteracy was the rule among first-wave Lithuanian immigrants, it seems that many of those who were educated gravitated to socialist organizing and publishing.

For example, according to *Wikipedia*, the *Amerikos Lietuvių Socialistų Sąjunga* (American Lithuanian Socialist Union or ALSS), was established in 1904 by Lithuanian immigrants, and did not affiliate with the Socialist Party of America until 1915. The ALSS-affiliated *Laisvė (Freedom)* newspaper was "one of the most influential and longest-running radical Lithuanian-language newspapers in the United States, issued daily from 1919 through 1958." The ALW had its own national publication, *Tiesa (Truth)*.

When the Socialist Party of America split in 1919, its communist-leaning Lithuanian Socialist Federation branch moved en mass into the newly formed Communist Party of America, and *Laisvė* became an organ of the CPA.

## Communists Down on the Farm

A local man who wrote for *Laisvė* during the 1930s under the pen name, "Urbana Farmer," was Joseph Pakutinsky (Lith. Pakutinskas), who owned the aforementioned 80-acre farm on Mechanicsburg Road with his son Frank Pakey. Joseph and his wife Anna Janusauskis were born in Lithuania in the 1880s, and immigrated to the U.S. around 1907. According to grandson Donald Pakey, Joseph was a coal miner in the Herrin area and later a farmer in Champaign County before settling in Sangamon County.

Don Pakey in playpen, sister Emily and "the goat." Pakey farm, 1950s.

What Don, a physics professor at Eastern Illinois University, remembers from family lore are his grandfather's radical writings for *Laisvė* and the lively summer picnics of the Lithuanian Lodge on the Pakey farm. The Pakeys even had a cement slab laid in the picnic area to create an outdoor dance floor.

When he was a toddler, Don joined the picnics in a play pen, where he was not alone. A goat that his older sister Emily had bought from one of the Lithuanian-American women for three cents was initially small enough to squeeze in through the bars of the pen and play with young Don. Although he was too young to remember, Don's guess is that the Lithuanian Lodge Pakey farm picnics ended when his grandmother Anna died in 1958.

"Then, in the early 1960s, my grandfather, whom we called 'Pa,' had the first of several strokes," Don recalled, "and he couldn't really talk after that. He lived with us on the farm till he died in 1969. I only have memories of my grandfather wandering around the farm and doing light work. However, Emily has good memories of talking to 'Mamita,' as we called our grandmother, and her flocks of baby turkeys. Mamita didn't know a lot of English, but she and Emily did talk."

Don's father Frank and Uncle Pete attended the University of Illinois in the 1930s and fought for the U.S. in World War II.

## Hard Times on the Left

Immigrant leftist organizations provided self-help and cultural resources, like libraries, choirs and drama clubs to impoverished workers and their families when few organizations did. But even more important, they served as vehicles, often in concert with labor unions and sometimes in competition with them, for the struggle against the shameless exploitation of unskilled immigrant workers in mines and factories.

"Mamita" (Anna Janusauskis Pakutinskas) with her baby turkeys, Pakey farm, 1950s.

To the extent that the U.S. government served more powerful corporate and national interests, immigrant socialist and communist organizations were feared, from their inception, as real or potential enemies of the state. During World War I, they organized pacifist opposition that was an open threat to the draft. As a result, Congress passed the Espionage Act of 1917, subjecting those who opposed or interfered with America's war effort to jail time and/or deportation.

In fear of the radical foreign language press, the Sedition Act was passed in 1918 to discourage and punish public expressions of opinion that cast the government or the war effort in a negative light. Although the Sedition Act was repealed in 1920, the Espionage Act was upheld by the Supreme Court. It was probably no coincidence that 1920 also saw the beginning of a succession of U.S. laws closing the spigot of mass immigration from Southern and Eastern Europe that had fueled the growth of the radical labor movement and the American left.

Outdoor dance floor at Pakey farm picnic of the "Lithuanian Lodge," 1950s.

After the Russian revolution, American leftists tied their leadership, philosophy and actions to that single existing example of communist government, the U.S.S.R. These ties were less of a perceived threat during World War II, when the U.S. allied with the Soviet Union to defeat fascism. However, with the beginning of the Cold War, organized communism in the U.S. was virulently suppressed.

Most of us have heard of McCarthyism and the Hollywood blacklisting of former Communist Party members and sympathizers. Additionally, according to Don, "The Internet tells us of the June 23, 1947 Taft-Hartley Labor-Management Relations Act, passed by Congress over President Truman's veto, which sharply curtailed the rights of organized labor while forcing unions to purge communists from their ranks.

"Likewise," according to Don, "on Nov. 2, 1949, the Congress of Industrial Organizations (CIO) voted at its national convention to revoke the charter of the United Electrical Workers, the CIO's third largest union, for failing to purge itself of communist influence. Ultimately, 12 left-leaning unions, and countless individual left-wing organizers, were booted from the CIO."

# Stalin and the Abuses of Communism

Leftist party ties (in most cases, slavish ties) to Soviet leaders and policies made them not only a perceived threat to the U.S. government, but also stubbornly blind to the horrific purges and the Siberian gulag of Soviet dictator Josef Stalin. The left's lockstep allegiance to the U.S.S.R., including the 1940 and 1944 Soviet re-conquests of Lithuania, was a fundamental cause of conflict and division in many Lithuanian-American communities, including Springfield's.

With the arrival after World War II of Lithuanian eye witnesses to Soviet brutality in the form of displaced persons (DPs) like my father Vince, it had to become increasingly precarious to remain a Lithuanian-American Stalinist. Yet decades of true-believer orthodoxy and a lifetime of struggle probably made it emotionally hard even to listen to such witnesses, let alone embrace what they said.

From left: brothers Frank and Pete Pakey in U.S. Army uniform, World War II.

For Dad's part, living through one Soviet occupation in 1940 and narrowly escaping a second in 1944–fleeing thousands of miles into exile and losing his homeland and way of life–only to encounter Lithuanian-American communists in Springfield parading around at one of their functions in Red Army uniforms, had to be nothing less than traumatic.

Dad recalled the sight well into his 90s. And I believe the large and devoted leftist contingent within the Lithuanian community here played a role in his estrangement from that community. It couldn't have felt safe to mingle with Stalinists who were hostile to all evidence of the rape of Lithuania, and who likely had overseas contacts that were a danger to our family back home in Soviet-occupied Lithuania. (In 1989, when our family was reunited for the first time in 45 years, I learned that my Lithuanian aunts, uncles and cousins were spied on and persecuted until the very end of the Cold War.)

## Brother against Brother

To this day, it strikes me as grotesque that the twentieth century's first two waves of Lithuanian immigration to the U.S. had to be divided, brother against brother, by two contradictory visions and experiences of communism. For many first-wave miners like Joseph Pakutinsky, communism probably was first and foremost about building a world where working people weren't oppressed by company bosses and their political hacks. (Joseph's leftist leanings also could have had roots in Lithuania's anti-czarist movements of the late 1800s.) Yet Lithuanian-American communists' hierarchical subordination to the Communist Party of the U.S.S.R, even to the extent of embracing the Soviet conquest of Lithuania, was the ultimate fatal flaw.

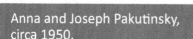

Political divisions pitting brother against brother were obvious from the beginning of the Lithuanian first wave, and may even have partially driven the building in 1908 of Springfield's St. Vincent de Paul (Lithuanian) Catholic Church. By the late 1910s, Catholics based at the church had organized the Knights of Lithuania and later, the Lithuanian Roman Catholic Alliance of Labor, likely as a bulwark against Lithuanian leftist organizing. For example, St. Vincent's and its branch of the Knights provided a rich array of the same kinds of cultural activities that leftist groups also used to attract, retain, and uplift their members. (See *Knights of Music, Baseball, Politics.*)

Anna and Joseph Pakutinsky, circa 1950.

During the 1950s, both Lithuanian Catholic and leftist groups contracted under the twin pressures of assimilation and a die-off of the first-wave immigrants who had formed their backbone. However, the decline of the leftist groups seems to have been more precipitous. This may have been partially due to leftist tendencies towards schism on the national level and the aforementioned Cold War-era attacks on the organized left. However, there can be no doubt that second-wave immigrants provided critical fresh blood for the parishes, while at the same time undermining the left's core reliance on the moral authority of the U.S.S.R.

America's prolonged and broad-based post-war economic expansion, trans-generational upward mobility through education, the success of labor unions, and increasing access to white collar professions in Springfield incrementally stole much of the left's thunder. Then in 1991 came the death blow: the break-up of the Soviet Union—ironically, on the force of peaceful and determined Lithuanian, Latvian and Estonian independence movements. The loss of the U.S.S.R. precipitated the ultimate crisis for the Lithuanian-American left, along with leftist movements around the world.

*All photos courtesy of Don Pakey.*

# Chapter 20
# Two Presidents Visit Springfield

Due to its large Lithuanian population, Springfield has played host to two Lithuanian presidents over the years: to be exact, one president-in-exile and one president-to-be. The first of these to visit was the most important leader of Lithuania's inter-war period of independence. The second was a World War II displaced person ("DP") who returned to lead Lithuania through the trials and triumphs of its early post-Soviet years.

On May 3, 1941, Lithuanian President **Antanas Smetona** became the first foreign president *ever* to visit Springfield, according to the *Illinois State Journal*. A life-long patriot who had worked for and signed the 1918 Act of Independence of the new Lithuanian republic following World War I, Smetona became Lithuania's first president in 1919 and subsequently, its longest-serving leader. He visited Springfield as a president-in-exile following the Soviet invasion and illegal annexation of Lithuania in the summer of 1940.

Antanas Smetona, President of Lithuania 1919-1920 and 1926-1940, *Wikimedia Commons. Owned by the National Museum of Lithuania.*

According to the newspaper, an official delegation including Springfield's mayor met Smetona's train from Chicago at the downtown depot, and police led his motorcade to the Illinois Capitol. (So the public could line the streets, the route of the motorcade was published in the newspaper in advance: west on Jefferson, south on Fifth, then west on Capitol Ave.)

## Likened to Lincoln

The official welcoming delegation included Fr. Stanley Yunker (Junkeris), pastor of St. Vincent de Paul (Lithuanian) Catholic Church, and William Yates (Yacubasky), chair of the Sangamon County Republican Central Committee. Several local women also helped arrange the visit and welcome the president: Mrs. Verona (Joseph) Welch (Wilcauskas), Mrs. Bertha (Yacubasky) Adams (Adomaitis), and Mrs. Julia (Gedman) Lukitis.

One newspaper report said Smetona proceeded to have an informal meeting at the Executive Mansion with Gov. Dwight Green. Other reports said he was met at the depot and introduced at a luncheon at the Leland Hotel (sponsored by Springfield's Mid-Day Club) by acting governor Lt. Gov. Hugh Cross. In his remarks, the lieutenant governor likened Smetona to Abraham Lincoln and spotlighted his achievement in establishing compulsory education and widely expanding Lithuanian literacy.

The importance of this cannot be overestimated in light of the devastating impact of illiteracy and zero formal education on the Lithuanians of the first wave. (Because of Smetona's policies, my father, who grew up on a subsistence farm in the Lithuanian countryside during the 1920s, had at least three years of formal schooling and learned to read and write and do math.)

LITHUANIAN CHOIR—Members of the Lithuanian choir, dressed in native customes, are shown above. The group sang yesterday during the Gold Star memorial service conducted at the Lincoln tomb under the auspices of the American Legion.

St. Vincent de Paul Church choir in performance dress, *Illinois State Journal-Register,* circa 1940. Ann (Tisckos) Wisnosky at center with necklace.

Prior to his own speech in English and Lithuanian, Smetona was honored by the singing of the Lithuanian national hymn by St. Vincent de Paul's choir (in costume) and the playing of the anthem and folk songs by George W. Killius on violin. According to the newspaper, members of the choir that day included: Bernice Bernotas, Agnes Bakunas, Genevieve Bugaveski, Frances Petrovich, Bernice Kurila, C. Turasky, Petronella Shimla, Ann Zintelis, Virginia Shadis, Bernice Rautis, Mary A. Shimkus, and Antocie (sp?) Zipnis.

The *Journal* reported that President Smetona's luncheon address detailed the brutality being suffered by the people of Lithuania at the hands of the Soviet

Union, pleading for the return of independence, justice and freedom to his homeland. (For more information about the remarkable life of Antanas Smetona, just search *Wikipedia*.)

Following lunch, the Lithuanian president toured Lincoln's Tomb, where he was greeted by other Lithuanian-Americans, and visited Lake Springfield, where he stopped at the home of Saddle Club owner Joseph Welch (Wilcauskas). Before returning to Chicago by train, Smetona was also feted at a public reception at the downtown Leland Hotel.

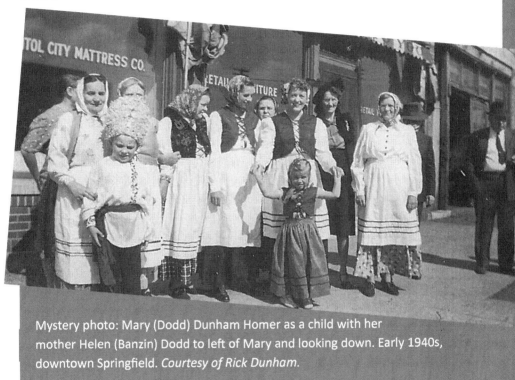

Mystery photo: Mary (Dodd) Dunham Homer as a child with her mother Helen (Banzin) Dodd to left of Mary and looking down. Early 1940s, downtown Springfield. *Courtesy of Rick Dunham.*

When I read that local Lithuanians lined the streets to greet President Smetona's motorcade, and saw the dirndl dresses likely worn by the choir at Smetona's luncheon, I wondered if this photo, owned by Rick Dunham, could have come from that day. (Note the boy in Cossack hat.)

## A Second President Visits

Fifty-six years and a long Soviet occupation later, Springfield was visited by **Valdas V. Adamkus**, a Lithuanian-born World War II refugee who had risen to power inside the U.S. Environmental Protection Agency (EPA) in Chicago. Adamkus arrived here on March 27, 1997 to give a talk at the University of Illinois at Springfield sponsored by the EPA's International Division. He was in the process of retiring from the EPA and moving back to Lithuania, after re-establishing his citizenship there in 1992. Adamkus also likely was already in the process of raising $1.25 million, with the help of Chicago friends, for his successful run for the Lithuanian presidency in 1998.

Members of Springfield's Lithuanian-American Club, some of whom knew Adamkus personally (I am thinking here of Ben and Vita Zemaitis), attend-

ed his March 27 talk and I believe, met him for dinner or a reception. Perhaps there was even a local fundraising event. Those photographed with Adamkus that day included: Romualda (Sidlauskas) Capranica, Rita Kupris, Vita Zemaitis, and Barbara Endzelis.

U.S. President George W. Bush shakes hands with President Valdas Adamkus of Lithuania, Feb. 12, 2007. *White House photo by Eric Draper.*

President Adamkus went on to lead Lithuania first from 1998 to 2003, and then 2004-2009, critical years for the country's admission to the European Union and NATO, its modernization and re-integration into the democratic world order. For more information about Valdas Adamkus, Lithuania's émigré president, who was also the longest-serving senior executive of the U.S. EPA and largely responsible for the clean-up of the U.S. Great Lakes, please visit *Wikipedia*.

*Post-script: In 1998, while I was working in Miami at a PR agency, I noticed a serious omission in an article on the front page of the Wall Street Journal. I promptly contacted the writer to inform him that the Valdas Adamkus whom the writer had cited for renouncing American citizenship had not done so in protest of U.S. policies or to evade taxes, but rather, to be elected president of Lithuania.*

*In 2005, while visiting relatives, I was taken to the Lithuanian Presidential Palace in Vilnius. It was interesting for me, while so far from home, to think of the fellow Lithuanian-American residing there.*

# Chapter 21
# Lithuanian by Many Names

One of my readers, Careen Jennings, recently submitted an extremely well-researched account of her Lithuanian immigrant great-grandparents, the Blaskie-Novicks, who lived in the Springfield area from the 1890s through the 1930s. Their son Billy Novick (1912-1928), Careen's great-great uncle, contracted polio. Until Billy died at 16, he had to crawl everywhere on his belly because his family couldn't afford a wheelchair. Unbelievable, but true.

In another section of her story, Careen shares no fewer than 13 different spellings of her paternal great-grandmother Mary's maiden name (probably originally Blaskavicius) uncovered through her research:

"On Mary's son Billy's 1912 birth certificate, the name is spelled Bluskonis. The Springfield city directories from 1917 to 1930 use the following spellings: Blesk, Blaskie, Blaski, Bluski, and Bluskie. The 1920 census uses Bluskie. The 1930 census gives three spellings: Blecki, Bleckie, and Bleakie.

"On daughter Margaret's marriage certificate, her mother's maiden name is spelled Bluske. *Ancestry.com* gives the spelling Blaskavicius, but cites no source for this spelling. And on Mary's death certificate, her father's last name is recorded as Blaskavich. The spelling that works on *Google* searches is Blaskovich. And there are probably more variations that I haven't found yet."

Mary (Blaskie) Novick with a grand-daughter. Circa 1930, two years after the death of Mary's crippled son Billy.

This huge variability in surname spelling is a common obstacle, if not also somewhat unique, to first-wave Lithuanian-American genealogy, compared with researching surnames more amenable to English translation and pronunciation (Italian, for example).

Where did such variability come from? Attempts at phonetic translation and truncation to comply with the norms of a new language and easy communication in the mines. Widespread illiteracy among first-wave Lithuanian immigrants and the lack of emphasis these impoverished immigrants, along with the officials who dealt with them, would have placed upon correctly recording their vital information. Maybe also once a surname was not really Lithuanian anymore, sense of ownership was diminished, being replaced with an "if you say so" attitude.

## Lithuanian or Pole?

For many Lithuanian immigrant families whose surnames were permanently converted to endings like "vich," "vitch," and "ski" or "sky," the issue was Polonization. Some of my readers have suggested that these transformations were made in the passenger registries of ships that were carrying mostly Polish immigrants. It is also a fact that for hundreds of years under the Polish-Lithuanian Commonwealth, and even under the Russian Empire that followed, Polish remained "high" culture vs. Lithuanian, and Poles the dominant force within both the nobility and the Catholic Church.

Under the circumstances, it would have made sense for lower-class Lithuanians, even in the process of their own national awakening, to reach for higher "Polish" status, or at the very least, to conform with it. Last but not least, there was the phenomenon of affinity. Both Polish and Lithuanian were targeted by the czarist 40-year language ban that prohibited publishing in the Roman alphabet.

As the Polish-Lithuanian Catholic Church and its village schools also came under Russian attack during this period (1863-1904), Poles and Lithuanians had rather a lot in common within the Lithuanian "province" of the Russian Empire. Perhaps that's why Poles and Lithuanians also tended to settle together in the same neighborhoods after immigrating to Springfield.

In any event, the incredible surname variability that Careen discovered is also an obvious tribute to the wide net she cast in her research, which involved many different dates and genealogy sources.

## Fetching Hot Water and Coal

The story of Careen's paternal great-grandparents shares many elements with other first-wave immigrants who arrived during Springfield's coal boom. Lithuanians Mary M. Blaskie (1869-1938) and her husband Edward Peter Novick (1865-1936), the son of Michael Novick (Lith. Navickas?) and Anna Bagdonis, both immigrated in the early 1890s.

The couple initially lived in a series of small mining towns north of Springfield: Spring Valley (Bureau County), Athens (Menard County), and possibly Cherry (Bureau County). By the time they arrived in Springfield in 1917, their 23-year-old (eldest child) Mary Louise had already married, after working from age 15 as a live-in domestic servant for wealthy Springfield families located on West Lawrence Street and South Grand Avenue.

According to Careen, the Novick family first appears in the Springfield City Directory in 1917, at which time they lived at 1919 E. Cook St., in a home that was owned by Mary Louise's new husband, August Schmidt. This indicates that the two families were probably living together. Then in 1918, the Novicks rented their own home at 1945 E. Lawrence St., where they resided until 1922, when records show they owned a home at 1808 E. Jackson St. Although the house on East Jackson had no electricity or running water, the Blaskie-Novicks lived there until around 1936.

Grandson John Edward Schmidt in front of the Novick house on East Jackson. 1980s.

Hot water for baths was fetched two blocks away at the entrance to the coal mine where father Edward worked. Careen writes, "Coal was used for cooking and heating, and during the winter Mary would go with her grandson John, a spry child, who would climb the coal cars on the railroad track and knock large chunks of coal to the ground for his grandmother to pick up and put into her wheelbarrow."

Elsewhere in this book, you will read of immigrants prosecuted and convicted for picking up coal that had fallen along the tracks from rail cars leaving the mines. However, Careen reports that even as a child, her father John could be sent by himself with a wheelbarrow to collect fallen coal. Perhaps enforcement was more lax with regard to children, and the family knew this. Or, maybe there was some trick or quick escape the Novicks could employ, living as they did only a distance of two houses from the tracks.

## Leaving School to Work

Like many coal-mining immigrant families of the time, the Blaskie-Novicks shared poor accommodations and needed every member who could possibly do so to work. Edward's mine operated only during the heating season, from October to April, so that is the only time he had a mining income. A whistle in the morning signaled that there would be work that day.

"During the summer, the family lived on odd jobs that Ed could get, what they could grow in their small backyard, and two-day-old baked goods," Careen writes. But it was necessary for all the children to work and contribute their earnings, as well. In addition to daughter Mary Louise's work as a domestic servant, which required her to leave school after fifth grade, son Edward, Jr., only finished sixth grade and was working as a truck driver by age 18 and a coal miner by age 20.

According to Springfield city directories, Stella (Vitalena), the youngest daughter, was working as a driller at Metor Work(?) in 1930, an operator at Sangamo Electric in 1931, and a nurse in 1934. Careen writes, "Tragically, Stella had a mental breakdown when she was still a young woman (schizophrenia?) and spent most of her life thereafter in the Jacksonville Insane Asylum, as it was then called."

## Polio without a Wheelchair

Young Billy Novick's grave, 1928.

Additionally, Careen draws for us perhaps the saddest picture I have yet encountered in this book. "Billy, the youngest surviving son (two of the family's children died in infancy), was paralyzed from polio. The family had no money to buy a wheelchair," she writes, "so he dragged himself around with his arms, holding his head up so he could see. His mother strained herself to lift and help her dear son many times a day. Especially as he grew into a teenager, this physical strain caused her to develop enlarged veins in her neck and arms.

"Tragically, Billy had no schooling, no tutoring, and no friends. But he taught himself to read from the newspaper comics. He died at 16 from complications of polio, loved by a family too impoverished to help him. Their feelings for Billy are clear almost a century later from this photo of his grave covered with flowers."

When I read this anecdote, I wonder if young Billy's fate might have been worse in Springfield than it would have been in Lithuania, where isolated in the countryside, he might never have contracted polio.

## The Blaskie-Novick Grandparents

Careen's father John Schmidt, son of August and Mary Louise (Novick) Schmidt, and his sister were often cared for by their immigrant grandparents Edward and Mary (Blaskie) Novick during the 1920s. Careen reports that this was while the children's mother Mary Louise, who had once worked as a domestic, now worked as a waitress at the Abe Lincoln Hotel, where many prominent politicians of the time dined.

The elder Novicks went to bed early, so unless the grandchildren were sleeping over, they never babysat after 6 p.m. (Possibly the lack of electricity had something to do with their early bedtime.) Careen's father John remembered that his immigrant grandparents never learned English, and when he was young he could understand Lithuanian.

Careen continues, "Even when John was 88, he still remembered a Lithuanian sentence that translates: 'Be good or I'll beat your bottom.' Children and grandchildren of immigrants had to learn that life was tough. John also learned to swear in Lithuanian, doubtless from his grandfather.

"My father John remembered that his grandparents, especially his grandmother, had a passionate hatred for Russians. Considering Lithuania's history, she had reason. Another vivid memory for John was of the delicious beet *barščiai* (borsht) that his grandmother made. Unfortunately, her particular recipe has been lost. Mary (Blaskie) Novick's entire life was built around her home and children, and her husband never 'let' her go anywhere except church."

## Death by Miner's Lung Disease

By the 1930 census, immigrant Edward was no longer employed due to mining-related lung disease. According to this census, although both Ed and Mary could speak English, neither could read or write. Neither had become naturalized U.S. citizens.

Careen writes: "John remembered his grandfather Ed sitting in a rocking chair on their small front porch on Sundays, happily drunk and singing Lithuanian songs. He made his own beer, skimming off the froth on top to taste it as it brewed. He had no social life ('never went anywhere') and probably had little else to bring him joy.

"When he spent the night at the Novick house, John remembered his grandfather Ed coughing all night and spitting into a bucket of ashes. After 20 years in the mines, Ed was disabled by several chronic lung diseases. He stopped working in July 1928—the same month that son Billy died—and lived for eight years unable to work.

According to his death certificate, Lithuanian immigrant Edward Novick died at about age 71 on April 11, 1936 from a lethal cocktail of lung diseases: mycocarditis, bronchitis, bronchiectasis with emphysema, and asthma. His death certificate states that his lung diseases were *not* related to his occupation. This is, of course, a transparent lie and may have influenced grandson John to become a lifelong pro-union Democrat."

Immigrant Mary's brother William was also a miner who registered for the World War I draft on June 5, 1917. His birthplace was listed as Marijampole, Lithuania, from which he arrived in the U.S. in 1911. On the 1920 census, he stated that he had applied for U.S. citizenship, could speak English and owned a home with no mortgage.

William Blaskie worked as a "shot firer" at the coal mine, or a "blaster" who used black powder to bring down the walls of coal from 5 to 11 p.m. at night so that chunks of coal could be sorted and loaded by crews on the morning shift. The dangerous nature of his job might have resulted in higher pay and could have accounted for his home ownership so soon after immigration, Careen writes.

"In 1940 William Blaskie's two sons were in their early 20s and still living at home, though one worked full-time and the other was looking for work. On his World War II draft registration dated April 27, 1942, William was 51 and still working for Peabody Coal."

*All photos courtesy of Careen Jennings.*

*Post-Script: Careen's father John Edward Schmidt (1916-2005) grew up in Springfield but spent his late childhood in Bluffs, Ill. He served in the Navy during World War II, and after the war, he built a motel in Decatur. He spent the rest of his working life in the motel business, his second and last motel being the Intown in Decatur. According to Careen, John retained strong ties to Springfield throughout his life because his parents August and Mary Louise (Novick) Schmidt remained here, along with his only sibling, a sister.*

*A Decatur native, Careen remembers many a Sunday spent with relatives in Springfield. She left Illinois for college and eventually ended up in small-town Eastern Connecticut, where she taught high school for nearly 40 years.*

# Chapter 22
# Sons & Daughters of Misfortune

## A Life Worth $20

On July 17, 1917 in Taylorville, the wife of a Lithuanian miner, Mrs. Victoria Abroms (Abromaitis?) committed suicide, leaving behind two small children. The reason? She had lost a precious $20 bill.

It is difficult to imagine the depths of poverty and domestic violence that left this young mother no other escape from the crisis of losing about five days of her husband's mining wages—likely saved from household expenses over weeks or months.

The *Illinois State Journal* reported that, "fearing her husband's wrath," Mrs. Abroms drank carbolic acid and died almost instantly. Derived from coal tar, carbolic acid, or phenol, was used back then as an antiseptic, especially in soaps. (Mrs. Abroms probably made her own soap and had a ready supply.) According to *Wikipedia*, during World War II, the Nazis used injections of phenol in individual executions of thousands of prisoners. Toxic to the central nervous system, it causes severe muscle spasms, then sudden collapse and loss of consciousness.

## Killed for Stealing Grapes

Many other Lithuanian immigrants of the first wave experienced not opportunity in new lands, but a stacked deck. It's likely most would have had an even tougher time back in the Lithuania of the same period. Nevertheless, it's important to remember that for some, immigration was not a panacea, or even, ultimately, a path to survival.

Also according to the *Journal*, in August 1906, Anton (Antanas) Garulis was shot to death while running with a basket of stolen grapes from the fruit farm of J.W. Cogdall east of Springfield. Probably a coal miner with no work for the summer, Garulis was with another unidentified man when caught in the act of grape thievery by 17-year-old Dwight Cogdall. Young Cogdall ordered the men to stop, and when they ran, he started shooting with a revolver.

Garulis was hit above the hip, and the bullet "went high," injuring internal organs and causing him to die later in the hospital. His young shooter posted bail on a warrant of manslaughter that was issued as "a matter of form." I believe the young shooter ultimately was not tried.

## Jailed for Scavenging Coal

In October 1905, Lithuanian immigrant Samuel Buckewitch (Buckevičius), of the Ridgely neighborhood on Springfield's north side, was convicted of larceny for picking up fallen coal along the railroad tracks running from the Jones & Adams mine.

Although the four bushels of coal found in his home, no doubt stored for winter, were worth only 28 cents, his fine and court costs amounted to $9.10. According to the *Journal,* this penalty was enough to have bought a whole wagon load of coal. It is not known whether Buckewitch was able to scrape together enough from friends and relatives to pay the fine, or whether he went to jail just for trying to stay warm.

## Stealing Flour for Hungry Children

"Their husbands were out of work, their children were hungry, and so they stole," reported the Jan. 23, 1918 *Illinois State Register*. But stealing from a railcar is a federal crime, and the railroad does not forgive.

Four Lithuanian women, "three with babies clinging to their skirts," pleaded guilty in federal court in Springfield, having been transported here from Granite City, where they were arrested for stealing flour from railcars "engaged in interstate traffic." Mary Kovich, Mary Savaoda, Katie Kranachivic, and Ann Artolian were their reported names (perhaps the newspaper was wrong and only two were Lithuanian: Kovich and Kranachivic).

Mrs. Kovich's 13-year-old daughter was brought along to act as court interpreter in English, Serbian, and Bohemian, in addition to Lithuanian. The four convicted women were each charged the minimum fine: $25 plus court costs, according to the newspaper. However, none could pay, so they were remanded to the county jail in Carlinville to serve 30 days.

On the bright side, federal authorities in Springfield treated the women and children kindly, letting them bunk in a courthouse conference room instead of the jail while they were here, and buying "stockings and dresses for the babies." (One can only wonder how poorly they were clothed.) Newspaper accounts also featured a charitable tone, suggesting "that the fines of the women may be paid for them by charitable citizens."

If not, I wonder if the children would have served 30 days with their mothers.

# Killed by Mentally Unstable Boarder

Lithuanian miners' wives were usually expected to earn extra income for the family by "boarding" multiple single miners along with their own families. This exposure in close quarters drastically raised the potential for domestic abuse of women and children, especially considering factors like alcoholism, criminal/vagrant tendencies and mental illnesses that might have kept many of the boarders perpetually single in a marrying culture.

According to reports in the *Journal*, on Feb. 9, 1926 Alice Tamoszaitis (Tamosaitis or Tamosaitiene), about 37, born in Lithuania, was shot and killed at 6:30 a.m. in her home at 1604 E. Carpenter St. The killer, Lithuanian Charles Kaziusis, was ruled by a coroner's jury to be "laboring under some delusion with murderous intent." After shooting his victim, Kaziusis subsequently shot himself through his left lung and died on Feb. 22, 1926, according to newspaper reports.

I first spotted the Tamoszaitis murder in a Sangamon County Coroner's inquest book in winter 2014 while I was looking up the facts of another immigrant's death. Almost a year later, while perusing a newspaper page shared by Tom Mann for information on a mine death, I spotted a column by A.L. Bowen that must have been referencing the same murder.

Grave of Alice Tamoszaitis, Calvary Cemetery, 2014. Headstone translation, correcting for misspellings: Alesė Tamošaitienė, June 1891 to February 9, 1926, Laukuvos Parish (Lithuania). Three Will Pray (or Pray Three Times), Rest in Peace. *Translation by Irena Ivoskute Sorrells.*

Dated March 11, 1926, just weeks after the crime, Bowen's column described how an un-named mother and wife was killed by a boarder who rushed into the dining room of her humble home, brandishing a revolver. "Pointing it at the mother, he accused her of placing poison in his food, and before the eyes of (her) husband and children, shot her down and turned the gun upon himself," Bowen wrote.

Besides timing, the fact that the killer subsequently shot himself also conforms with the facts of the Tamoszaitis murder.

## Mental Illness Recognized but Not Treated

In lamenting the tragic death of a wife and mother, Bowen noted, in language familiar to our own time, that the husband and neighbors had noticed the shooter acting strangely. "Underlying symptoms of a dangerous (mental) disease," he wrote, "were recognized but not understood." Bowen went on to draw parallels between mental/nervous illnesses more rampant than tuberculosis, yet much less understood, diagnosed and treated.

"Isn't it strange how much attention we give to physical disease, but how little we give to mental?" he asked. "The killing of this woman adds another accusing finger at our failure to understand that part of our health which means the most to us."

I shudder now to think how the scant reserves that many Lithuanians brought to the daily rigors of the mining life were progressively eroded, likely in combination with alcohol. The steady mental and physical decline of the men around them could only have endangered countless immigrant women and children where they should have been safest: inside their own homes and neighborhoods.

*Alice Tamoszaitis grave photos courtesy of Genealogics.*

## Stereotyping Lithuanian Crime

In the early twentieth century, local newspapers reported Lithuanian ethnicity in crimes of violence, much as media later in the century reported race. As a newspaper reporter in the early 1980s, I remember how the practice of race identification in the news was debated before it was changed, along with the custom of identifying all women as Mrs. or Miss.

Nevertheless, it's easy to see why a "Lithuanian" brawl could have seemed relevant to U.S.-born readers back when there was frequent immigrant-on-immigrant crime in the impoverished neighborhoods, often called "patches," where immigrant miners lived, socialized, drank and fought. It's also easy to see how such a wave of crime came to stereotype Lithuanian immigrants in the news.

July-December 1906, the *Illinois State Register* covered a "Riverton Riot," allegedly by three related Lithuanian saloon-keepers, that resulted in grievous injuries to the local marshal, John A. Cline. The prosecution side of the story was that Cline ordered Lithuanian immigrant Maude (Martha) Grigiski (Lith. Grigiskis) to close her Riverton saloon, which was illegally open on a Sunday.

Maude reportedly refused, pulled a gun and backed Cline out of her yard. Then her husband, William, arrived, seized the officer's club and started beating him over the head. Maude reportedly joined in the beating with the butt of her pistol, while brother-in-law Peter (Simon) Grigiski arrived and allegedly started beating Cline with a brickbat.

The three Grigiskies were charged with assault and battery with intent to kill, and "riot." They made bail of $1,200 each, apparently after William exited first and sold some property to bail out his wife. Marshal Cline received 56 stitches to close wounds on his scalp.

## Lithuanians to the Defense

According to newspaper reports "almost the entire village" was subpoenaed in the case to witness either to the events or the defendants' characters. Those who had not been subpoenaed came along to observe the proceedings, so that the courtroom was full long before the trial began. The paper also reported, "Most of the witnesses in this case will be Lithuanians, and an interpreter will be necessitated."

When the defense took the stand, the Grigiskies proceeded to make a case for their actions based on the alleged "immoral character" of Marshal Cline, which was attested by many (presumably Lithuanian) witnesses. William Grigiskis then testified that the assault was the result of Cline first attacking his wife. Maude testified that she had closed her saloon as ordered, but then Cline insisted they go back inside to see if anyone was still there, at which point he made advances and knocked her out with his revolver.

## Battling Sunday Alcohol Bans

The real issue probably was a law closing saloons and taverns, frequently operated by immigrants for immigrants, on Sundays, which could have been the best day of the week for the saloon business, since miners got paid on Saturday. Certainly, Sunday was the only officially designated day of rest for working people.

In New York City back when Teddy Roosevelt was police commissioner, more than 10,000 German immigrants marched to oppose a similar law closing taverns on Sundays. Such bans were not only likely a precursor to Prohibition; they were almost undoubtedly aimed squarely at hard-drinking immigrant workmen and tavern-keepers. In fact, Simon Grigiski had been fined $25, along with six Italian tavern-keepers, back in 1902 for the same offense, according to the newspaper.

## 'Rioters' Convicted

After weeks of trial, on Dec. 29, 1906, the *Illinois State Journal* reported, Simon was acquitted, and William and Maude Grigiski were convicted, denied a new trial, and fined $100 plus costs, each: a total judgment amounting to $400. (One has to wonder at a fine, only, for assaulting a lawman—maybe it was a compromise of some sort based on Cline's previous actions or reputation?) It's unknown if the Grigiskies were allowed to re-open their saloon.

Lithuanians Ralph Patkus, Tony Gabriel and Peter Soto were also reportedly arrested or charged with participating in the assault on Cline. One can almost imagine the whole Lithuanian neighborhood joining in a fight apparently in defense of their countrymen against a despised representative of the law. (However, these three men were not tried.)

## 'One Carved at a Christening'

My favorite example of Lithuanian immigrant stereotyping in the news is: "Lithuanian Celebration in Devereaux 'Patch' Results in the Usual Quota of Cracked Pates." This *Journal* article from January 1910 goes on to report "a miniature riot, such as usually accompany Lithuanian christenings."

"Devereaux Patch" was a poor immigrant neighborhood near the Devereaux Heights Peabody coal mine four miles north of Springfield. Lithuanian immigrant Charles Rokinh reportedly beat Tony Shodwit with a blackjack and cut him with a knife at the home of the christened infant. The paper also reported, "Several swollen pates and blackened eyes are said to have resulted from the Sunday night celebration."

- Lithuanian-American Luke Terlis testifies he did not mean to shoot countryman Joe Timmis, critically wounding him in the gut on July 4, 1906. "Terlis declares that the shooting was accidental, as the ball pierced his own hand before it struck his friend." Both men are coal miners. "Their knowledge of the ways of this country is exceedingly limited, and they speak very broken English."

  According to various *Journal* reports, Terlis offered a bribe of $20 not to be arrested when accosted at his Devereaux Patch boarding house by a deputy. In police reports, victim Timmis and witnesses agree that the shooting was accidental and occurred when Terlis was trying to prove to a group of miners standing at the corner of Peoria Road and Sangamon Avenue that the gun he was carrying was unloaded.

  In a dramatic twist, Timmis's wife later testifies that Terlis had made advances and wanted to do away with her husband, and so had probably planned the shooting to look like an accident.

- Mike Krizonoski is charged with conducting a "blind pig" (operating a speakeasy) in Devereaux Patch, November 1911.

- Lithuanian Mike Rester is charged with stabbing fellow Lithuanian Frank Kerns during a brawl at the Jacob Usman saloon in March 1907.

- Charles Yotus pleads guilty to selling liquor in Devereaux Patch for three days before he was caught, September 1911.

- Peter Akulaitis shoots and kills Joseph Linc in self-defense in the Ridgely neighborhood, September 1906. Linc was wielding a two-bladed pocketknife and had cut Akulaitis severely before he was shot. Akulaitis's gun was believed to have been passed off to a friend in the crowd "who secreted it."

- John Lawrence and Eva Adamitis are both charged with assault with intent to kill in April 1946. Eva reportedly shot John in the face after he beat her in her home.

- Lithuanians Charles Shadwich, Charles Tyrones, Pete Zolden, Joe Savage and Robert Skeets are arrested Christmas Eve 1911, for gambling (a dice game) on East Washington Street.

## Outlaws & Outliers

With the help of loving and intact families and their church, most Lithuanian-Americans here were able to rise above generations of harsh oppression in the old country and harsh conditions in the new to achieve a kind of impoverished respectability. Not all, however. I would wager that almost every Lithuanian-American family in Springfield has at least one outlaw or outlier in the closet not too many generations back.

The majority, I would guess, had never known a family or community life unmarred by unnatural death and spontaneous acts of violence: crimes of passion, temporary insanity or inebriation. At the turn of the twentieth century, there was little help for the disease of alcoholism, let alone the full spectrum of mental illnesses and criminal tendencies: no welfare and no social safety net.

Insecurity—physical, economic and social—was the rule for unskilled immigrant workers, and early death smote the upstanding as unexpectedly and frequently as the morally or criminally deranged. I can't even imagine what it would have been like to face a grinding struggle to survive every day for a lifetime—with no hope of relief. Not only would some pressure release have been required; at the same time, fear of punishment would not have exerted its normal deterrence. With so much hardship, anger and bitterness surrounding them, it seems remarkable that so many could rise above and not give in to bitterness or take their revenge on society.

## Bootlegging

At the most practical level, property crime to support the family after the injury or death of a father in the coal mines launched more than one disadvantaged youth into the Illinois penal system.

But small-scale bootlegging—a victimless crime—was perhaps the most common illegal activity. According to Wally Surgis, Prohibition provided an almost irresistible temptation—and pathway—to illegal activity for Lithuanians and other immigrants for whom alcohol consumption and production was a way of life. In fact, pervasive alcoholism and crimes under-the-influence in burgeoning immigrant communities drove much support among mainstream Americans for the Christian Temperance movement and Prohibition, which was quite popular in many quarters.

Wally reports that his Surgis (Sudrius) grandparents in Auburn were illiterate but owned a still. During Prohibition, Wally says that his father Walter and Walter's sister were employed by their Lithuanian immigrant parents to haul illegal, home-made alcohol to customers. Grandfather Frank Surgis actually became quite rich from his bootleg trade, according to Wally, and later went to live with his daughter on East Mason Street in Springfield. Over time, however, medical treatment for his mining-related black lung disease ate up all his earnings, so that he died in the same poverty he had escaped.

## Running with the Birger Gang

Frank's son Walter continued on the wrong side of the law, eventually running with the famous Southern Illinois bootlegging gang headed by immigrant Charlie Birger, and serving sentences at Menard (Chester) Penitentiary for bank robbery and bootlegging. Wally adds: "During Prohibition or the Depression, my father and a friend from Auburn got hold of some phony deputy sheriffs' badges and went into the bars in Springfield under the guise of being officers of the law. They confiscated the slot machines, took them somewhere and broke them open for the money inside.

"It didn't take long for the big boys in Chicago to come downstate to put a permanent stop to this. My dad's friend got wind of this and left town, but my dad was caught and taken out to Lake Springfield to be done away with. He somehow managed to escape when they stopped the car, dove into the lake and swam away. He didn't say, but I assume he was probably under fire as he swam to safety.

"Dad then got out and walked the railroad tracks back to Auburn to stay off the road. He said he packed some clothes, went hitch-hiking and didn't care which direction, as long as it was far away. He ended up in Oklahoma, worked the coal mines there for a while and then rode the rails to Colorado. Dad stayed gone for three years and figured it was safe after that to come home. I doubt if he ever stole a slot machine again."

Walter's criminal career did not later prevent him from working for Pillsbury Mills and the City of Springfield, according to Wally. He was also famous for fishing and gardening and sharing produce with the poor Lithuanians of East Reynolds Street through friend and barkeep Tony Romanowski (Lith. Ramanauskas).

## Untimely / Violent Death

To see just how pervasive crime and unnatural death were in the Lithuanian immigrant community here, one only need look at the Sangamon County Coroner's inquest book from a 12-day period in February 1926. First came the aforementioned murder on February 9 of Alice Tamoszaitis in her home on East Carpenter.

Then on February 18, John Blazis, 45, of 2565 S. College St., was cut in half by a train on the Wabash tracks between the Wits and Iles junctions at 6:15 a.m. No speculation was offered as to whether the death was intentional, but it appeared Blazis had fallen or was lying across the tracks.

Finally, on February 21, my father's paternal uncle by marriage, Frank Orback, Sr., died after consuming 55-proof alcohol with traces of poison wood alcohol. The widow, Dad's paternal aunt Anna (Baksyte) Orback, sued Antanas and Ursula Lawrence (Lith. Launikonis) for $10,000, allegedly for providing the alcohol that killed her husband. Her civil suit appears to have been dropped after a couple of years.

## 'All in the Family' Violence

Whenever searching local newspaper archives for other information, I frequently stumble over Lithuanian-on-Lithuanian crime. For example, in 1910, the *Journal* reports, Lithuanian immigrant William Gurski was charged with stabbing his countryman and North 15th Street neighbor Tony Krodok in the right lung as he stepped off a streetcar following a dispute between the two men earlier that night in a downtown bar. Krodok was described as a boarder. Both men were probably miners. According to the paper, Lithuanian Mike Karinanski also was held for complicity in the stabbing.

The case of Anthony (Antanas) Laugzem (1891-1938) is an example of the alcohol-fueled violence that could erupt at immigrant social gatherings. Despite his pleas of innocence, Laugzem was found guilty of murdering a fellow Lithuanian-American, Tony Pachules, by a Sangamon circuit court jury on Oct. 18, 1922, according to the *Journal*.

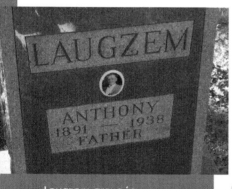

Laugzem grave in Calvary Cemetery, 2014. *Courtesy of Genealogics.*

Party guests had placed bets on an informal dancing contest at the Laugzem home on East Black Street in the Ridgely neighborhood. Laugzem testified that a dispute erupted between the victim and another man over their bets, and he asked both men to leave. Pachules, the victim, was shot in the back while walking away from the house. His deathbed statement claimed he turned and saw Laugzem firing from the porch, but Laugzem never wavered in his testimony that he had remained inside the house and that the other man who was asked to leave must have shot Pachules.

## All the Way to the Supreme Court

Laugzem's lawyer, Edmund Burke, a prominent former state's attorney, appealed the conviction, unsuccessfully, all the way to the Illinois Supreme Court after being denied a new trial. Burke's insufficient evidence appeal might have been based on the "X" signature by the illiterate victim on the written statement naming Laugzem. The convicted killer's 14-year sentence was upheld, though he continued to deny guilt. Laugzem's daughter Stella Laugzem (Lang) later became the first of three wives who all pre-deceased John Nevada (Lith. Nevardoskus—also Nevidauski), who earned a purple heart in World War II.

It seems clear that the same language and economic barriers that ghettoized immigrants also made violent crime largely an "all in the family" affair. Many individuals could survive and succeed only by cutting themselves loose from the lifelong dead weight of relatives who consistently drank away all their earnings, then begged for money, or who descended into a life of crime. Clearly Lithuanian-on-Lithuanian violence, including domestic and sexual abuse, added significantly to the minefield of risks and burdens Lithuanian immigrants and their offspring had to walk as they tried to survive and thrive in the United States.

## Shooting to Kill During the Depression

What do the deaths of 12-year-old African-American Gilmore Johnson and 15-year-old Lithuanian-American Joseph Donner (also Donnor), both of Springfield, tell us about crime and punishment during the Great Depression? I was surprised to learn that even petty property crime by youths back then was often met with fatal gunfire, both by police and by family business owners.

This no doubt speaks to the high frequency—and the high stakes—of property crime as families struggled to survive the greatest economic calamity in American history. This, at the same time that local coal mines were conducting mass layoffs and the Progressive Miners of America (PMA) were on strike.

## 'Haves vs. Have-Nots' When Nobody Had Much

The nature of crime and punishment during those trying years of wholesale unemployment and bread lines definitely seemed to pit struggling families against each other—just as the "Mine Wars" pitted the United Mine Workers against the Progressives.

I say that because the taverns and groceries being targeted for break-ins—and occasionally, armed robbery—were owned and defended by working families living on the premises. And, the policemen shooting to halt, maim or kill were often laid-off miners distinguished from the people they were shooting at mainly by the luck of having secured jobs on the force.

The fact that men on both sides of the "Mine Wars," as well as child burglars and the family business owners they targeted, pretty universally seemed to own or to be able to steal firearms underscores the fact that our seemingly crime-ridden times may not be unique.

## Shot by Police

Joseph Donner, Jr., of North 19th Street was born on May 8, 1917 in Piston, Penn., to coal-miner Joseph and his wife Anna (Zacarosky) Donner, both born in Lithuania. Only a few months after I learned of this young man's death, I stumbled upon his graduation photo from Ridgely Grade School at age 15 in 1932.

From left: Joseph Donner with friend John Shaudis at their Ridgely Grade School graduation, 1932. *State Journal-Register.*

According to the *Journal*, young Joe apparently began participating in a string of petty burglaries and larcenies starting two months after his grade school graduation on July 4, 1932, when he reportedly entered the Woodland Avenue home of Walter Hanson with an older boy, Joseph Orback, 17. Orback was the son of the aforementioned Frank Orback, Sr., and Anna (Baksyte) Orback, my father's paternal aunt.

On Dec. 1, 1932, according to the newspaper, Orback, Donner, Charles Jedrosky, 17, and George Sotak, 17, all–except Donner–of North 17th Street and likely all Lithuanian-Americans, broke into the Voyzel lunchroom on R.R. 8, taking a small quantity of tobacco and candy to sell. Then, the paper recounts, Orback, Jedrosky and Donner, minus Sotak, broke into the Frank Mason Grocery at Walnut Street and Calhoun Avenue. Police waited in ambush.

## Ambushed at Grocery Break-In

Young Donner was shot in the back and the side when he ran away instead of obeying the order to halt. While initial reports indicated he was improving, young Joe died of his wounds at St. John's Hospital on December 3, and was buried in Calvary Cemetery on December 6.

A *Journal* article dated Dec. 1, 1932, states that Patrolmen John Rooney and William Cellini, and Detectives Edward Hagan and Samuel Phoenix, were the officers who had fired their service revolvers. The coroner's inquest reportedly did not determine which officer fired the shots that hit and killed young Donner.

According to William Cellini, Jr., grandson of Patrolman Cellini, "Sam Phoenix (1903-73) was one of the few African-Americans on the force at that time. He must have joined at the same time as my grandfather, because on the 1930 census, Sam is listed as a coal miner at 520 N. 12th St. Then by 1931, he's on the force. It's remarkable that he got to be a detective in the short span from 1931-32."

According to Cellini, Edward Hagan, despite his Irish-sounding name, was another African-American detective. Patrolman John Rooney was from England, and the 1930 census shows he immigrated to the U.S. in 1910.

Probable juvenile ringleader Joe Orback went on to violate the probation he was granted for the 1932 break-ins and was sent to Menard for two years in 1933, according to newspaper reports. This seems to have launched him into a life of crime, since the 1940 Census finds him in prison at Marion. I sometimes wonder if young Donner might not have ended as he did if it hadn't been the Depression, and he hadn't fallen in with the wrong older boys.

## Shot by Tavern Owner

Gilmore Johnson, 12, of North 14th Street, was breaking through the window of a side door at Lapinski's Tavern near 10th and Washington at 5:50 a.m. Dec. 20, 1937--while his 13-year-old accomplice Griffin Clark kept watch–when Lithuanian-American Simonas (Sam) Lapinski, who slept upstairs, was awakened by the noise and grabbed his gun. After Lapinski ran down the stairs and shouted at the boy, he took off south down 11th Street.

Dad's first cousin Joe Orback on a better day, circa 1945. *Courtesy of Sandy (Orback) Pecori.*

Lapinski ran into the street and fired three shots in warning, while ordering Johnson (never having seen Clark) to halt. Then he fatefully fired a fourth shot that he testified he *did* intend to hit the fleeing burglar. Lapinski also testified that in the darkness, he didn't know the criminal he was shooting at was just a boy. Unfortunately, young Johnson was fatally wounded.

## 'Colored' Jury Wants Investigation

According to the *Journal*, an unloaded .38 caliber pistol and a watch were found on the boy, which the newspaper said had been taken from the Starlight Tavern at 1230 E. Washington, which the boys had previously broken into. The newspaper also reported the two boys also had broken into the Edward McCann tavern at 917 E. Washington and the Leon Stuart filling station at 14th and Jefferson streets, and had been apprehended three times before and released, due to their youth. This time the surviving boy was turned over to juvenile authorities.

An "all-colored" coroner's jury unanimously recommended that Sam Lapinski be turned over to a grand jury, and he was held for investigation by a grand jury, but I could find no further articles about what happened next. Sam was active at St. Vincent de Paul Lithuanian Catholic Church and its chapter of the Knights of Lithuania. His son Sam, Jr., a former miner, had recently joined the Springfield police force and later seems to have taken over Lapinski's tavern.

# Chapter 23
# Veterans: World War I

As many as 50,000 Lithuanian-Americans fought for the United States in World War I. This remarkable number was later leveraged to lobby U.S. President Woodrow Wilson to recognize the newly independent Lithuanian state that emerged from the war's aftermath.

Ironically, the vast majority of the young Lithuanians who served America in World War I were fighting for a country they barely knew. Most were very recent, impoverished immigrants—not yet citizens–who barely spoke or read English. Ironically, many had fled Lithuania to escape long-term military conscription by the Russian czar.

This is the reality we must face when we think of **Jonas (John) Kedis, Joseph (Juozas) Kowlowski, Walter Rauktis, and Stephen Shvagzdis,** four young Lithuanian immigrants to Central Illinois who died in the War to End All Wars. Like most of the war's victims, these four died violently, far too young, and so very far from family and home.

John Joseph Straukas, Riverton. WWI "doughboy" portrait, 1918. *Courtesy of Nancy (Kaylor) Betz.*

However, the fact that these young Lithuanians were shipped back across the Atlantic to die so soon after they had crossed the Atlantic with so much courage and hope strikes me with a special poignancy. That they died in the climactic bloodbath in which so many American lives were sacrificed to finally bring the war to an end seems particularly tragic.

## The Meuse-Argonne Offensive

According to the *New York Times*, during the late summer and fall of 1918, 26,277 Americans died during the Meuse-Argonne Offensive. For 47 days, American units threw themselves against the densest, most sophisticated and deadly fortifications in history, turning the tide of the Great War against the Germans.

"It remains, to this day, the deadliest battle in American history," the *Times* says. The reason? "The Germans had had four years to set up their defenses in the area, and they didn't waste a single day of it: Everywhere you go in the Argonne, you'll find (evidence of) German trench works, pillboxes, block-houses, and artillery pits (once complete with officers' villas, rest camps, waterworks, and electrification)."

*The Times* also noted that the American Cemetery at Romagne-sous-Montfaucon, Lorraine, France, where Pvt. Jonas Kedis is buried, is the largest American cemetery in Europe from either World War I or II, holding 14,246 dead. To read more about how dug-in the Germans were, and how Americans still managed to prevail at Meuse-Argonne, see the *New York Times* article dated Dec. 28, 2014 entitled, "Travel in France: Vestiges of the Great War's Bloody End."

*(Thanks to exhaustive research of U.S. Census, draft and service record databases by our Lithuanian-American friend Tim Race of Elmhurst, Ill., as well as information and photos uncovered by Genealogics and Mike Kienzler of sangamonlink.org, we have the partial stories of Kedis, Kowlowski, Rauktis and Shvagzdis. Let us now honor them in memory.)*

**Jonas (John) Kedis**, born about 1890 in Kaltinenai, Lithuania, arrived in the U.S. in April 1910 from the Dutch port of Rotterdam on the ship Rijndam. Although he lived in the 700 block of East Washington Street in Springfield in 1916, Kedis was living and working in Chicago as an iceman for Commonwealth Ice Co. by the time he registered for the draft on June 5, 1917.

About 27 years old of medium build with light brown hair and blue eyes, Kedis was an alien who had sworn an oath of loyalty to the U.S., placing himself on an accelerated track to citizenship specially created for immigrants who fought in the war. On his draft papers, he declared no dependents.

Unfortunately, Kedis was killed on Oct. 10, 1918 while serving as a private with the U.S. Army's 1st Engineer Regiment, 1st Infantry Division, and is buried in the just-mentioned Meuse-Argonne American Cemetery. Ironically, if he had survived another five weeks, he would have made it to armistice.

"Stanley Kedis,
"330 North Fifth Street,
"Springfield.
"Dear Sir: It is with regret and sorrow that I inform you of the death of your brother, Private John Kedis, Company C, First United States Engineers, who was killed in action on October 10, 1918.
"He participated in the battle October 8 and 10, when the victory that he fought for was nearly won. He was buried where he fell, on the field of battle.
"His loss is deeply felt by all.
"F. BILLBY,
"Col. Engineers, U. S. A."

**Walter A. Rauktis**, born in Veikanus (possibly Viekšniai), Lithuania, in 1891, was mining for the Jones & Adams Coal Co. on Rural Route #8 and living at 2518 Peoria Rd. in Springfield when he registered for the draft on June 6, 1917. He described himself as single, but with a mother and father who depended on him for support.

Rauktis had blue eyes and light brown hair, and was not yet a citizen, either, when he was killed in service to our country as a private with the U.S. Army 47th Infantry Regiment, 4th Infantry Division on July 29, 1918. He is buried in the Oise-Aisne American Cemetery in Fere-en-Tardenois, France.

Pvt. Rauktis is in the back row, right edge, in this photo from the *Illinois State Journal-Register. Courtesy of sangamonlink.org.*

Young coal miner **Joseph (Juozas) Kowlowski**, born in Marijampole, Lithuania, in 1893, migrated from the Pennsylvania coal fields to Pana, Ill., sometime after 1910. He would have been in Christian County for seven years or less when he was drafted in 1917. (I hope to get a few more details about Kowlowski's life, death and burial place.)

**Stephen Shvagzdis** was born in 1890, the son of Mrs. and Mrs. Michael Shvagzdis. He was living at 1413 E. Adams St. in Springfield when he entered the service in April 1918. He trained at Fort Dix, N.J., was shipped overseas in June 1918, and served as a private with Company K of the 148th Division of the U.S. Army in the famous Meuse-Argonne Offensive.

Private Shvagzdis was killed in action Nov. 11, 1918, Armistice Day of the War to End All Wars. He could have missed only by minutes or hours being honored as the very last soldier in the entire war to be killed. But according to the *Times*, that honor went to U.S. Army Private Henry Nicholas Gunther of Baltimore, 23, shot through the head at 10:59 a.m. on Nov. 11, 1918—one minute before the peace treaty took effect. A small monument still stands on the spot where Pvt. Gunther was killed, probably not far from where Pvt. Shvagzdis fell, near the tiny village of Chaumont-devant-Damvillers, France.

## STEPHEN SHVAGZDIS

Private, Company K. 148th Division, U. S. A. Son of Mr. and Mrs. Michael Shvagzdis. Born June 25, 1890. Resided at 1431 East Adams street, Springfield, Ill. Entered service April 29, 1918, in Springfield, Ill. Received his training at Camp Dix, N. J. Sailed overseas June 25, 1918. In action in Meuse-Argonne Offensive. Killed in action November 11, 1918.

From the Sangamon County Honor Roll. *Courtesy of Mike Kienzler and sangamonlink.org*

### CHARLES KRISTUTE

U. S. A. Son of Charles Kristute, Lithuania. Address, Pawnee, Ill. Entered service at the age of twenty-four years. Entrained for Camp Forrest, Ga., September 4, 1918.

### STANLEY PATRILLA

Private, Company K, 45th Infantry, Ninth Division, U. S. A. Son of Mrs. Isabella Patrilla, Lithuania. Born December 24, 1890, in Lithuania. Address, Auburn, Ill. Entered service May 30, 1918, in Springfield, Ill. Received his training at Camp Gordon, Ga., and Camp Sheridan, Ala. Was at Camp Sheridan, Ala., when the Armistice was signed. Discharged June 14, 1919, at Camp Taylor, Ky.

### JOSEPH PAULAUSKAS

Private, Infantry, U. S. A. Son of Mr. and Mrs. Frank Paulauskas, both deceased. Born July 25, 1888, in Lithuania. Address, 1031 Wheeler avenue, Springfield, Ill. Entered service February 23, 1918, in Springfield, Ill. Received his training at Camp Taylor, Ky., and Camp Sevier, S. C. Sailed overseas June 6, 1918. In action at Ypres, Voormezeele, Bellicourt, Busigny, St. Souplet, Macenghien, and Ribecourville. Was in France when the Armistice was signed. Discharged April 14, 1919, at Camp Grant, Ill.

### FRANK PETROWICH

Private, Company C, 119th Infantry, 38th Division, U. S. A. Son of Mr. and Mrs. Joe Petrowich, Lithuania. Born December 24, 1893, in Lithuania. Address, Auburn, Ill. Entered service February 23, 1918, in Auburn, Ill. Received his training at Camp Taylor, Ky., Camp Sevier, S. C., and in France. Sailed overseas May 11, 1918. In action at Ypres and Hindenburg Line. Was in Amiens, France, when the Armistice was signed. Discharged April 14, 1919, at Camp Grant, Ill.

### CHARLES M. RACZAITIS

Private, Company B, 105th Engineers, 30th Division, U. S. A. Born March 1, 1889, in Lithuania. Address, Diverson, Ill. Entered service September 23, 1918, in Springfield, Ill. Received his training at Camp Taylor, Ky., and Camp Sevier, S. C. Sailed overseas May 18, 1918. In action at Bellicourt, Monthpalain, Brancourt, Premont, Busigny, LaSalle River, Vaux Andigny and Maurehioy. Gassed in action. Was in Brancourt, France, when the Armistice was signed. Discharged April 22, 1919, at Camp Grant, Ill.

### JOHN JOSEPH STRAUKAS

Private, Company P, Fifth Battalion, 22nd Engineers, U. S. A. Son of John Straukas, Lithuania. Born August 25, 1892, in Lithuania. Address, Riverton, Ill. Entered service June 23, 1918, in Springfield, Ill. Received his training at Ft. Benjamin Harrison, Ind. Sailed overseas September 15, 1918. Was in action in Meuse-Argonne Offensive when the Armistice was signed. Discharged July 7, 1919, at Camp Grant, Ill.

Local Lithuanian-American soldiers from the Sangamon County Honor Roll. *Courtesy of Genealogics.*

*Below is a list of WWI draft-registered Lithuanians from Central Illinois who survived the war. Their names and counties are from research by Tim Race of Elmhurst, relatives, and a database developed by Genealogics in much-appreciated voluntary assistance to my blog and book.*

*Each man is from Springfield unless otherwise noted. Many other Lithuanian-Americans from our area no doubt were drafted and served in World War I, but their service could not be verified because their surnames did not appear Lithuanian to the eye, and/or they listed their country of origin as Poland or Russia. (Lithuania and Poland were part of the Russian Empire until after WWI.)*

*It is plausible to assume that most of the men on this list not only registered, but served. Two survived service in the Great War only to die in our local coal mines.*

## The List

William Blaskie, Joseph Damkus (came to Springfield in 1898, worked as a policeman after 1906 and lived with his wife Isabel Adomaitis at 1809 N. 10th St.), Mike Bubnis, Frank Embrolitus (Macoupin, killed in coal mining rock fall, Gillespie, 1941), Andrew Fraier, Joseph Gedman, Anthony Glemza, Charles J. Grigas, John F. Gurgens (Army, Camp Wadsworth, limited duty), John Kalvatis (Montgomery County), Mike Kavaloski (Macoupin County), Franciscus J. Krasauskis, Charles Kristute (Pawnee), John Kukowich, John Kunski (Montgomery County), Jurgis Lanauskas, Stanley Norbut, Stanley Patrilla (Auburn—also lived on Jefferson Street in Springfield with the Papir family), Charles Paulanski (Logan County), Joseph Paulauskas (moved to Detroit after the war), John Petkus, William Petraits (Christian County), Joseph Petrushunas, Stanley Petrokas, Anton J. Petrouch (Divernon), Frank Petrowich (Auburn), Joseph Plaskas, Alex Potsus, Charles Raczaitis (Divernon–gassed in action and came home disabled), George Ragoznice, Charles Rumsas (Sangamon County), Sylvester Senkus, John Joseph Straukas (lived in Riverton as a nephew of the Grigiski family), George Stravinski, Frank Tonelis, John Treinis, Mike Trumbit (Macoupin County), Frank B. Vinson (Christian County), Ignatz Wecksnis, Paul Widowski (killed in a Madison Coal Co. mine explosion, Divernon, 1923), John Joseph Yacubasky (Yates), Stanley (Junkeris) Yunker (probably did not serve--went on to become the long-time pastor of St. Vincent de Paul Catholic Church), Andrew Zelowski (Christian County), Joseph Zvingilas.

# Chapter 24
# Veterans: World War II

Back in 2013, I was intrigued to learn of a memorial plaque honoring the war dead of St. Vincent de Paul (Lithuanian) Catholic Church. Various informants mentioned it was made of bronze or some other metal and located at the back of the church, though no one seems to know where it went when the church was closed and torn down in the 1970s.

I owe my first knowledge of the missing memorial plaque to the devoted memory of Maria (Fry) Race, granddaughter of Agnes (Tonila) Gooch, who often spoke of her brother Johnny, Maria's great uncle, who was honored on it. On Nov. 9 and 11, 2014, the *State Journal-Register* carried two brief items about our quest for the plaque. If it survives and can be found, the Lithuanian-American community could then ask the Cathedral, where Lithuanian Catholic immigrants first organized themselves more than 100 years ago, to re-mount the plaque in a sacred place of honor.

In the meantime, I have tried to reconstruct the stories of Springfield's Lithuanian-American dead from World Wars I and II. Melinda McDonald of Rochester also used her talents to design a graphical re-creation of the plaque for my blog.

## Springfield Lithuanian-American World War II Deaths

Whereas the Lithuanians who fought for the U.S. in World War I were recent immigrants, World War II was fought by the immigrants' U.S.-born sons. Sixty-eight members of St. Vincent de Paul Church served their country in World War II, according to the *Journal-Register*.

**John F. Miller** (Milleris), 26, of Springfield, died in military service in 1944. He was killed in an automobile accident in the Savannah Beach, Ga., Eighth Army Air Force camp where he had been stationed since 1942. Corporal Miller had completed basic training at Seymour Johnson Field, Tenn. He was the brother of Jeanette, Florence, Louise, and twin Peter S. Miller (who was serving as a sergeant with the U.S. Army in Corsica, France when John was killed.) All were children of Sylvester and Mary (Moskers) Miller. Sylvester was born in Lithuania and the family operated Miller's Market at 121 W. Jefferson St. for many years. John had been employed at

*Killed*

CORP. JOHN F. MILLER

*Illinois State Journal-Register*, 1944.

the market before working at the Wright Aeronautical Co. in Dayton, Ohio, at the time of his enlistment.

**George Sneckus, 20,** of Springfield, was the son of Lithuanian immigrants George and Nellie Sneckus. After graduating from Lanphier High School, he earned the rank of staff sergeant in the U.S. Army Air Force, 100th Bomb Group. George was a "waist gunner" on his first mission on a B-17 bomber when he was shot down and killed over Germany only a few weeks before the Normandy invasion. George's body initially was recovered by the Germans from a farmer's field and buried in the local cemetery.

Many years later, George's niece Teresa (Sneckus) Gregoire, daughter of George's older brother Julius, learned of her uncle's brave sacrifice, and of the retrieval and re-burial of his remains in Belgium with many other U.S. aviators. In August 2001, Teresa took her mother, aunt, and two cousins to visit and decorate George's grave in the Ardennes American Cemetery at Neupre, Belgium. Teresa says it was a very moving experience because no one from George's family had ever visited his grave.

U.S. Air Force Staff Sergeant George Sneckus. *Courtesy of Teresa (Sneckus) Gregoire.*

**John P. (Johnny) Tonila** was one of nine children of Lithuanian-born coal miner John George and Agatha (Mankus) Tonila, who each emigrated from Lithuania separately around 1900. A local Golden Gloves boxing champ, Johnny drove a delivery truck for a living. He was not quite 32 and engaged to be married when he gave his life in the Battle of Monte Cassino near Rome, Italy, in May 1944. He was killed during an artillery strike while serving as a cook in a mess tent with the U.S Army 338th Field Artillery Battalion.

Johnny Tonila, circa 1940. *Courtesy of Maria (Fry) Race.*

A technician fifth grade, Johnny was not drafted—he enlisted in 1939 and served in the Philippines before the U.S. entered WWII in December 1941. Beloved and never forgotten by his many sisters and brothers, Johnny is also remembered by great-niece Maria (Fry) Race, whom he never met.

Johnny Tonila, Golden Gloves champ. *Courtesy of Maria (Fry) Race.*

**Steven E. Buckus**, 22, of 1403 Osbourne, Springfield, was a private first class in the U.S. Army who had fought in North Africa, Italy, France and Germany when he was reported MIA in Germany on April 8, 1945, the very closing days of the war in Europe. His remains were not recovered and returned to his mother, Mildred Veronica (Peleckis) Buckus, for burial in Calvary Cemetery until January 1949.

According to newspaper reports, six months prior to enlisting in the fall of 1942, Steven spent two weeks in the hospital as the result of an auto accident in which he was a passenger. He had been employed by the Cudahy Packing Co. and had five sisters. His sister Helen Sullivan was informed her husband Henry had been killed in Belgium just a few months before the family learned of Steven's death.

**John Z. Urbis, Jr.,** of Riverton, a technical sergeant with the U.S. Army, is buried in the Cambridge Permanent Cemetery in Cambridge, England. An aerial engineer on a "Flying Fortress," John was shot down over Hamburg, Germany. His parents, John and Anna (Zebrawskie) Urbis of Riverton, received notice of his death on August 20, 1943, according to the *Illinois State Journal*.

John had been a bookkeeper for eight years at Yelton-Weaver Supply Co. when he enlisted in December 1941. Posthumously, he was awarded the Distinguished Flying Cross and the American Legion Gold Star. Prior to his death, according to newspaper reports, he had been cited for "extraordinary achievement in bagging three enemy planes" and received the Air Medal with three oak leaf clusters. He was Riverton's first casualty of the war and an only son with one sister: Helen Shattuck Callan.

## Veterans Not Killed in Action

Second Lieutenant Frank I. Makarauskas of Springfield was the U.S.-born son of immigrants Stanley and Agnes Makarauskas and the much younger brother of Lithuanian-born Michael and John (Makarauskas) Mack, Springfield's self-made McDonald's restaurant mogul. Frank's widow Dorothy (Roth) Makarauskas, formerly of Springfield, reports that Frank was drafted into the U.S. Air Force right after he graduated from Feitshans High School in 1943 at age 18. Due to his lengthy training to learn changing navigation parameters for the B-24 bomber, World War II was over before Frank saw combat. But that training changed his life. After the war, Frank

Frank I. Makarauskas, *courtesy of Dorothy Makarauskas.*

earned an electrical engineering degree at Michigan State University on the G.I. Bill, becoming the first in his family to attend college. He later worked as an engineer for Central Illinois Power Co. in Mattoon and Marion, and for the Michigan Department of Commerce in Lansing.

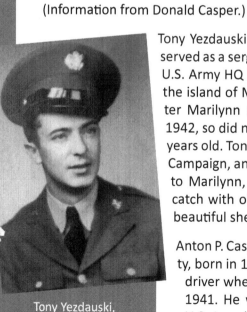

Stanley J. Yanor of Springfield was the son of a Lithuanian immigrant who worked at the coal mine at the corner of Chatham Road and West Washington Street. After attending Du Buois Grade School and Springfield High School, Stanley enlisted in the U.S. Army and served as a sergeant in the famous Battle of the Bulge. Stanley's Lithuanian language skills later gave him a role as a translator after the Allies invaded Germany, where tens of thousands of Lithuanian refugees had fled as the Red Army reached their country in the summer of 1944. After the war, Stanley owned an insurance adjusting business briefly in Springfield, then in Champaign. (Information from Donald Casper.)

William J. Urban of Springfield served in the U.S. Navy. *Courtesy of Debbie (Davis) Ritter.*

John P. Yuskavich, Jr., *courtesy of Pat (Yuskavich) Towner.*

Tony Yezdauski of Springfield served as a sergeant with the U.S. Army HQ BTRY 229 AAA in New Guinea, specifically the island of Morotai, beginning in March 1942. Daughter Marilynn reports that she was born in September 1942, so did not meet her dad until she was almost four years old. Tony participated in the Asiatic Pacific Theatre Campaign, and made the most of his time off, according to Marilynn, who says her dad fished and shared his catch with other soldiers, and came home with many beautiful shells.

Anton P. Casper of Sangamon County, born in 1910, was a bus or truck driver when he enlisted in August 1941. He was a private with the U.S. Army's Field Artillery.

Tony Yezdauski, *courtesy of Marilynn (Yezdauski) Doherty.*

William J. Casper of Sangamon County was born in 1921. He enlisted as a private in the U.S. Army Air Corps in July 1941.

Thomas J. Kasper of Sangamon County was born in 1909. He was married and a meat-cutter by trade when he became a U.S. Army warrant officer (private) in December 1942.

John Nevada (Lith. Nevardoskus) was awarded the Purple Heart for his service as a ski trooper in the Italian Alps with the famous U.S. Army 10th Mountain Division.

*State Journal-Register* photo picturing Broneslaw Dedinas, center, 1944.

Bernice Bernotas, World War II "Wave." *Courtesy of Susan (Bernotas) Potter.*

Charles Galman, son of Jonas Galminas (John Galman) in center. *Courtesy of David Black.*

*Following is a list of many Sangamon County Lithuanian-Americans who served in World War II, based on painstaking research of public records by Tim Race of Elmhurst, Ill., as well as submissions from descendants and other sources. Those who lost their lives are in bold.*

Leo Ambrose, Frank L. Arnish, William J. Augustitis (Army, Bronze Star), Edward J. Babeckis, Joseph J Babeckis, Clement J. Banaitis, Veto (Vytautas) F. Banaitis (Army), Adam Bender, Anthony P. Bernotas (Army), Bernice Bernotas Stevens, Vetout (Vytautas) C. Bernotas, Joe Bestudik (Navy), Thomas Bestudik (Navy), William V. Blazis, John F. Brazitis, Walter Brazitis, **Steven E. Buckus**, Anton P. Casper, William J. Casper, John Chenski, Edward C. Chernis, Joseph J. Chernis, Alfred F. Cizauskas, Broneslaw Dedinas, Domenick Detrubis, John G. Dombroski, Charles Dumbris, Florie J. Evinsky, Joseph J. Evinsky, Charles J. Galman, John Grigiski, Frank W. Grinn (Army–Asiatic-Pacific Medal with two bronze stars), Frank Gudausky (Navy), Charles Gurgens (Marines), Thomas J. Kasper, William Kavirts, Joseph P. Kellus, Stanley Klickna, Al, John, and William Klutnick, Barney J. Kurlytis, John Kutselas, Albert T. Kwedar (flight surgeon, Army Air Force), Thaddeus Lamsargis, Joseph J. Lauduskie, William J. Laukaitis, Frank I. Makarauskas, Edward J. Masus, Victor Matula, Joseph Martinkus, John W. (Guoga) McCaskey, Thomas L. Micklus, William J. Micklus, Walter J. Mikelonis, **John Miller (Milleris)**, Peter S. Miller (Army), William D. L. Morris, Joseph R. Morris, John T. Nevada (Nevardoskus–Nevidauski)–Army 10th Mountain Division, Purple Heart; Frank and Pete Pakey (Pakutinsky), George A. Patkus (Army), Ralph M. Patkus (Navy), Frank W. Pupkis (leader of the UMW local), Tony Rachkus, George A. Rackauskas, Jack R. Relzda, Joseph J. Repske, George E. Rudis, Stanley O. Senalik (Army, two bronze stars), George Rudis, John F. Rumsas, John Edward Schmidt (Navy–his mother was a Blaskie-Novick), Alban C. Shadis, Frank Shadis, William J. Shaudis, Felix Shimkus (four battle stars, WWII and Korea—union leader at Peabody #7 in Taylorville), Frank S. Shimkus, John D. Shimkus, Joseph J Shimkus, Stanley Shimkus (U.S. Marine, owner of Stanley Supply and Stanley's Plumbing and Heating for 26 years) William C. Shimkus, Anthony G Sirtout, **George Sneckus**, Julius Sneckus, Anthony Sockol, Edward J. Stanks, Dominick J. Stankus (Army), Anthony P. Stockus, Charles J. Stockus, Martin Stockus, Frank J. Surgis, Albert J. Swinkunas, William J. Tater, Adolph W. Tisckos (Navy), Charles G. Tisckos (Navy), Martin Tisckos (Army), **John P. Tonila**, William J. Urban, **John Z. Urbis**, Anthony F. Usalus, Joseph J. Usalis, Joseph P. Welch (Wilcauskas)–Navy, George J. Wisnosky (Army), Joseph Yacubasky (Yates), Walter Yakus, Joseph Yamont (Jomantas), Stanley Yanor, Stanley Yuscius (Army), Tony Yuscius (b. 1923, served with the Army in the Middle Eastern theater and earned three bronze service stars), Anthony J. Yuskavich, John P. Yuskavich.

*Post-script: Records discovered by Genealogics show that 62-year-old coal miner Frank Meszeikis, who lived on South Walnut Street, also registered for the WWII draft. A resident of Springfield for 45 years and a member of Progressive Miners of America Local 63, Frank was crushed by a roof fall in Panther Creek No. 5 on Dec. 23, 1947.*

# Chapter 25
# Honoring an Uncle Lost in World War II
*By Teresa and Ron Gregoire*

Staff Sergeant George Sneckus was one of two waist gunners on a 10-man Boeing B-17 heavy bomber in World War II. Only 20 years old, he was assigned to the famed 8th Air Force 100th Bomb Group. The media had given this group the ominous nickname of "The Bloody 100th" due to its high casualty rate in dangerous bombing raids over German-occupied territory.

Unfortunately, the story of young George, like so many other airmen in the 100th, reflects the group's lethal reputation. On May 24, 1944, George's bomber flew out of Thorpe Abbotts Field, England, headed to Berlin. It was his very first—and his last—mission.

The remains of all 10 airmen on the plane, including George's, were found along with the wreckage of his B-17 in a farmer's field near Itzstedt, Germany. The German Air Force brought the remains of the "flyers" (as they came to be called by our allies) to the South Cemetery in

U.S. Air Force Staff Sergeant George Sneckus, 20, at completion of his training to be a waist gunner on a 10-man B-17 bomber, 1944.

Neumunster, Germany. There, they were given military honors and buried in plain wooden caskets.

## Buried as an 'Unknown'

Due to the condition of George's body and the unauthorized removal of dog tags, his remains could not be positively identified when he was later disinterred from the Neumunster cemetery, by a special U.S. military team, for reburial in one of the U.S. military cemeteries in liberated countries.

So George initially was buried as an "unknown" in Ardennes American Cemetery in Neupre (formerly Neuville-en-Condroz), Belgium. It was not until September 1948 that his parents, Lithuanian immigrants George and Petronella (Nellie) Sneckus, received a letter notifying them their son had been positively identified by forensic technicians utilizing dental records.

Initially unable to accept this news, it wasn't until January 1949 that George's parents agreed with his identification and gave their approval for the inscrip-

Teresa (Sneckus) Gregoire with flowers and photo at her uncle George's grave, Neupre, Belgium, 2001.

tion on the cross marking their son's grave to be changed from Unknown X-955 to S/Sgt. George Sneckus.

Teresa Gregoire (nee: Sneckus) of Springfield never knew her father Julius's only sibling, her Uncle George. "When I was a little girl, during the summer months, I would often see my grandmother sitting for hours in solitude in her backyard. Her tulip chair facing west, she would watch the sunset while my grandfather tended to his very large vegetable garden," Teresa recalls. "I believe she suffered from depression, which was probably true of so many parents who lost their sons and daughters in World War II."

## North Side Pride

Over the years when the family would reminisce, there were few details to complete George's story. He was a graduate of Lanphier High School, where he had been an outgoing, musically talented first-chair violinist. Along with his brother, he had been a member of the self-proclaimed north-end boys' club "The Vultures" from 1935-1942. The club consisted of 14 youngsters, many of whom were Lithuanian-Americans like George.

So strong were his ties to "The Vultures" that the club's name was etched into his violin. Teresa still treasures that violin and other relics of her uncle's life, including a large, framed portrait taken of the young airman with his 50-caliber Browning machine gun upon his induction into the U.S. Air Force. She still remembers the picture hanging above her grandparents' television until their death in the early 1960s.

## The Search Begins

Then one day in the late 1990s, a friend of Teresa's mother, Jim Graff of Middleton, a U.S. Army veteran who had fought in the infamous Battle of the Bulge, suggested that the family should have the military medals due George. Very active in veteran-related events honoring the lives of his fallen comrades, Jim provided Teresa with the address and information needed to claim George's medals. More importantly, he introduced her to an extremely helpful and thoughtful contact in England, Robert (Bob) Watkins.

## A Brit in the 'Blitz'

Early in WWII Nazi Germany waged a relentless campaign of night-time bombing raids of several U.K. cities that became known as the "Blitz." These destructive and deadly raids lasted from September 1940 through May 1941. As a child, Bob was one of thousands of Londoners who regularly sought shelter in the tunnels of the Underground subway system during these raids. Due to those wartime experiences, Bob was dedicated to helping American families learn more about their loved ones lost defending England.

Robert and Teresa became friends by corresponding via the Internet. He provided links to various websites, including the 100th Bomb Group at Thorpe Abbotts Field, where George had been stationed. With Robert helping Teresa gather information from veterans and families on both sides of WWII, the two followed every possible lead.

## German vs. American Information

Amazingly, Robert tracked down a lead from a German veteran providing new information conflicting with official records about George's death. American records state that a thousand-pound bomb was accidentally dropped on George's plane from a B-17 flying above. This was, unfortunately, not an uncommon accident in formations that included hundreds of B-17s. However, German records indicate something different happened.

They describe George's bomber as the lead plane in the second tier of a B-17 formation. Though armed with ten 50-caliber machine guns and able to sustain considerable damage and keep flying, the B-17 lumbering giants were easy targets for the Luftwaffe fighters.

In theory, a bomber group's survival depended on flying in tiered "box" formations massing the B-17s' guns against German Me-109 and FW190 fighters. German fighter pilots typically attempted to break the B-17 formation by flying into it from the front, where less defensive firepower could be directed. This could also force the B-17 pilots into evasive maneuvers. Once out of formation, the more vulnerable individual bombers could be shot down.

In the case of George's ill-fated mission, it was reported that a German pilot attacking from the front had flown directly into George's B-17. As the fighter pilot approached, neither pilot veered. The German account of the crash mentioned that the fighter pilot had lost an eye on an earlier mission. He may have been shot on approach, or crashed head on into George's bomber unintentionally, due to impaired depth perception and poor visibility due to heavy cirrus clouds and smoke coming from the B17 engines.

## Making the Pilgrimage

Using Internet links provided by Bob Watkins, Teresa located George's grave in Belgium. Then in August 2001, Teresa, her mother, Josephine Sneckus, and three other family members made plans to visit both Thorpe Abbotts Air Force Base in England and George's final resting place.

During her research, Teresa had been contacted by daughters of two crewmen on George's plane. Born while the two men were at war, neither woman had ever met her father. Teresa promised to take photos and decorate both men's graves on their behalf.

Thorpe Abbotts Air Force Base in East Anglia is where George was stationed for two weeks prior to his fateful mission. Complete with a memorial museum staffed by volunteers and a website, this former base has been restored to honor the 100th Bomb Group and all the airmen of the 8th Air Force. It is the most complete surviving example of the 122 WWII airfields constructed in the rich farming region northeast of London.

While there, Teresa and her mother envisioned a young George living, training and taking off in his heavily ladened bomber from the main runway, just 30 minutes by air from targets on the continent. The women continued their pilgrimage across the English Channel, making their way to the Ardennes American Cemetery in Neupre, Belgium, and George's gravesite.

They were humbled by what they saw there: more than 5,000 white crosses in perfect formation, one for each fallen airman. Before leaving on her trip, Teresa had filled a large container with soil from the backyard of her uncle's boyhood home on North Bengel Street in Springfield. She brought the very soil that George once played on as a child to spread over his grave.

Since he had never been able to return home, she wanted to bring his "home" to him. Teresa also left a fragment of the Thorpe Abbotts' runway, given to her by the base's caretaker, next to George's cross. The family then placed large bouquets of fresh flowers on the graves of George and his two brothers-in-arms, said prayers, and sang patriotic songs. Finally the graves of the fallen had been  visited, honored and decorated by people from back home.

## Facts Confirmed by Eyewitness

Once home, Teresa decided to contact the Thorpe Abbott's online discussion board and posted the following: "Researching my uncle's death, I discovered that the German and American records present conflicting accounts of this air battle. Can anyone tell me which story is accurate?"

Within a few minutes she received a response from a Robert Black, who had been a radioman/gunner on the second Lt. Clarke T. Johnson plane shot down during the same battle, crashing in the same field as the first Lt. Martin T. Hoskenson plane that George was on. One of only three survivors of the B-17s shot down that day, Robert confirmed that it had happened as the Germans said: "I was in the plane behind your uncle's and witnessed the collision."

Having two sons of her own, both now older than George when he died, Teresa says she can't imagine how his mother (her grandmother) Nellie must have suffered. "George closely resembled my father Julius, who served as a staff sergeant in the Marines during WWII, fighting in the Pacific at the same time George was fighting in Europe. I sometimes wonder if he had lived and grown older along with my father, if they would have shared their war stories with us," she muses.

"Now whenever I look at our country's flag, I think of George's ultimate sacrifice, and that of his family. To me, this sacrifice defines the meaning of patriotism. The memory of George and how he died is something my family and I will carry with us and honor for the rest of our lives."

*Photos courtesy of Teresa Gregoire.*

# Chapter 26
# Our Sports Hall of Fame

According to the *Illinois State Journal-Register*, Lithuanian-Americans have contributed their share of Springfield sports greats. Names like **Rudis, Blazis, Banaitis, Wisnosky, Gurski, Darran, Gvazdinskas, Bestudik and Alane** have graced the columns of the paper's sports pages over the years—as well as its annual Sports Hall of Fame.

However, even in this exalted company, the **Urbanckas** name stands out.

On left: Al Urbanckas, D.D.S., being named to the *Journal-Register's* Sports Hall of Fame, 1992. *Newspaper glossy.*

**Al (Alfred) Urbanckas, Jr.**, who later became a Springfield dentist, played basketball for Cathedral Boys High School, becoming the first Cathedral athlete to lead the city tournament in scoring the same year (1954) that he won the state high jump title. Dr. Al was all-city in basketball in both 1953 and 1954. Later, he set the Big Ten high-jump record on behalf of the University of Illinois (6 feet and 8 and ¾ inches) that stood 1954-64. In 1957, he won the high jump in the Big Ten outdoor and indoor track and field conferences.

After he also tied for first place in the NCAA high jump competition that same year, Dr. Al was named Midwest Track Athlete of the Year (1957) by *Coach and Athlete* magazine. His jumps routinely boosted U of I's rankings at Big Ten track and field events throughout his college career.

Dr. Al's uncle **Peter Urbanckas**, Springfield High School Class of 1934, played SHS basketball and football as offensive and defensive left tackle. Known as the "Bone Crusher" on the gridiron, Peter later helped bring Golden Gloves boxing to the Illinois State Armory in Springfield.

Still later, he was known as "Pistol Pete" for recruiting thousands of new members for Springfield's YMCA 1968-94. Peter was also a charter member in 1956 of Lake Springfield's TRN Club. He was inducted into the *SJ-R's* Sports Hall of Fame (as a "Friend of Sport") at age 85 in 2000, nine years after the induction of his nephew, Dr. Al.

Al Urbanckas, Jr., in high jump competition, 1950s. *Courtesy of same.*

Not to be outdone, **Debbie (Urbanckas) Jemison**, Dr. Al's daughter, was inducted into the *SJ-R's* Sports Hall of Fame in 2014 for her outstanding career in Sacred Heart Academy (SHA) and University of Missouri (Columbia) volleyball.

According to newspaper reports, Debbie graduated from SHA in 1981 after being named to the "All City Volleyball" lineup in 1979 and 1980. At Missouri, Debbie was a starting outside hitter for four years and captain of the team during her junior and senior years. She set the university's record for service aces in a four-game match, and held the record for kills–23 in one match—for five years. Debbie even made the final cut for the U.S. Junior Olympic Team.

Debbie Urbanckas in high school. *Courtesy of Al Urbanckas, D.D.S.*

One more Urbanckas, Dr. Al's father and Peter's brother **Alfred Urbanckas, Sr.**, completed four decades of "chain gang" service at high school football games in Memorial Stadium at age 86 in 1997, serving alongside his Lithuanian-American friend Peter Kurila. Al, Sr., had played football for SHS and was a member of the class of 1928. In 1947, he became a founding member of Lake Springfield's Postal Club.

Photo of chaperone Mary (Rudis) Bestudik of the AAGPBL. *From the official website of the AAGPBL.*

In addition to the four Urbanckases just mentioned, the *SJ-R's* Sports Hall of Fame also includes Lithuanian-Americans **Joe Bestudik** (2003), and **Ed Gvazdinskas** (2004). Bestudik was a U.S. Navy veteran of World War II who was drafted by the Brooklyn Dodgers baseball team prior to the war. He played for several teams in the American League after the war, as well.

Other Lithuanian-American names in the Sports Hall of Fame belong to "Friends of Sport" **Rich Lamsargis** (1999) and **Bill Maslauski** (1997).

Inducted in 1993, **Mary (Rudis) Bestudik** (Joe Bestudik's wife), was a multi-talented athlete (basketball, baseball, diving, bowling) who played women's basketball at the regional and national levels, and captained the 1934 Amateur Athletic Union (AAU) All-American basketball team.

According to the newspaper, nine years later, she teamed with Marge Tapocik to win the scratch and handicap doubles titles in the women's city bowling tournament. An early champion of women's sports, in 1948 Mary chaperoned away games for the "Springfield Sallies" All-American Girls Professional Baseball League (AAGPBL) team. Remember the film, "A League of Their Own?"

**Other Notable Lithuanian-American Sports Men and Women:**

**Dick Alane** was a triple threat on the Griffin High School baseball, basketball and football teams.

**John Gurski** won the Springfield Public Links Golf Tournament in 1948.

Coal mine union leader **Felix Shimkus** was a national amateur bicycle race champion and organized bicycle races in Springfield.

From age 68 to 88, **George Rackauskas** was a committed volunteer organizer for The State Farm (LPGA) Classic at The Rail Golf Course (1980-2000).

L to r: Gordon White and Dick Alane holding the trophy for the Colt League World Series, 1958. *Courtesy of Elaine Alane.*

**Matt Banaitis** was a baseball catcher and winning quarterback (2014) for the Chatham Glenwood Titans.

**Enoch Blazis** and **John Wisnosky** played football for Griffin High School. After four years on the Griffin team, Enoch also played for the U.S. Naval Academy in Annapolis, MD. (He's now a development executive for St. Olaf's College in Northfield, Minn.)

**Dianne (Darran) Warren** was the first Southeast High School swimmer to go to state in 1978. Swimming for Southeast in a city meet, her younger sister **Kristen** broke the record for the 500-meter freestyle that's still on the board at Eisenhower Pool. She also went to state in the 200 and 500 freestyle, placing fourth in the 500.

As president of Lake Springfield's Anchor Boat Club, Dianne and Kristen's father **Bud Darran** spearheaded a Sports Night each year that featured a whole series of pro athlete speakers, including Coach Mike Ditka of the Chicago Bears. Bud also served as a high school swim "starter" for 37 years.

Dick Alane, #35, knocks the ball down for Griffin High School, 1958. *Courtesy of Elaine Alane.*

Peter Urbanckas, "Friend of Sport" Hall of Famer with his trophies, *State Journal-Register*, Dec. 25, 1997.

# Chapter 27
## Who Put the 'Mack' in McDonald's, Springfield?

John Mack on far right at ribbon-cutting for his (second) McDonald's, South MacArthur Boulevard, 1961. *Sangamon Valley Collection, Lincoln Library.*

Anybody who's eaten a McDonald's hamburger in Springfield has feasted on a bit of local Lithuanian-American history involving a family aptly named "Mack" (Lith. Makarauskas). McDonald's first local franchisee, the late John Mack, came to the U.S. from Lithuania in 1922 at age 10 speaking no English, and left school at age 14 to mine coal. He weathered first the precipitous decline of coal mining and the Central Illinois "Mine Wars," and then the decline of the corner grocery business before making his risky and revolutionary leap into fast food.

At the peak of the Mack fast food empire in the 1980s, John's family owned all eight of Springfield's McDonald's restaurants, according to the *Illinois State Journal-Register.* According to sister-in-law Dorothy Makarauskas, John changed his surname to Mack a full 16 years before he went into fast food. He had no way of knowing he would one day be the man responsible for bringing "Mack-fries," "Mack-cheeseburgers" and "Big Macks" to Springfield, not to mention some of the city's prime teen hangouts.

Despite paying minimum wage, the McDonald's on South MacArthur Boulevard was not only THE place for teens to work. It also became such a popular hangout in the '60s and '70s that the packed parking lot required its own bouncer. Hot rods cruised around the parking lot and up and down MacArthur a la "American Graffiti" every Friday and Saturday night during the school year, and every night during the summer. Thousands of local youth–boys, only, at first–earned their first paycheck at one of the restaurants.

What a fantastical vision all that would have seemed to the boy who grew up in shattered and impoverished Lithuania during and after World War I. As you will read, John's remarkable life embodied almost all of the major forces that shaped first-wave, early twentieth-century Lithuanian immigration to the U.S. coal belt.

Makarauskas family reunion day, 1922. Left to right, back row: Stanley and wife Agota, and Agota's uncle. Front row: sons Michael and John. *Courtesy of Dorothy Makarauskas.*

## Coming to America

Starting in 1890, two to three thousand Lithuanian immigrants began making their way to the Springfield area via Scotland and Pennsylvania. John Mack's father, Stanley, had arrived in the U.S. to mine coal just before the outbreak of World War I in 1914. He was not reunited with 10-year-old John and the rest of the family until they joined him in the U.S. in 1922.

Because of the decline in local coal mining, John was forced to follow his father and older brother Michael into the mines at age 14 after completing sixth grade. Working days were so hard to come by starting in the 1910s that most miners secured only two-three per week. Yet under the time-honored communal tradition of job-sharing, each family was perversely incentivized to maximize its headcount in the mines, further contributing to the problem of limited hours.

Even worse, mines shut down for the entire summer when there was no need for coal, and during protracted biannual contract strikes.

## Mine Wars

According to Carl Oblinger's book, *"Divided Kingdom: Work, Community and the Mining Wars in the Central Illinois Coal Fields during the Great Depression,"* increasing coal mine mechanization during the 1920s led to mass layoffs. This eventually culminated in one of the most important labor conflicts of the 1930s, the so-called Central Illinois "Mine Wars" (1932-36). The trouble began when mine owners tried to slash wages at the height of the Great Depression. This launched a bitter strike that soon pitted the United Mine Workers against a competing new union formed by members who refused the UMW's order to return to work under a 20 percent pay cut they had roundly rejected.

Michael Makarauskas and Adella Klimaitis wedding, 1933. Brother John Mack just behind Michael and Mary Gidus (Mack) just behind Adella. *Courtesy of Dorothy Makarauskas.*

Lithuanian immigrants and their sons were represented on both sides of the conflict, but mainly, it seems, they sided with the new union called the Progressive Miners of America (PMA). And so did John Mack.

## Feeding Striking Miners' Families

Having arrived in mining in 1926 as a boy of 14, Mack seems to have become something of a hero to the PMA just six or seven years later by organizing or operating part of the commissary system that fed the strikers' families.

According to the *Journal-Register*, one such commissary was operated in the basement of Lithuanian immigrant Simonas (Sam) Lapinski's Springfield tavern. At the same time, many family-owned corner groceries, already accustomed to "carrying" underemployed miners on credit ("on the book"), stepped up to do the same during the protracted strike by the Progressives.

It's not certain what kind of commissary Mack operated when he was cash-poor and only in his young 20s. It could have been something akin to today's urban farming or food pantries. On page 92 of Oblinger's book, PMA miner Tom Rosko exclaims: "He carried them all [the strikers] in Springfield, John Mack!"

Younger brother Frank carries a block of ice from John's South First Street grocery to a customer's car, 1943. *Courtesy of Dorothy Makarauskas.*

## From Commissary to Grocery

Mack's commissary activities seem to have grown into a Mack grocery store operated from 1941-43 on First Street. In 1943, Mack closed the First Street store and opened a larger corner grocery at 1501 Keys Ave. Dorothy, wife of John's much younger, American-born brother Frank, remembers that the Keys Avenue store, which sold meat, bread, milk and dry goods, was Springfield's first "self-serve" corner grocery.

This meant that customers picked up their own items and brought them to the cashier, instead of, as at other groceries of the time, the staff moving about the store to fill customers' orders. John Mack was also a butcher, a trade that no-doubt proved handy both in his commissary and grocery activities.

Left to right, back row: daughter JoAnn, John and his wife Mary. Middle: sons Tom, John, Jr., and Jim. Front: daughter MaryAnn. Late 1940s. *Courtesy of JoAnn's daughter Colleen Shaughnessy.*

Mack's son Jim remembers the financial squeeze his father faced as he continued to broadly extend store credit well into the 1950s. To make matters worse, the first supermarket chains had begun eating the small independent grocers' lunch.

## Enter McDonald's Founder

Then one day, Ray Kroc drove by the huge Allis-Chalmers construction machinery factory right across from the Mack family's South Sixth Street home. Kroc considered the real estate across from the factory's main gate the perfect site for Springfield's first McDonald's restaurant (the nation's 69th).

It was serendipity that brought together a new fast-food business model based on churning out hundreds of ground beef patties a day with Mack, a butcher able to provide the ground beef, but struggling to survive in the dying corner grocery business.

The plan Mack devised with Kroc was bold. It required moving his family home around the corner to clear a lot for constructing the new drive-up restaurant and parking lot. This would require money--lots of it (including a McDonald's franchise fee).

Mack needed to borrow $100,000 in an era when credit and large loans were extended much less frequently than today. Daughter MaryAnn (Mack) Butts recalls: "Mary, our mother, was in the meetings with Dad when he went to the banks. They literally laughed at him and said, 'You have a sixth-grade education and you want to open a restaurant?'

"Mother said it was embarrassing and she really felt bad for him. The banks also said, 'Who would want to buy a 15-cent hamburger?' They thought it was ridiculous because that was kind of expensive back then," MaryAnn recalls.

Who, indeed?

John Mack refused to give up. Illinois National Bank, where one of the executives was proud Lithuanian-American Augustus "Gus" Wisnosky (Vysniauskas), and where much of the Lithuanian community did business, finally agreed to make the loan.

McDonald's employees,
1825 South MacArthur Blvd., 1964.
*Sangamon Valley Collection, Lincoln Library.*

## Teen Hangouts

Mack's first McDonald's across from the Allis-Chalmers main gate on South Sixth Street opened in 1957. The second opened in 1961 on South MacArthur near Laurel. These were small, open-air drive-ups without eat-in capacity. Because customers were expected to eat in their cars, the McDonald's parking lots were much more extensive than the restaurants.

According to Glenn Manning of Rochester, in the 1960s, hot rods would scoop a fast-food loop bracketed on either end by one of these first two McDonald's. The loop ran north from the MacArthur drive-up, then east on South Grand Avenue to a Top's Big Boy car-hop restaurant on or near Fifth Street, then down Fifth (one way) until Fifth ran together with Sixth to the Sixth Street McDonald's. Then cars would loop back up Sixth to South Grand, and on to MacArthur.

## Local Sourcing Rules

In the early years, all the burgers, fries and buns were fresh and sourced locally. According to Mack daughter MaryAnn, her father had a ground-beef patty-making machine made specially in St. Louis so he could keep his long-time Keys Avenue grocery employee Frances Trello busy churning out fresh patties for his new restaurants. Corporate dictated the lean and fat content of each patty, along with the recipe followed by a local contract bakery that delivered fresh-baked buns daily.

HUNGRY? DRIVE OVER TO McDONALD'S

### McDonald's famous 15¢ hamburger

2849 So. 6TH ST.

JUST OPPOSITE ALLIS CHALMERS MAIN GATE          SPRINGFIELD, ILLINOIS

| | |
|---|---|
| HAMBURGERS | 15 CENTS |
| CHEESEBURGERS | 19 CENTS |
| TRIPLE THICK SHAKES | 20 CENTS |
| FRENCH FRIES | 10 CENTS |
| COKE | 10 CENTS |
| MILK–COFFEE | 10 CENTS |
| ORANGEADE | 10 CENTS |
| ROOT BEER | 10 CENTS |

Mack McDonald's ad for South Sixth Street drive-up, circa 1957.
*Sangamon Valley Collection, Lincoln Library.*

Mack son Jim recalls that potatoes came in 100-pound bags on a rail car. They were peeled with the help of a peeling machine, then sliced by hand into fries—and after being washed and rinsed a total of three times— were blanched at low heat till they were finally ready to be deep-fried.

The soft ice cream for shakes was sourced locally, but the shake flavor mixes came from headquarters. John Mack reportedly used to joke that the mixes were created in a lab by Gary Butts, daughter MaryAnn's husband, who had been a chemist (and was sometimes seen tutoring teen employees with their chemistry books).

Many of the Mack kids and grandkids worked in the family business, including son John, Jr., and daughter JoAnn (Mack) Shaughnessy's husband and the couple's daughter Debbie (Shaughnessy) Blazis. The magic starting age for most of the Mack kids seemed to be 15—one year older than John when he followed his father Stanley and brother Michael into the coal mines in 1926.

## Premature Death and Future Expansion

Paterfamilias John died of cancer in 1974 at the age of 61. "Dad didn't have a long life, and he only had so much education, but he had guts and he was really smart—very good at math," daughter MaryAnn says. "He only had a sixth-grade education, but he died a millionaire, and we are forever proud of him."

After Mack's death, his widow Mary and sons Tom and Jim and daughter MaryAnn and her husband Gary Butts went on to open five more locations in Springfield. (Mary is said not to have been involved in day-to-day operations but left this to the younger generation.)

According to Jim, though stressful, the frequent expansions were considered a superior option to having corporate open competing new locations by bringing in a non-Mack franchisee. Not all of the new locations that corporate wanted were profitable, and Jim remembers that growing and operating the business took a heavy toll on the family over the years. But at least if a new location cannibalized customers, the "business" gained from the Macks would still belong to the Macks.

Along the way, according to MaryAnn, the family retained its loyalty to INB, which had

1975 artist's rendering of a Mack photo that was placed inside the family's restaurants in memoriam. *Courtesy of Dorothy Makarauskas.*

made the loan for John Mack's first franchise, and did all its banking there. In 1989, after more than 30 years in fast food, the family sold all eight of their Springfield restaurants, repaid all outstanding INB balances, according to Jim, and totally exited the business.

## The Man Who Was 'Larger Than Life'

John Mack is remembered as a larger-than-life personality who "would light up the place" when he visited one of his franchises to sit down and enjoy a burger, according to Don Gietl, who worked at a "Mack McDonald's" just like brothers Jim, Charlie and Terry. Great corporate citizens, the Macks carried on in John's altruistic footsteps by sponsoring innumerable local fundraisers and giving generously to Goodwill, among other charities

The Mack family also organized the creation of Springfield's Ronald Mc-Donald House after experiencing a family tragedy. Ronald McDonald houses are erected near hospitals to provide lodging for the families of seriously ill children undergoing treatment far from home.

John's youngest brother Frank and wife Dorothy had an 18-year old son, Robert, who was fighting brain cancer at Sloan-Kettering in New York City.

Mary Mack, John's widow, visited a Ronald Mc-Donald house nearby. She was so impressed that she dedicated herself to donating and raising the funds necessary to provide such a house for the Springfield community, which still stands today.

*Dedicated to the memories of Mary and John Mack, their children JoAnn (Mack) Shaughnessy and John Mack, Jr., as well as John's brothers Michael and Frank, and Frank and Dorothy's son Robert.*

John Mack's younger brother, Second Lieutenant Frank I. Makarauskas as U.S. Air Force B-24 bomber navigator trainee, circa 1945. *Courtesy of wife Dorothy.*

# Chapter 28
# The Chepulis Champion Garage

Founded by brothers Joe and William Chepulis, Champion Garage at 820 E. Black St. celebrated 50 years in the auto body and auto repair business in 1986. Back in 1936 when the business opened, cars were metal-plated tanks compared with today's alloy and plastic-bodied vehicles. They were also mechanically simple compared to today's mechanical-electrical-digital marvels.

Champion Garage, 1939.

Remember chrome bumpers? Those were not just crash-resistant, but demolition derby-worthy. Remember when cars had faces, with headlights for eyes and grin-like front grilles?

Over the years, Champion saw it all, while providing a livelihood for the Chepulis brothers' families. One of the most interesting photos of the business, to me, shows Champion's tow-truck from a simpler time with homemade lettering on the door.

Siblings Mary Ann and Bill Chepulis with tow truck, circa 1940.

Joe, Bill and Mary Ann were the children of Lithuanian immigrants Carl (Karalius) and Mary Eva (Lelesius) Chepulis. Carl was a coal miner born in 1884 in the Marijampole area. Also born in 1884, Mary Eva came to the U.S. when she was 18 with a cousin name Kurila. The couple married in 1908 at St. Vincent de Paul (Lithuanian) Catholic Church. Their first child was born in 1909. The family lived on North 15th Street for many years, across the road from the Sluzalis family.

Sons Joe and Bill ended up working in the area's coal mines, at first to take their father Carl's place on days when he couldn't work. (Carl suffered for years from black lung disease, and died of it at age 66.) Joe and Bill later took up auto body work at Gietl Brothers Garage on Second Street near the Illinois Capitol. They learned the trade and opened their own garage, Champion, in 1936, right in the middle of the Great Depression.

Mary Eva Lelesius and Carl Chepulis wedding, 1908, St. Vincent de Paul's.

*Here are a few comments on my blog post about Champion and its founders: — "I worked at Marine Bank for years re-possessing cars, and Joe was our tow truck driver. He could hook and snatch a repo car before people even knew what happened to them!"*
*— "I remember (Joe's son) Joey and his family from my many visits to the shop as an auto claims rep long ago. Stepping into their shop was like a step back in time...Joe and Mrs. Chepulis were very kind. I remember Joey and his mom running the place after Joe died."*

Cash-poor immigrant families had to pull together, and in many cases, live together, to survive. Not surprisingly, they also had to cooperate to capitalize and operate a family business. This may explain why immigrant son Joe didn't marry and leave home until he was 35, Mary Ann until she was 40, and Bill until he was 50. Additional insight is given by Ann (Tisckos) Wisnosky in her essay at the beginning of this book.

Champion Garage, 1940.

Ann points out that language barriers and being different from mainstream Springfield "gave us a strong sense of not belonging in the outside world. Our real world was the family, neighborhood, and church." Aging immigrant parents in declining health who had literally given their all for their children also commanded a tremendous sense of filial obligation and loyalty.

Daughters (or youngest daughters), in particular, were expected to stay home and not marry as long as a parent needed help. And it was not uncommon for mothers to say they couldn't imagine anyone loving their sons more than Mom did—or any other woman coming close to Mom's cooking! In fact, economic and emotional interdependence in functional (as opposed to dysfunctional) immigrant families was so strong that I believe it actually depressed rates of marriage and reproduction for many immigrant sons and daughters.

One example of an immigrant mom taking charge is related by Joe Chepulis's daughter Mary. "Dad had an Indian Motorcycle, a really famous brand. If anyone had one today, it would be worth a fortune. However, he was a bit of a daredevil and he had an accident with it and had to go to the hospital. While he was in the hospital, his mother sold it."

Joe Chepulis, 18, on his Indian motorcycle, August 1928.

Additionally, Mary remembers visiting grandparents Carl and Mary Eva after they moved to North Peoria Road, just east of old Gate 3 of the Illinois State Fairgrounds. "I'd go over there and my grandmother would braid my hair, pulling the two braids together at the back of my head and tying them together with a ribbon. There were chickens and a cow, and every once in a while, the cow would have a calf. I remember having to walk home to our house on North 15th Street through cow pastures.

"I also remember that we parked cars at Grandma's during the state fair: Cars were 50 cents for the day, motorcycles, a quarter. I was so impressed as a kid when my Uncle Bill built a stand to sell sodas to the fairgoers."

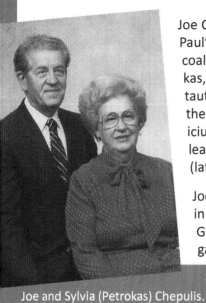

Joe and Sylvia (Petrokas) Chepulis.

Joe Chepulis married Sylvia Petrokas at St. Vincent de Paul's, where they had met. Sylvia was the daughter of coal-mining Lithuanian immigrant Stanley W. Petrokas, who was the son of Ignatius and Barbara (Gestaut) Petrokas. Sylvia's mother Catherine Rice was the daughter of Adam and Anna (Senkos) Rieskevicius. Catherine had died in 1924 at the age of 25, leaving Stanley with two daughters, Sylvia and Ruth (later Lustig), whom he raised by himself.

Joe and Sylvia Chepulis had four other children, in addition to Mary, who all attended St. Aloysius Grade School: Joe, Jr. (Joey), who took over the garage when his dad became ill in 1987; John, an electrician; Bernadine (Chepulis) Dombrowski, who studied music at the American Conservatory of Music in Chicago; and Patricia (Chepulis) Wade, who retired from the state and also earned a nursing degree. All the girls attended Ursuline Academy.

Mary holds bachelor's and master's degrees in education from SIU-Edwardsville and has worked for decades as an advocate for the disabled. She also is a former secretary and long-time member of the Lithuanian-American Club. Joe, Jr., (Joey) has two children and five grandchildren; John has two children and one grandchild; Bernadine has two children; and Mary has a daughter.

Back row, l to r: Joe, Jr., Mary, Patricia. Front row: John and Bernadine.

As for Champion Garage, Joey operated it until about 2006, and then began renting it out to another auto body operator.

*All photos courtesy of Mary Chepulis and Bernadine (Chepulis) Dombrowski.*

# Chapter 29
# The Blazis Muncheonette Diner and Magnolia Court Motel

ULTRA MODERN ROOMS :: PHONE 522-6941 :: WILLIAM BLAZIS, Manager

Passers-by on East Cook Street may not know that today's Kings Court Apartments, operated by an arm of Abundant Faith Christian Center, were once part of a Blazis (Blazavich) family-owned hospitality complex. In the heyday of old U.S. Route 66, the Magnolia Court Motel and Muncheonette Diner (what a clever name!) welcomed thousands of vacationers, salesmen and legislators to Springfield.

The complex was built from nothing by Lithuanian immigrant and Blazis family matriarch Mary (Chunis) Blazis (later Stulzinski or Stulginski) and her American-born general contractor son Bill with help from Mary's other grown children: Enoch, Ann Ackerman, Helen Summers and Mary Yazell. Billed as "ultra-modern," the Magnolia Court had 48 one- and two-bedroom guest units and true to its name, had many magnolias planted on the property. A new family home on nearby White City Boulevard was also part of the ambitious Blazis complex in the 2600 block of East Cook Street, the main artery connecting Route 66 to the Lincoln sites downtown.

Part of Magnolia Court motel complex, 1957.

## Personal Memories

I have a personal connection to this story. In the 1950s, my father worked part-time on the construction of another Blazis family real estate development: the Regency Court duplex apartments, also on East Cook. In 1963 or '64, when I was six or seven, Dad took me to what I now know was the Bill and Irene (Pietrzak) Blazis home, though for decades I only remembered playing with two little girls while Dad visited the parents.

Bill and Irene (Pietrzak) Blazis, 1958.

Even though I met her only once, I never forgot sweet, little Mary Agnes, who was severely disabled by cerebral palsy. I also never forgot how kindly Mary Agnes was taken outside by her able-bodied sister Barbara to join me and my older sister Terry on the family's swing set. It took 50 years, but suddenly, thanks to an interview with (mother) Irene, I finally know who young Mary Agnes really was—her family story.

## From Mining to Real Estate

Lithuanian immigrants William and Mary (Chunis) Blazis (born about 1884) moved to Springfield from the coal town of Dubois, Penn., in the early 1930s. They came to join Mary's brother Julius Chunis, who was already working in the mines here, bringing with them their five children. The family settled in a large home on the corner of 18th and Jackson streets. Mary worked to support the family as a housekeeper at the Cathedral of the Immaculate Conception.

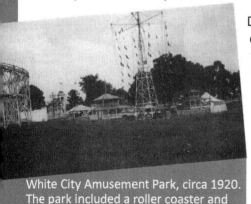

White City Amusement Park, circa 1920. The park included a roller coaster and dance hall. *State Journal-Register* and Sangamon Valley Collection.

During the late 1930s or early 1940s, according to daughter-in-law Irene, Blazis family matriarch Mary launched the family into real estate development. Her first move was a big one. Using money from the payout on her husband's life insurance policy and taking out a loan from Illinois National Bank (INB), she bought a major parcel out of foreclosure. The so-called White City Property had been owned by the Hoogland family and was the site of the defunct White City Amusement Park, modeled after New York's Coney Island.

## A Hospitality Complex for Route 66 Travelers

Then, after sons Bill and Enoch returned from serving in World War II, Mary and her children saw new opportunity in booming family vacation travel on Route 66 (now Dirksen Parkway) and the advent of the motor inn or motel. So in the late 1940s or 1950, Mary sold much of the White City Property to become the site of single family homes and Springfield's Washington Middle School and Jaycees Park. (Orlandini Distributors bought the nearby Blazis White City Tavern and Blazis family home to become the family's offices.)

Next, on the remaining parcel, the Blazis clan began to build their Route 66 hospitality complex. Like other entrepreneurial immigrant families, they did this with almost nothing but their ability to work hard and take risk.

Bill in World War II
U.S. Army uniform.

## Blazis Right-Hand Man

On the construction project for the Magnolia Court and the Muncheonette, Bill was his mother's right hand, taking care of all the construction hiring, ordering, supervising, and even stepping in to help perform the manual labor, according to wife Irene. Matriarch Mary held the family purse strings, taking a second loan from INB to cover construction costs and payroll.

Mary's daughters Helen, Ann, and Mary helped with all the bookkeeping and chores like keeping work crews fed. Once the Magnolia Court Motel and Muncheonette Diner opened, Bill and his brother Enoch managed the motel (Bill personally did all the maintenance) and sisters Helen Summers and Mary (and husband Fred) Yazell operated the diner.

Ann (Pazemetsky) Traeger remembered that the sisters made and sold delicious pies there. Trained butcher Bill Blazis cut a hindquarter of meat for the diner every week, according to Irene. Family members took modest salaries while their mother kept ownership of the properties and the bank loan.

Then disaster struck: son Bill died of lung cancer in 1967. Son Enoch managed the complex on his own for a while. But in 1972, with Howard Johnsons and Holiday Inns taking the Magnolia Court's business, matriarch Mary sold the

family's motel, diner and home complex to the Kresse family of Riverton. After a long slide into dilapidation and crime, in 1998 the motel was rehabbed down to the bricks and converted into the one- and three-bedroom Kings Court Apartments in a $1.5 million project.

King's Court rehab project, *State Journal-Register*, 1998.

## Sponsoring 'DPs'

While it's sad to ponder a family's dream fading into oblivion about the same time it was realized, the Blazis immigrant achievement lives on in memory. In addition, Mary Blazis and son Bill sponsored the families of two Lithuanian displaced persons ("DPs") after World War II: Joseph Petrakus, M.D., with his wife and two children, and Walter and Tamara Danelevich and their daughter. According to Irene, Dr. Petrakus became the first foreign doctor to intern at Memorial Hospital, which paved the way for others, such as Dr. Chatara from Soviet Georgia.

The Blazis family also were proud members of St. Vincent de Paul (Lithuanian) Catholic Church, where Bill sang in the choir, where he married Polish "DP" Irene in 1954, and where all six of Bill and Irene's children (Mary Agnes, Barbara, twins Fred and John, Vincent and Enoch) were baptized. When young Mary Agnes died of pneumonia in 1965, followed by her father's death in 1967, both were memorialized at the church. Matriarch and immigrant Mary (Chunis) Blazis passed away in June 1976 at the age of almost 92.

Irene Blazis holding Barbara, Bill holding Mary Agnes, and matriarch Mary (Chunis) Blazis in center, 1958.

*All family images courtesy of Irene Blazis.*

# Chapter 30
# Tisckos Furniture Story

One Lithuanian-American business that touched many of our homes and lives was Tisckos Furniture Barn (or Store), which operated just north of downtown from the 1940s to the early 1990s. I recently found out that my mom and dad bought our family's first couch and living room rug there.

Coal miner's sons who made good, Martin and Charlie Tisckos (pronounced TISH-kus) opened their store at 522 N. Fourth St. just after World War II–right in time for the post-war baby boom. (Brother Charlie, a lawyer, was a silent partner.) In the late 1950s, Martin purchased the old McCoy Laundry building at 322 N. Fourth and moved the store to this much larger four-story building.

Chuck Tisckos, Charlie's son, recalls that Tisckos Furniture carried quality home furnishings, bedding, appliances and carpeting: brands like Heywood-Wakefield, Flexsteel, and Hotpoint appliances. The store was also an exclusive Broyhill distributor. I recently learned I have another personal connection with the store: my late father-in-law Ray Gietl laid carpet that customers purchased there.

Immigrants John and Alexandra (Alice Urbas) Tisckos. Circa 1960.

## From Tailor to Coal Miner

Martin and Charlie's father was Lithuanian immigrant John (Jonas) Tisckos, born in 1888, who came to Springfield via Scotland, where he was an apprentice tailor. In Springfield, John Tisckos was a career coal miner, retiring from the New North Mine in 1952, around the same time the mine closed. His wife was Lithuanian immigrant Alice Urbas. John and Alice belonged to St. Vincent de Paul Church, which John likely helped excavate and build. In addition to Martin and Charlie, the couple had children Adolph, Ann (Tisckos) Wisnosky, and William (Vance).

Della and Charlie Tisckos wedding day, circa 1939, in front of St. Vincent de Paul Church.

# Coal Miner's Son Becomes Lawyer

Tisckos son Charlie graduated from the now-defunct University of Illinois and Lincoln College of Law. He married Della, the daughter of Lithuanian immigrant John Grenowage (pronounced GREN-a-vitch), born in 1888, and German immigrant Mina Schiller, born in 1891.

John Grenowage, later Green, was a coal miner who came to Springfield via Pennsylvania and worked the mines here until the 1930s, when mass layoffs prompted strikes and the local "Mine Wars." While their dad John was mining, Della and her siblings John, William, and Edward lived next to the Springfield circus grounds at 11th Street and Black Avenue. Later, the family farmed southwest of Taylorville on Scrapeford Road.

The beautiful Della (Grenowage) Tisckos, my mother's best friend, with husband Charlie and daughter Nancy. Circa 1942.

Tisckos son Martin and wife Marinella (Marni) had three children: Leslie Candace, Marty, and Scott. Martin died in 1996; his brother and silent partner Charlie in 1998. Although they worked with their fathers in the store, the Tisckos descendants did not carry on the business after Martin and Charlie died.

Charlie Tisckos's son Chuck married Beryl Jean (Parish) and has one son, Ben. Ben and wife Kathy have a daughter, Chelsea. Charlie and Della's daughter Nancy married Richard Vicars and has a daughter, Lisa, and sons Richard, Jr., and Patrick.

Marni and Martin Tisckos, circa 1975.

*Information and photos courtesy of Chuck Tisckos.*

# Chapter 31
# Remember the Kwedars?

After writing about the Mack/Makarauskas fast food "dynasty," I was reminded by Barbara Endzelis of another local Lithuanian-American family that's almost as big with the letters "M.D." as the Macks were with "Mc."

How many of our families were treated, over the years, by now-deceased Springfield general practitioner and surgeon Albert Kwedar, M.D., his deceased ophthalmologist brother Edward Kwedar, M.D., or his retired ophthalmologist son, Stephen Kwedar, M.D.? How many of us are currently patients of Dr. Edward's son John Kwedar, M.D., a long-time ophthalmologist with the prestigious multispecialty group, Springfield Clinic?

In 2014, I spoke briefly with Kwedar (Lith. Kvedaras) family matriarch Helen, the 97-year-old sister of Drs. Edward and Albert Kwedar (and Drs. Stephen and John's aunt).

John Kwedar, M.D., ophthalmologist, Springfield Clinic. Undated.

## From Steel to Coal

Helen told me that the family got started in America when Thomas Kwedar immigrated from Lithuania, probably around the turn of the century. Helen said Thomas was 21 when he came to America, first to Pittsburgh, where he worked in a steel mill. He married Pennsylvania-born Lithuanian-American Victoria Shupenus, daughter of Anthony and Helen (Zwinak) Shupenus.

After the steel mill where Thomas was working closed, he and Victoria moved to Springfield because of relatives here, and because of the availability of work in the local coal mines. However, the sporadic and seasonal nature of mining in Springfield soon put pressure on the family's finances.

Thomas and Victoria put their heads together and decided to buy a small farm near Pana that Thomas could work during the long summer months while the mines shut down. This would ensure that the family was never hungry or in debt for food, since they would grow their own vegetables and raise milking cows.

Helen says it was called a "truck farm," maybe because produce could be trucked to Springfield for sale. She says she was only two when parents Thomas and Victoria moved with Helen and her siblings Albert and Anna to the farm in 1918. (Edward Kwedar was not yet born.)

## College Ambitions Unusual for Immigrants

Helen also says her parents were diligent savers because they planned for all their children to go to college. Unfortunately, the Pana bank holding the family's accounts failed after the 1929 stock market crash, when Helen was 13. Her two brothers somehow still managed to graduate from college and the University of Illinois medical school. Helen attended night school at Springfield College in Illinois.

Kwedar daughter Anna (also now deceased) has an interesting story, according to maternal cousin Jim Shupenus. He says, "Anna was single and apparently worked as a disbursement officer with the CIA in the Washington, D.C. area. When she came to visit in Springfield, she was preceded by the FBI, who interviewed any person she might talk or have contact with on her trip. Also, I was told by my parents that when there were air raid drills in Washington, a helicopter would go to CIA headquarters and she would board it (probably along with others)."

## Delivering Triplets Outside a Hospital

According to Edward's son, Dr. John Kwedar, Dr. Albert was a classic GP of his era, working 80 hours a week and rarely seeing his family as he made house calls all over Sangamon County, setting broken bones and delivering babies—in between office hours, hospital rounds and performing emergency appendectomies and other types of surgery. Dr. John says Dr. Albert's most cherished memories were his home deliveries of two sets of triplets—all of whom survived. One set of triplets he delivered on a farm had to be placed in the family's oven to keep warm.

Another interesting fact about Dr. Albert is that he secretly married his sweetheart Ruby, whom he met growing up in Pana, while he was a resident at the U of I's Chicago Medical Center. Ruby was accomplished in her own right and later served as president of the Illinois State Medical Society Auxiliary.

## Re-Activating Eye Department

Dr. Albert's son Stephen "re-activated" the eye department at Springfield Clinic (which had been dormant for eight years) when he joined the Clinic in 1972. A graduate of Northwestern University Medical School and residencies at the University of Oregon and Barnes Hospital in St. Louis, Dr. Stephen preferred practicing in a large multispecialty group.

He brought many new techniques to Springfield, including: intraocular lens implantation, photocoagulation of diabetic retinopathy and retinal holes, the YAG laser and laser iridectomy. Dr. Stephen also helped Springfield Clinic's eye department found its optometry section.

Dr. Albert's son Michael, who died at 51, had a successful career as an administrator for the City of Springfield and the Illinois Department of Corrections, and held advanced degrees in political science and public administration.

Dr. Albert's brother Edward W. Kwedar, M.D., taught at the SIU School of Medicine. Born on Thomas and Victoria's farm near Pana in 1931, he married Dorothy Lashmet in Evanston in 1957. He died in his home in Springfield at age 79 in 2011.

## Too Many House Calls

Dr. John says ophthalmology appealed to the Kwedar M.D.s who followed in Dr. Albert's footsteps. They preferred that specialty's fine surgical motor skills and its predictable hours after witnessing the strain on Dr. Albert and his family as he worked 80-hour weeks in his office, at the hospital, and on innumerable house calls–day and night–all across the county.

In the 1960s and '70s, the extended family endured several tragic accidents that took the lives of several Kwedar children. However, the proud family medical tradition continues today not just with Dr. John, but also Dr. John's two daughters.

# Chapter 32
# Y-T Packing and Turasky Meats

The Turasky family in Springfield started with Joseph Turasky, born in 1881 in Lithuania. He married Katherine Yakst, born in 1891 in Lithuania (daughter of Paul Yakst and Anna Jucevicius).

Katherine and coal-miner Joseph, Sr., had seven children: John Turasky, born in 1909 (wife Della), Joseph Turasky, Jr., born in 1910 (wife Catherine "Cassie" Ambrose), and Agnes (husband Lindell Walthers), Helen (husband Ed Price), Charles (wife Louise), Betty (husband Joseph Fitzpatrick) and Frances Turasky (husband Joseph Dowd).

Immigrants Joseph and Katherine (Yakst) Turasky, 1921.

Joseph Turasky, Jr.,'s wife Cassie Ambrose, born in Springfield in 1916, was the daughter of Antanas Brazas (Ambrose), born in Lithuania in 1880, and Victoria Stockus, born in Lithuania in 1882.

Immigrants Antanas and Victoria (Stockus) Brazas (Ambrose). Undated.

## Meat, Not Mines

When Joseph, Jr., was young, his father took him into the mines to see if he wanted to be a miner. Sent alone down a long, narrow shaft to work, young Joseph was cast into total darkness when his lantern went out. "He had never seen darkness like that, absolutely no light at the bottom of a coal mine," recalls his son Joe. "He crawled and crawled, following voices until he made it back to the other miners, and he never went down into a mine again."

Instead, Joseph, Jr., founded Y-T packing in 1949. The company began as a slaughterhouse that supplied neighborhood groceries. The Turaskies shut down their slaughtering operation in 2004 to focus on ready-to-eat meats. Now in their third generation of Turasky family ownership, wholesale meat business Y-T Packing and retail arm Turasky Meats sell custom cuts and other signature products to local restaurants, grocers and individuals.

## Supporting Their Club and Church

A long-time member and leader of St. Vincent de Paul (Lithuanian) Catholic Church, Joseph, Jr., served as a trustee and a member of the church's 50th anniversary Jubilee Committee in 1956. According to newspaper accounts, Joseph, Jr.'s wife Cassie was a member of the choir that sang during the Springfield visit of Lithuania's president-in-exile Antanas Smetona in 1941.

Joseph, Jr., and Cassie's son Joe, born in 1941, served as an altar boy at St. Vincent's. Joe Turasky also has been an officer and generous supporter of Springfield's Lithuanian-American Club since serving as one of the club's founders in 1988.

Joe married Carolyn Ann Mazzier in 1967. Their son, Bradley Joseph Turasky, born in 1981, now heads day-to-day operations at Y-T and Turasky Meats, though Joe still works in the award-winning family business. Brad recently served as 2014-2015 president of the Illinois Association of Meat Processors, the second Turasky, counting his father, to do so.

Joseph (Jr.) and Cassie (Ambrose) Turasky, undated.

Joe and Carolyn (Mazzier) Turasky with Brad and Dana (Ervin) Turasky, circa 2010.

Born in 1949, Joseph, Jr., and Cassie's son Anthony ("Big Tony") also was an altar boy at St. Vincent de Paul. He married Jeanne Hemstock in 1969 and they had four children: Anthony ("Little Tony"), Lisa, Luke, and Jill. "Big Tony" was a partner with his brother Joe in Turasky Meats, Y-T Packing Co., and Turasky's Catering until his untimely death in 1999. As of July 2015, he has six grandchildren. "Little Tony" took over Turasky Catering after his father's death and also operates Trail's End Saloon in New Berlin.

Born in 1944, Joseph, Jr., and Cassie's third son Richard also was an altar boy at St. Vincent's, and later was a member of the church choir with his wife Margaret Mary (McCue.) Richard's early musical experiences at St. Vincent's led to a lifelong avocation and career. And even though his wife Margaret was a career employee of United Airlines, both were constantly involved in musical activities. Margaret is an accomplished classical organist and Richard was dedicated to the field of choral music as a singer, director, and teacher.

Victoria (Stockus) Ambrose, 1975.

Before leaving Springfield, Richard, Sr., taught music at Griffin High School for four years and was music director at the Cathedral of the Immaculate Conception. He then proceeded to teach music in the Chicago suburbs for 30 years and to serve as assistant organist at Holy Name Cathedral, Chicago. Presently, Richard, Sr., spends part of the year with his wife in Phoenix, Ariz., and sings with the Phoenix Symphony Chorus. He formerly was a member of the Chicago Symphony Chorus, Grant Park Chorus, and Ravinia Chorus—and even once sang with the Lithuanian Opera Company-Chicago in its presentation of the Verdi Requiem.

Married in 1967, Richard, Sr., and Margaret had three children: Regina, Richard, Jr., and James Hunter. As of July 2015, they have five grandchildren.

*Photos courtesy of Richard Turasky, Sr., and Joe Turasky.*

# Chapter 33
# Taking a Spin at the Cara-Sel Lounge

Interior of the Cara-Sel Lounge, Seventh Street and North Grand Avenue. Circa 1955.

One of the more colorful Lithuanian-American businesses in Springfield was the Cara-Sel Lounge, Seventh and North Grand Avenue, which was operated for 17 years by World War II veteran Tony Yuscius. Tony, who died at 86 in 2009, was the son of Lithuanian-born coal miner Joseph and his wife Marcella (Radavich) Yuscius.

After Joseph died of black lung disease, Tony's mother Marcella and her many children fell on hard times. (The Cohen family, who operated a grocery on Peoria Road, and later, The Mill tavern and restaurant, are said to have assisted Marcella—and many others—with grocery credit.)

## Growing up Poor

The hard times known by many Lithuanian families in Springfield, generated by death in or from the mines, not to mention mass mine layoffs, led youngsters like Tony and his siblings to work from a young age to help support their families. The same conditions led many to launch their own small businesses.

Tony's business opportunity did not come until sometime after he graduated from Lanphier High School and served in the U.S. Army in the European-Af-

rican-Middle Eastern Theatre during World War II, earning three bronze service stars. It's hard to know how Tony got the idea for the Cara-Sel Restaurant and Bar, a play on the word "carousel," with its colorful circus décor and circular bar. ("Follow our bar round 'n round—you will certainly find your friends here.")

Tony Yuscius serving Joe Saputo in dark sweater, according to Sandra Coffee. Joe and his brother Frank operated the Saputo Twins Corner, a downtown tavern.

Announcing

# OPEN HOUSE

TODAY, SUN., OCT. 24

At the Startling, New and Beautiful

# CARA-SEL
RESTAURANT and BAR
North Grand at 7th

{ Follow our bar round-n-round
You will certainly find your friends here!

DON'T MISS THIS
GREAT NEW THRILL ➝➝➝

NEW, ENLARGED KITCHEN
Complete DINNER SERVICE 11 A.M. Till CLOSING

## UNIQUE

We guarantee you have never seen anything like the colorful beauty and gay atmosphere of our completely new establishment.

Undated ad,
*State Journal-Register.*

Phone 2-0685

The CARA-SEL

625 E. NORTH GRAND
SPRINGFIELD, ILLINOIS
*Tony Yuscius*

CLOSE COVER BEFORE STRIKING

Cara-Sel
matchbook cover.

# From Circus Theme to 'Go-Go' Bar

Tony and his wife Carol operated the Cara-Sel from sometime in the 1950s until the early 1970s. There were many neighborhood taverns and corner restaurants in Springfield during that period, so one can imagine it was a challenge to find a niche. After a more family-oriented start indicated by its circus theme and enlarged kitchen, the Cara-Sel hopped on the "mod" train sometime during the 1960s, with mini-skirted dancing "go-go" girls at night, like

Cara-Sel A-Go-Go, 1967.
Sangamon County tax files.

those on popular TV shows *"Rowan and Martin's Laugh-In"* and *"Hullaballoo."*

The establishment really made an impression on those who still remember it today:

—*"When I went there, it was a nice place for a couple of girls to go, have some drinks and maybe meet a couple of guys. I also went there on dates, like after a movie."*
—*"Go-go girls would dance on the bar and in front of the bar—also in the back room."*
—*"I used to walk by the Cara-Sel on my way to Edison Middle School, and then Lanphier High School."*
— *"When I was a boy, my father drove a truck and would arrive home on Saturday mornings, at which time I would accompany him to the Carousel (sic) for lunch. Late at night, there were cages and go-go girls, and still being in grade school, I would not have been welcome. The Teamsters had their office directly across the street. One block to the east was the Pantheon Theatre, and next door was Palazollo's Soda Shop, where all the Lanphier students gathered. Noonan Hardware and Ben Franklin Five and Dime were on the same block."*
—*"They had a left-handed/right-handed drinking club. You had to drink with whichever hand behind the bar was lighted. We paid to join and there was a fine for getting caught drinking with the wrong hand. The reward was a free eat-and-drink party once a year for the members. Neat place."*

In an ironic twist, sometime in the 1970s or maybe early 1980s, Tony Yuscius and his wife Carol completely changed direction, closed the Cara-Sel and converted the premises into the Northtown Child Care Center, a day care they operated for 20 years. Tony had two brothers: Stanley and John Yuscius, and five sisters, Mary Yuscius, Ann Asher, Josephine Pavletich, Ardella Dodd and Patricia Bietsch.

Cara-Sel exterior in tamer times, 1954.

## Second-Generation Entrepreneur

Tony's son, Tony J., a 1979 graduate of Griffin High School, is a second-generation entrepreneur as founder and president of another cutting-edge local business, Advanced Digital Media. Advanced offers video crews for hire, and more note-worthily, a website called blueroomstream.com that live-streams unedited footage of virtually every news conference in the Blue Room of the Illinois Statehouse. The live-streaming service also includes other political and government events, as well as some committee hearings and rallies. Tony J.'s innovative business grew out of his many years with the Illinois Information Service, helicoptering around the state at a moment's notice with Illinois governors Thompson and Edgar, in order to record public appearances and speeches with his trusted minicam.

Tony J. Yuscius, President, Advanced Digital Media.

The late Tony Yuscius, Sr., also had a daughter, Susan Yuscius (husband, Larry O'Brien) of Springfield, and three grandchildren: Jewel and Megan O'Brien and Tori Yuscius (Tony J.'s daughter), as well as several nieces and nephews.

*All photos courtesy of Tony J. Yuscius and public sources.*

# Chapter 34
# Lithuanian Tavern Life

Family-owned corner taverns where coal miners ate, drank and socialized proliferated throughout Springfield during the first half of the twentieth century. Keeping the tavern going was a family affair, with wives often doing the cooking and cleaning and husbands, sons, and sons-in-law mainly tending bar. This leads me to believe that a goodly number were founded by formerly single miners after they married, as a step up the economic ladder—and like the corner grocery store, a safer line of work.

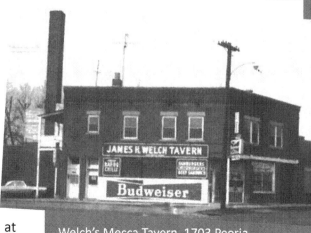

Sam Lapinski Beer Parlor 1030 E Washington
Joe Meiron in front
John Lazdauskas
in rear. 1935.

Sam and Mary (Mankus) Lapinski (Lapinskas) behind the bar, 1030 E. Washington St., 1935.

Owning one's own dual-purpose tavern/grocery provided steady access to the twin staples of Lithuanian-American existence—food and alcohol—without the need to rely on credit or go "on the book" at any other establishment when mine work dried up for extended periods. Almost always, the tavern family owners lived behind, above, or next door to their business.

## Lithuanian Tavern 'Ground Zero'

The following local taverns, most now defunct, were owned by Lithuanian immigrants and/or their offspring: Lapinski's (1030 E. Washington), Bernie Yanor's and Jim Casper's taverns (opposite corners of 11th at Peoria Road), (Kostie) Welch's Tavern (11th and Laurel–later at 1827 Peoria Rd.), James Welch's Tavern (formerly the Mecca) at 1701 Peoria Rd., Peter Yumbras's tavern at 2126 Peoria Rd., the (John Re-

Welch's Mecca Tavern, 1703 Peoria Rd., 1967. Sangamon County tax files.

The 2102 Peoria Rd. home of my great aunt (*Teta*) Mary Yamont. Circa 1965. Sangamon County tax files.

kesius) Welcome Inn (11th and Washington), Tony Romanowski (Antanas Ramanauskas)'s Railroad Tavern at 1729 E. Reynolds St. (later owned by Frances Casper), Alby's (Alby and Vera Stasukinas's) tavern (14th and Carpenter), Bozis's tavern on East Mason, Enoch and William Blazis's White City Tavern on East Cook, Carl Pokora's tavern at 22nd and South Grand Avenue East, and the Lazy Lou at 1737 E. Moffatt, not far from Pillsbury Mills, which was owned by Frank W. and Mary (Gerula) Grinn. Other taverns were Wally's, operated by Walter Kerchowski at 716 North 14th St., and drinking establishments owned by Nancy (Kensman) Zakar around 16th and Carpenter and Anna (Leschinsky) Kasawich on East Reynolds after their husbands died. *(Read on for Lithuanian-owned supper clubs.)*

For pure Lithuanian tavern density, we need look no further than Peoria Road near its intersection with Sangamon Avenue at the southeast corner of the Illinois State Fairgrounds, "ground zero" for Lithuanian immigrant density. There, in addition to two Welch-owned taverns, we find Bernie Yanor, Jim Casper, and Peter Yumbras watering holes.

## From Beer to Soda to Supper Club

Some taverns started out serving beer to miners in the early 1900s, then became grocery stores or soda fountains, exclusively, during 1920s Prohibition—then reverted to taverns again in the 1930s. The ancillary restaurant/grocery functions of taverns were perhaps not as important as their provision of alcohol. But many are still also remembered for their food. Fish dinners on Friday were extremely popular, due to a heavily Catholic customer base. An ad from 1956 for Alby's mentions "Homemade Chili, Hamburgers, Hot Tamales and Cheese." In 1940, one of the Welch taverns had chicken and potato salad dinners for 10 cents and boneless fish dinners for 5 cents.

Over the decades, the basic tavern "hole in the wall" with simple food and drinks evolved into the larger and more ambitious "supper club" that featured live music with dancing and a more extensive—and expensive—menu for sit-down dining, drawing customers from a wider area. One of the first of these was The Blue Danube, built on Keys Avenue near Converse by the Yates/Yacubasky family in 1933.

Some of the best-known Lithuanian-owned supper clubs were:  the Cara-Sel Lounge (Tony Yuscius) on North Grand Avenue, the Skyrocket Inn (Kostie Welch) on Sangamon Avenue near the fairgrounds, and the Fairview (Alex and Alice Palusinski) and Butch's (Frank Gudauski's) Steak House--both further east on Sangamon Avenue. Other dinner and dancing establishments were Bogden's Grove (Harmony House?) on West Washington, (Stephen) Benya's Supper Club in Nokomis, and the upscale Saddle Club (Joe Welch) at 307 S. 6th St., which was also a local newspaper watering hole.

Lapinski extended family, 1940s.

## Striking Miners' Commissaries

Taverns served an important, little-known function during the infamous "Mine Wars" 1932-36, when they were neighborhood "commissaries" for striking members of the Progressive Miners of America (PMA), storing and distributing food to

Lapinski tavern ad, undated.
*State Journal-Register.*

hungry families. A Dec. 4, 1937 article in the *Illinois State Journal* describes character testimony given by Lithuanian-born tavern owner Sam (Simonas) Lapinski in defense of Sam's Lithuanian-American son-in-law Anthony Chunes, who was on trial in federal district court in Springfield for strike-related railroad sabotage.

The article states that Anthony had been a bartender at Lapinski's, and that the basement of the tavern functioned as a PMA commissary. Chunes was convicted and imprisoned in the 1937 mass trial of 36 PMA strikers, despite the testimony of his Lapinski in-laws and wife Monica (they later divorced). (Lithuanian-Americans Charles Mostaka and his son-in-law Joe Biernoski testified in defense of accused PMA miners Sam and Tony Profeta in the same mass trial.)

Distributed, as they were, throughout Springfield's neighborhoods and built on an intimate scale, corner taverns were the neighborhood watering holes, restaurants, and entertainment centers of their time: an era when social life took place on the scale of the family and the neighborhood, and "people knew each other." Along with adult socializing, taverns offered juke box music, pinball, shuffleboard, punch boards, slot machines—and later, when it was a real novelty, TV.

On the bad side, taverns presented a temptation to alcohol and gambling (both during and after gambling was legal) on every corner for those who could least afford it. To my knowledge, the potentially rougher side of tavern life and their core miner clientele made them generally off-limits for children at night.

## Gambling as an Ancillary Business

Punch boards were a form of gambling in which a key was purchased and used to push in a circle on a board to see if there was a prize behind. During the height of the Depression (before gambling became illegal within Springfield's city limits in 1939), even grocery stores had punch boards with candy prizes for children. The price of the key was commensurate with the value of the potential prize.

One family of Lithuanian-American tavern-keepers was prominent for decades in the business of distributing punch boards to taverns and social clubs throughout the county, according to newspaper reports. I am not revealing that family surname in deference to a descendant's sensitivity to the illegal nature of gambling in the city after 1939 and the county after 1948 (though local bans were often not enforced).

However, I can refer interested readers to several articles in the *Illinois State Journal*. One, dated Oct. 21, 1948, gives the names of Sangamon County's three main illegal punch board suppliers as reported by a grand jury investigation. Another, dated Sept. 6, 1963, describes gambling arrests arising from a raid on a (non-Lithuanian-owned) tavern called The Press Box. Last but not least, a March 12, 1964 *Journal* article describes an anonymous tip and police raid on a garage behind a well-known Lithuanian-American tavern on Peoria Road that netted 5-10,000 punch boards and tip boards, resulting in the owner's arrest.

Not the punch-board family: Back row, l to r: Antonia and Bernie Yanor, owners of Bernie's tavern at 11th and Peoria Road, with daughter Josephine (Stankavich). Front row, l to r: Yanor children Joe, Anna (Carver), and Bernie, Jr., 1920s.

## Growing up in a 'Tavern Family'

And now, we have the fond childhood memories of growing up in a tavern family from Georgeann (Carver) Madison. Georgeann is the granddaughter of Bernie and Antonia Yanor, who owned Bernie's tavern. In early childhood, she lived with her parents George and Ann (Yanor) Carver above Lithuanian immigrants Peter and Helen Klim's Shoe Repair shop, next door to Klim's son Jim Casper's tavern, and across the street from Bernie's tavern.

The Klim's Shoe Repair building where the Yanor-Carvers lived upstairs. 2009 N. 11th St. Circa 1965, Sangamon County tax files.

Little Georgeann Carver (of the Yanor clan) in a home-made swimming pool, 1940s.

Georgeann recalls: "My Uncle Bernie tended bar there, and after school, I was allowed to sit at the end of the bar and watch 'Pinkie Lee' on TV instead of practicing my piano lessons like my mother sent me across the street to do." (Before TV ownership was common, television was another major draw of the corner tavern. In 1956, an Alby's ad enticed customers to come in and "Enjoy Television Tonight.")

Georgeann continues: "My Uncle Bernie cooked the best cheeseburgers, tamales, chili and barbecues. He would make a cheeseburger for me even though my mom wanted me to eat dinner at home. Almost every time I was there, my grandfather would hand me a silver dollar out of his pocket. I would be at the tavern in the early evening before the coal miners came in from work at the mine at 11th and Ridgely."

Georgeann also remembers that on Christmas Eve, Father Stanley Yunker, pastor of St. Vincent de Paul's (Lithuanian) Catholic Church, would come to the Yanor living quarters at the tavern and distribute Holy Communion. "He would have a drink of whiskey or wine or two and some holiday food with the Yanor-Stankavich-Carver families." (Georgeann's beloved maternal aunt Josephine Yanor and husband Bill Stankavich lived across Peoria Road, one block south on 11th Street.)

*Here are some additional recollections and information from Georgeann, Sharon Darran, Chuck Tisckos, Ann Traeger, Scott Welsh, Joe Turasky, Frank Mazrim and William Cellini, Jr.:*

**Casper's:** Still standing–now Dudes Saloon. Helen Klim, mother of owner Jim Casper, used to make the best chili. Klim's Shoe Repair was just north on 11th Street from the tavern, which was at the corner of 11th and Peoria Road. The Casper and Yanor families were related by marriage; hence, it's no surprise that Casper's and Bernie's taverns were on the same corner near Klim's.

George and Anna (Yanor) Carver, baby Georgeann, circa 1945.

**Lapinski's**: Adolph Kelert and Sam Lapinski, Jr., also a Springfield policeman, ran the tavern after parents Sam (Simonas) and Mary Lapinski retired. The St. Vincent de Paul Church choir used to go there for beers and fish dinners on Friday nights after choir practice. Constance Kelert, Adolph's wife, was a talented soloist in the choir when she died suddenly at age 44 while attending a funeral in LaSalle. During the 1940s, customers would drive up, buy carp sandwiches and eat them in their cars.

Sam, Jr., and his wife had a house on Lake Springfield, and St. Vincent de Paul's held its annual *didelis iškylą* (big picnic) there in the 1950s and 1960s, according to Chuck Tisckos. Sam, Sr.'s, brother George Joseph (Jurgis Juozas) Lapinski was in Central Illinois for a while, but his branch of the family moved to Michigan in the early 1920s to find factory jobs.

Sam and Mary Lapinski also rented apartments in the East Washington Street neighborhood, including above their tavern, to WWII displaced persons or "DPs," including the Abramikas family.

**The Fairview**: Some of the St. Vincent de Paul choir members would go there in the 1950s and '60s for the fried chicken (half a chicken) special on Thursday nights. Alice Palusinski was the daughter of the original owners Lithuanian immigrants Kaston and Caroline (Compardo) Stockus. Ownership changed when the Palusinskis retired in the 1980s, and in 2013 or 2014, the establishment re-opened after a fire.

Bouser Viele also owned the Fairview for a least a time. He is listed as owner in the 1956 St. Vincent de Paul Jubilee book.

**The Saddle Club**: Owned by Joe Welch (Wilcauskas) who also, at various times, owned the Capitol Food Market, Raydine Corp., Empire Hotel and Independent Novelty Co., according to articles in the *Illinois State Journal.* Some sources also indicate ownership by Al Miles.

**The Mecca**: Joseph Yucus is listed as the owner from at least 1933-37. Around 1948 into the early 1950s, Andrew Corcoran is listed as the owner. Became James Welch's tavern in the 1960s.

The Lazy Lou, 1737 E. Moffat St., 1965. Sangamon County tax files.

**The Welcome Inn**: Great 5-cent fish sandwich. According to John Rekesius, part of a three-lot property owned by immigrant John Frank Rekesius, Sr.

**Boggens (Bogden's) Grove (Harmony House)**: A huge establishment with music and dancing. Picnics were also held on the grounds. *(Only minimal/ sketchy information about this establishment.)*

**Bernie's**: According to Georgeann (Carver) Madison, Antonia Yanor cleaned the tavern at night, but never entered the premises during operations. The Lithuanian-born daughter of Michael and Margaret (Shalunas) Razuskinas, Grandma Antonia was introverted and spoke only Lithuanian. Her son Bernie, Jr., was affected by polio and never married. Son Joe was a welder and married Monica (Monty) Yanor, a long-time officer of the Springfield Lithuanian-American Club.

**The Skyrocket**: At 2202 Peoria Rd., perhaps the most storied Lithuanian tavern of them all (though Lapinski's had more continuous ownership by a single Lithuanian-American family). Started as Chick's tavern, owned by Lithuanian-American John F. Gurgens with son John, Jr., working the bar back in the 1930s. By 1945, it was owned by Kostie Welch and his brothers. (Maybe the Welches took over while the younger Gurgens went off to fight in the war and his father, born in the 1880s, couldn't handle all the work?)

Carver-Madison wedding inside St. Vincent de Paul Church, 1962.

The Welches first offered dancing on Sunday nights to the music of The Rocket Trio, and later featured dancing every night except Monday and "really good" steak dinners, according to one newspaper ad. (Starting in 1953, William Cellini, Sr., had gigs playing piano there with his uncle's band.)

After the Welch era, the Skyrocket was owned for 17 years by Ules Rose, whose daughter Barb married Charlie Foster, Jr., the son of Charles, Sr., and Ann Mosteika Foster, the long-time music director and organist at St. Vincent de Paul's Church.

Peter Welsh bought the Skyrocket in 1963 from Rose. According to Peter's son Scott, all seven Welsh children and their mother Barbara worked in the bar at one time or another, and its position next to the Illinois State Fairgrounds attracted a cast of characters few places in town would see. "It was an interesting education for all of us. The stories of the Skyrocket are legend, including visits from the Hell's Angels, dignitaries hanging out late night, and many 'disagreements' between patrons handled with flying fists," Scott recalls. "My dad Pete ran a tight ship and was respected by most for not putting up with a lot of problems."

The Skyrocket served food until the late 1960s, then only during fair week, when Barbara Welsh ran the kitchen. Thornton Oil purchased the land in the early 1990's.

**The Blue Danube**: Founded in 1933 by the Yacubasky/Yates family next to their grocery on Keys Avenue near Converse. The tavern was managed by Joseph Yates, as his brother William spent most of his time in Republican politics. The Blue Danube had a kitchen, a dance floor that was "well sanded and waxed," and an ample area for tables and booths–but its claim to fame was its "magic bar." One *Journal-Register* writer described it as "electrically charged in such a way that when specially-treated glasses are placed on it, they are illuminated in many colors. This gives the appearance of nothing short of magic, and has proven a very popular source of entertainment."

Casper's tavern, 2001 N. 11th at Peoria Road. Circa 1965. Sangamon County tax files.

According to newspaper ads, The Blue Danube's motto was, "where courtesy prevails." It featured festive New Year's parties and Sunday dinners of either roast young duck, fried milk-fed spring chicken, T-bone steak, frog legs, breaded veal cutlet, or roast loin of pork with many different sides, including "Chinese" celery salad and lime and grapefruit salad, plus a full spread of desserts—all for just 65 cents. Also on the menu were "fancy mixed drinks, the finest of wines, liquors and beer, good music and dancing."

The Yates were involved in a protracted dispute with the city's liquor board for allegedly operating without a liquor license, hosting dancing without a permit and serving alcohol after hours. They sold their supper club in 1938. *(See the chapter on the political rise of the Adams and Yates families).*

**Alby's:** Alby Stasukinas, a former coal miner, was born in Springfield, the son of Joseph Adam and Rose Anna (Poskevicius) Stasukinas. The tavern served a chicken lunch.

**Bozis's Tavern**: Owned by Tony and Mae Bozis, who lived next to the tavern on East Mason in a small brick bungalow. "Several Lithuanians lived around there, and across the street on the corner, Tony's mother owned a grocery store," according to Sharon Darran. She recalls going to a dinner at the tavern after a funeral, and being served the hot Lithuanian spiced honey and whiskey drink *viritos*, and lots of Lithuanian food.

Tony was also a plumber with his brother John, who lived in Riverton. At Bozis's, beer was served in glass jelly jars. "They had a couch in the bar and Tony would lay on it and take a nap while his wife Mae did the bartending," Sharon remembers.

*Detailed tavern research and public image retrieval courtesy of Genealogics.*

*Lapinski tavern and family photos courtesy of Diana Barbour. Yanor family photos courtesy of Georgeann (Carver) Madison.*

# Chapter 35
# Lithuanian Taverns: Holding up, or Holding Back the Neighborhood?

My first *Taverns* post struck a rich vein of local lore, which I will continue to mine. Wally Surgis (Lith. Sudrius) tells me about another interesting tavern-keeper, immigrant Tony Romanowski (Lith. Antanas Ramanauskas), who owned a grocery store/tavern on East Reynolds Street from what appears to be the 1920s to the mid-1950s.

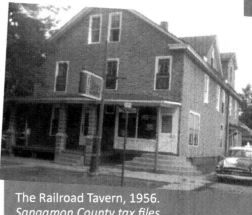

The Railroad Tavern, 1956.
*Sangamon County tax files.*

According to Genealogics, the 1924 Springfield City Directory lists Tony as a grocer at 1729 E. Reynolds with wife Mary (later, also his brother John). Wally describes Tony as only about 5-foot-3 and very round, with "Peter Lorre eyes." While operating the Railroad Tavern and living in the attached house at #1729 for many years, Tony reportedly cooked food and gave out drinks to poor Lithuanian immigrants in the area. Wally recalls: "Tony would feed and house the poor of the neighborhood, and even bought enough life insurance to bury the ones who had no family."

## Communalism on the Neighborhood Scale

Tony's service to his fellow Lithuanians was no doubt part of a larger fabric of immigrant communalism in the neighborhood between 16th and 19th streets on East Reynolds that rivaled the fairgrounds area for its concentration of Lithuanian residents.

We already know that during the infamous 1932-36 "Mine Wars," when thousands of Progressive Miners went on strike, corner groceries and taverns acted as food collection and distribution points or "commissaries" for hungry mining families. According to Wally, mutual aid in the neighborhood long after the 1930s included sharing personal fishing catches and canned garden produce. As the social center of its neighborhood for many years, the Railroad

```
REYNOLDS E—Contd
1700½  Fisher John E 2-8574
1701   Urbanckas Anton @
1704   Bierbaum Fred D 3-0540
1705   Bernotas Anna Mrs @ 6478
1708   Romanotto Pete T @ 8-0860
1709   Tisckos John @ 3-4456
1709½  Seaborn Wm
1711   Kosavick Tony @
1712   Kerchowski Boltrus @
1715   Ocrey Vern 3-5379
1716   Vacant
1718   Sivels Carl
1719   Hatchett Robt 8-0233
1720   Wright Chas E @ 3-9846
1722   Mitchell Anna Mrs @ 8-5388
rear   Vacant
1723   Wilson Harrison
rear   Vacant
1725   Koslowski August
1728   Chinn Willard D @ 4-9673
1729   Rialroad Tavern 2-0589
       Casper Frances Mrs
rear   Ramanauskas Tony @
1729½  Hinds L F
       Orback Anna Mrs
1729 1/3  Vaughn Shirley H
```

Springfield City Directory, 1956.

Tavern also reportedly held regular Sunday picnics on a nearby vacant lot.

To get a sense of the persistence of the East Reynolds Lithuanian community from the year 1900 or so up through the 1950s, take a look at these snap-shots taken by Genealogics from two Springfield city directories (image for 1956 followed by 1951). In both, we see many likely Lithuanian names, such as: Genewitch, Valatkas, Brazitis, Kerchowski, Ramanauskas, Sockel, Turasky, Al-ane, Casper, Urbanckas, Bernotas, Tisckos, Kosavich, and possibly others: Sivels, Kostinence(?), Gorda(?), Koslouski(?)--and Orback(!)

REYNOLDS E—Contd
1520 Cherry Ethel Mrs
1521 Atkins Jas O 8-7455
1522 Genewitch Ike 7749
      Spfld Tobacco & Candy
1526 Valatkas John 8-1901
1530 Krushall Robt 8-4186
1532 Apartments
      E Romanotto Leo
      W Houston Thos 2-8125
1535 Fowler Hersey E 8-4897
1537 Cason Frank 9606
1538 Washington Arth
  —16th Intersects
1600 Brazitis John
1605 Liggins Clarence 3-2
1606 Sockel Anthony
1608 Tinsley Thos 7909
1609 Seitz Jos 3-4046
1610 Turasky John V 3-863
1612 Day Jas R 7823
1614 Hayes Danl E 8-4903
1617 Richards Homer 8-605
1625 Brennan Thos P 6041
1628 Richey Jos 2-3482
1629 Alane Victor 9690
1630 Casper Wm
1631 McCormick Elbert

—17th Intersects
1700 Apartments
    1 Jordon Rebt
    2 Krueger Ewald 8-3339
1700½ Brandle Don 3-2638
1701 Urbanckas Anton
1704 Bierbaum Fred D 3-0
1705 Bernotas Anna Mrs
1708 Shedko Jacob H 9710
      Romanotto Peter
1709 Tisckos John
1709½ Vacant
1711 Kosavich Tony
1712 Kenney Jessie Mrs
1715 Murrell Bernice 3-537
1716 Conely Mattie Mrs
1718 Sivels Carl
1719 Viola Silvio
1720 Wright Chas E 3-984
1722 Mitchell Anna Mrs
      8-5388
rear Kostinence Andrew
1723 Stufflebeam Geo 3-8020
rear Gorda Clara Mrs
1725 Koslouski Louise Mrs
1725 Chinn Willard D 967
1729 Railroad Tavern 2-0589
      Romanauskas Tony
rear Peters Jos
1729½ Hinz L F
—15th Intersects

Springfield City Directory, 1951.

## Finding My Lost Orback Relatives

Here is where my passion for the stories of other families—and the commu-nity—gets unexpectedly personal. The Anna Orback living at 1729 ½ E. Reyn-olds in 1956, right next to the Railroad Tavern at #1729, is a name I suddenly recognize. Although I only heard her name once or twice as a child, I believe that Anna is my long-lost Lithuanian great aunt!

In 1956, Tony R. is listed as still living at the rear of the Railroad Tavern, #1729 East Reynolds, though he has since sold the tavern to a Mrs. Frances Casper. Does this proximity to big-hearted Tony mean that my great aunt was one of the very poorest of the poor that he was helping? Given Tony's reputation, I would say that my widowed great aunt Anna was almost surely one of those whom Tony housed, fed, and possibly even buried.

My other Lithuanian great aunt, "*Teta*," officially Mary Yamont (Marija Baksyte Jomantiene) was like our grandmother. She, herself, was of extremely modest circumstances in a three-room house at 2102 Peoria Rd, where my family used to visit on Sundays. Dad and his aunt and her grown children Joe and Mary would sit in the kitchen and speak Lithuanian. Maybe Anna Orback and her family came up in their conversations. But they never spoke of Anna and her family or introduced them to my sisters and me.

The two Baksys sisters. On left, Anna Orback, son Frank, Jr., and daughter Elizabeth. On right: Mary Yamont, daughter Mary and son Joe. Missing from photo: sons Joe Orback and Benny Yamont. Circa 1940. *Courtesy of Sandy (Orback) Pecori.*

Sometime in the years after *Teta* died in 1978 at age 94, I remember hearing maybe once or twice of a second great aunt in Springfield—someone of very close blood, considering how we had so few relatives on our Springfield Lithuanian side—yet someone who had been unmentionable for decades.

## Anna Orback's Story

I have since looked up Anna Orback's granddaughter Sandy (Orback) Pecori. I learned that even she had been shielded by her father, Frank Orback, Jr., from her Orback relatives—growing up almost exclusively with her mother's Frasco family. However, there were occasions when the two Lithuanian Baksys sisters and their families were together, witnessed by some photos that Sandy shared.

Frank Orback, Jr. *Courtesy of Sandy (Orback) Pecori.*

The rift that separated immigrant sisters Mary Yamont and Anna Orback might have had something to do with Anna's long-term alcoholism and emotional and economic decline after the death of her husband, Frank, Sr., from alcohol poisoning in 1926. It seems that Anna also welcomed her sister Mary's divorced husband Benedict, Sr.—another sure cause of bad blood.

It's likely that Anna welcomed financial support from almost anyone who could render it. In fact, according to granddaughter Sandy, Anna pressed her son, Frank, Jr., so relentlessly that he had to cut ties with her to insulate his own family. I imagine that Anna's loss of family support is why she ended up living with a man named Hinds, according to the 1956 directory, and depending on long-time tavern-keeper Tony R.

## Leaving the 'Old' Neighborhood

The story of Tony helping the aged, poor and alcoholic immigrants left behind on East Reynolds by the 1950s is the flip-side of the success story whereby the young, educated and more successful American-born of the 1920s-1940s left their immigrant neighborhoods.

I personally can attest to the depressed state of the Peoria Road/fairgrounds neighborhood where *Teta* lived when my family visited there from the 1960s through the early 1970s. Anyone can see as much from photos in the Sangamon County tax files.

The truth is, the poverty of the neighborhoods where immigrant families had struggled through the decline of coal mining, the "Mine Wars," and the Depression caused these enclaves to be abandoned during America's long, post-war economic boom. And to the extent that the old neighborhoods conserved the bleak first-wave Lithuanian immigrant experience, they were a major disappointment to second-wave immigrants who arrived not understanding the hard times the first-wavers had endured, and expecting to find them in much better circumstances.

## Blaming, and Escaping, the Taverns

Here's how Lithuanian Springfield must have looked to my father Vincas Baksys when he arrived from the "DP" camps of Germany in June 1949: substandard, ramshackle housing (slapped together by struggling miners, initially without indoor plumbing) and everybody on a tavern stool or awash at home in so-called "jug" beer.

Drinking may have been fine for those left behind, defeated. But the new immigrants still had their big plans and dreams: families to start, fortunes to make. So when these second-wavers arrived in the old neighborhoods that conserved the poverty of the first wave, but not the causes of that poverty, the culture of taverns and alcohol could easily have seemed to blame.

And that is how most of the second-wave immigrants or DPs who arrived after World War II, like my father, ended up renouncing tavern life and living outside the old neighborhoods as soon as they could afford it. Of course I am a direct beneficiary of my father's decision to work hard instead of whiling away hours on a tavern stool. We are so lucky he didn't have a drinking problem. Perhaps most important, we are lucky that Dad found the right opportunities in Springfield in the 1950s, '60s, and '70s to work and lift himself up—along with his family.

At the same time, I can't really condemn the taverns that were important means of support and the first visible nodes of economic progress for the first wave. Certainly taverns persevered through the 1950s and '60s as the most Lithuanian, and numerous, of neighborhood institutions.

Alcoholism was an ugly reality of European immigrant life all over Springfield (not just for Lithuanians, but all the "drinking" cultures, such as the Irish, Italians, Germans and Slovaks.) And as a counterweight to the dead weight of alcoholism, the story of Tony Ramanauskas demonstrates how tavern-keepers probably shared some of their modest success with the surrounding neighborhood. Such sharing likely grew out of a sense of ethnic communalism, as well as something even more basic: customer loyalty.

## The Earliest Taverns

Scrolling back in time, the 1906 Springfield City Directory lists quite a few Lithuanian-owned taverns that apparently did not make it to the 1930s, roughly the beginning of my tavern and supper club coverage in the previous chapter. For example, according to Genealogics, in 1906, William Anskis owned a tavern at 1931 Peoria Rd.; John Brazis, a tavern at 805 E. Washington; Michael Dunkus, one at 729 E. Washington; Charles Gedmin (Gedman?) at 800 E. Washington; George Kamiczaites (Kamizaitis), at 1800 S. 11th; Messrs. Kaslavsky (Kazlauskas?) & Burezik, at 1428 E. Reynolds; and Messrs. Yuris & Kalosky, at 112 S. Seventh St.

Why did more of these very early taverns not survive?

- Those in the infamous "Levee" district just east of downtown might have been burned or sacked in the 1908 Springfield (white) Race Riot; and

- Other taverns could have passed into new hands or been put out of business by 1920s Prohibition.

The impact of Prohibition on Lithuanian taverns was somewhat muted, according to one of my informants, by the ongoing practice of serving illegal alcohol discreetly, behind closed doors. Once Prohibition was repealed in 1933, the taverns simply applied for city liquor licenses and re-opened their doors.

Last but not least, as we leave the topic of how alcohol was carried on as a business by immigrants with lots of know-how and few other opportunities, let me not neglect a certain specialized role for women. Widows, alone or with children to support, could not go down into the mines after their husbands were killed or injured there. According to one informant, Lithuanian widows who boarded unmarried miners would home-produce and sell hard liquor with the help of their boarders.

## A Positive Role in the Second Wave

By 1949, at least one "tavern family," the Lapinskis, had gone into real estate, and used its apartments to house several newly arrived DP families. Violeta (Abramikas) Abad remembers that her immigrant family, including her parents and baby sister Regina, lived in a third-floor apartment above Lapinski's Tavern on East Washington Street for several years after their arrival in the U.S. under the U.S. Displaced Persons Act of 1948.

Violeta says, "My father then sponsored his brother and family to come to America in 1951 from the displaced persons camps in Germany, and they also lived with us above Lapinski's until my Uncle Vincas was able to save enough money to move to their own apartment."

After reading my first *Tavern Life* blog post, Violeta says she shared memories with her first cousin Laima (Abramikas) Milaitis of moving their mattress out on the porch/balcony on summer nights because it was too hot to sleep inside the third-floor apartment. However, it wasn't long after the Abramikases' first years above the Lapinski tavern that this second-wave family made its way to middle class success in America. "Making it" in only one generation was a velocity that the first wave of coal-mining immigrants had, in most cases, been unable to achieve.

## The Path of Hard Work and Opportunity

Immigrants Stephanie and Walter Abramikas, circa 1985. *Courtesy of Regina Buedel.*

Violeta's father Walter Abramikas, who had been a forestry professional in Lithuania, worked a union job at our local Allis-Chalmers factory, which hired many immigrants after World War II. This allowed him and his wife Stephanie to save enough money also to get into rental real estate—and send their two daughters off to college. In my own immigrant family, again thanks to hard work, saving every penny, and an Allis-Chalmers union job, my two parents who had never gone to high school managed to send five daughters through college straight to the middle class.

As for the first generations of coal-mining Lithuanian immigrants and their American-born children who faced many harsh decades of minimal opportunity in Springfield, I am now convinced that institutions like the church and neighborhood taverns and groceries fulfilled ironically similar social functions. They built and preserved the social safety net of their time: the communal bonds that could often be a desperate family or individual's last means of support.

*With appreciation to Genealogics for in-depth public records research.*

# Chapter 36
# A Second Wave of Immigrants

As a result of the 1939 Molotov-Ribbentrop Pact between Nazi Germany and the Soviet Union, in 1940 the U.S.S.R. brutally annexed Lithuania. In just the first nine months of their reign of terror, the Soviets imprisoned, tortured, executed and deported to their deaths in Siberia tens of thousands. In late June 1941, the Russians were driven out by a Nazi invasion. This, in turn, resulted in a massive Jewish Holocaust in which a minority of Lithuanians participated and a minority helped Jews hide or escape.

Three years later, during the summer of 1944, the Red Army re-approached from the east, driving the Nazis before it. About 60,000 Lithuanians who could not endure a second Soviet occupation made a desperate choice. They fled their homeland on foot and by horse-drawn cart, falling back on the same shelled and congested roads as the German army with Russian forces in full pursuit.

Sophie and son Hank (Vytautas) Endzelis, displaced persons from Lithuania, prepare to board their ship to the U.S. in Tubingen, Germany, 1948. *Courtesy of Barbara Endzelis.*

At the same time, about 40,000 Lithuanians of all ages and both genders became partisans or "Forest Brothers" valiantly committed to fighting the second Soviet occupation of their country. Without outside help, most were captured and killed by 1954.

Once back on Lithuanian soil, the Russians resumed in earnest the mass deportations they had launched in June 1941, just before the Nazi invasion. In the late 1940s and early 1950s, an estimated 200,000 Lithuanians were shipped to the farthest, frozen reaches of Siberia, most never to return.

Although they were subsequently smeared as "fascists" by the Soviets, the Lithuanian refugees who fled west into German lands in 1944 were mostly teachers, civil servants, members of the intelligentsia, successful farmers like my father, and employees of the Lithuanian state. As the nation's backbone and patriotic "brain trust," those who fled came from the same ranks as those targeted for deportation to Siberia, underscoring why they felt no choice but to leave.

## From Teachers to *Dypukai*

Lithuanian refugees who escaped repatriation to Soviet-occupied Lithuania ended up in United Nations' displaced persons camps in western Germany. Several thousand of these later immigrated to the United States under the U.S. Displaced Persons Act of 1948. And several dozen of these so-called

"DPs" or "*Dypukai*" arrived in Springfield under the sponsorship of first-wave relatives who had come here during the coal-mining boom. (Others immigrated to Canada, Australia, and South America.)

Among Springfield's second wave of traumatized war refugees were Lithuanian orphans Vytautas and Romualda Sidlauskas. You can read about the arrival of these two children in Springfield, probably in 1948, in the newspaper clipping below.

# WAR ORPHANS ARRIVE

Vytautas, 8, and Romalda Sidlauska, 10, arrived yesterday at the Gulf, Mobile & Ohio station from Mattenberg, Germany. After the disappearance of their father in Lithuania and their mother's death in 1944, the children were placed in a displaced persons camp in Germany. Through the efforts of an uncle and the war relief services of the National Catholic Welfare conference the children were brought to this country to live with their second cousins, Mr. and Mrs. George J. Wisonsky, of 511 W. Canedy St. Left to right are front row, Georgann Wisnos-

—Staff Photo.

ky, Vytautas, Romaulda; back row, Mr. and Mrs. Wisnosky, Monsignor William Cassin and Miss Mary Henry, train hostess.

*State Journal-Register,*
circa 1948.

In addition, the Paulionis family was sponsored by a branch of the Urbanckas family, their distant relatives, and my paternal great aunt Mary Yamont (Marija Jomantiene) sponsored my father Vincas Baksys after spotting his name among lists of DPs that were printed in Lithuanian newspapers. This may be how many displaced relatives were located.

## One Generation Helps the Next

All across the United States, first-wave immigrants and their beneficial organizations were heavily involved in resettling refugee relatives and those to whom they had no relation, and are to be forever commended for their patriotism and humanitarianism. (Every DP individual or family had to be sponsored by a U.S. citizen who certified the new immigrants would have homes and jobs once they arrived.)

Among other second-wavers resettled in Springfield at this time were the Abramikas, Danelevich, Uzgiris, Petrakus, and Lelys families. Some DPs who were initially settled here later moved to Chicago to find a larger Lithuanian community and more opportunities for employment.

## Professionals No More

These so-called "second wave" immigrants were often displaced professionals and other highly educated individuals who felt a moral imperative to preserve Lithuanian identity and culture abroad while their homeland was wiped from the map. Most had left never intending their absence to be permanent, never believing the U.S.S.R. would be permitted to occupy Lithuanian for more than 45 years.

Once here, most had to accept manual labor and factory jobs due to language barriers and foreign degrees that were not recognized in the U.S. Very few climbed back up to the same levels they formerly had occupied in their professions, or worked in the same professions again.

They married and started families, or raised to adulthood the small children they had brought with them through the camps of Germany. And always, they carried with them the memory of everything they had loved and lost.

My paternal grandmother Petronėlė (Jarmoskaite) Baksiene, a.k.a., Petronella Baksys, in German DP camp, circa 1947. Grandmother died in Connecticut in 1957 without ever again seeing children Stasys, Isidorius, and Antanina, left behind in Lithuania.

# Chapter 37
# Obituary for an Immigrant:
# Constance Lelys

*(This piece was written and distributed by Mike Lelys at his father's wake.)*

Constantine and Helgi
(Lilles) Lelys, circa 1988.

Constantine (Connie) Lelys was born in Musnikai, Lithuania on October 22, 1919, the son of Ramualdas Lelys and Salomeja (Szeffer) Lelys. After fleeing Lithuania during World War II, he married fellow Baltic refugee Helgi Lilles of Estonia in 1948 in Linz, Austria, where their first son Michael was born.

During the family's 1950 transatlantic voyage to the U.S., two-year-old Michael was vaccinated for smallpox with a contaminated needle. He became gravely ill on the ship and was hospitalized upon arrival in New York with an extremely high fever. As they dreaded news that their son might not survive, Connie and Helgi's new life in the land of opportunity was almost shattered before it began.

## Bicycling Across Town to Stoke Furnace

Fortunately, with God's mercy, Michael survived and the family moved to Springfield, Ill., with the assistance of a loan from Catholic Charities. Connie took his first Job as a custodian for St. Patrick's Parish under pastor Father Haggerty. He maintained the buildings and kept the school and church furnaces stoked with coal, even when that required getting up at four in the morning and riding a bicycle across town to St. Pat's during the winter months. It wasn't always pleasant work, but Connie took pride in the fact that he had been given a job, and he did that job to the best of his ability.

Connie also joined the Lithuanian Catholic parish of St. Vincent de Paul, where he was very active in the church choir and all the social events. He was a close friend of the pastor, the Rev. Stanley O. Yunker, and even became Father Yunker's personal barber, once Father learned that Connie had somewhere acquired the skill of cutting hair (probably practicing on his son Michael).

## From Factory to Office Work

Like many local displaced persons from WWII, Connie later was employed by construction machinery manufacturer Allis-Chalmers, where he thought he had done a bad job when he was laid off after one month, not realizing that lay-offs at factories were quite routine. Later, Connie went to work at Gothard's Manufacturing on Clear Lake Avenue. After a short time, Gothard's moved to South Carolina, but offered some employees like Connie transfers to Sangamo Electric.

However, unlike many displaced persons, Connie didn't spend the rest of his working life in a factory or at manual labor. He had his sights set on office work, and after working at Sangamo Electric for only a brief period, with the help of Alan Smith, D.D.S, his dentist, Connie was hired as an office assistant to the Illinois Supreme Court.

There, he befriended Clerk of the Supreme Court Mrs. Earl Searcy, who admired his beautiful handwriting and great work ethic and suggested he apply to the State of Illinois Highway Division (now IDOT) for a draftsman position. Fearing he could not pass the civil service exam (in English, of course), Connie studied intensively, and with the help of Mrs. Searcy, he passed the test.

At that time (1960), Helgi and Connie's second son, Mark, was born. After five years, Connie transferred to the Illinois Department of Conservation and retired from that department in 1984 after 20 years of service as an engineering technician.

## God and Family

Connie loved and lived his 80 years to the fullest. He enjoyed spending time with his family, particularly his grandsons Christopher, Matthew, and Joseph. In the late 1990s, grandson Christopher purchased the home next door to "Grandpa Connie" and it wasn't uncommon to see the two talking to each other about the status of Grandpa's garden, fishing, or just about anything two guys would talk about.

Connie set a high work ethic for his sons Mike (wife Mary Ann) and Mark (wife Jennifer) and reminded them constantly that he wanted them to have a better life than his own. He loved God and his family, and reminded everyone of that at family gatherings.

Mike Lelys and Mary Ann Wilk wedding, June 1970, St. Vincent de Paul Church.

## Man of Music

Connie could play the accordion, violin, mandolin, guitar, organ, and probably any other instrument he picked up. He could also speak multiple languages, including Lithuanian, German, Polish, Russian, Ukrainian, Latin, and some Estonian.

During his earlier years, he played the accordion for many different gatherings, including Lithuanian and Estonian picnics and any other occasion where a "squeeze box" might liven things up. When Connie was invited to a party, the "squeeze box" was always the first item loaded into his car, "just in case."

After his heart surgery in 1992, Connie decided to allow his son Mike to take over the accordion playing. He would accompany on mandolin and coax Mike to play the many European and American folk songs familiar to him. He never criticized Mike for not being as proficient as him on the accordion (probably because he didn't want to admit that his years of investing money and time in Mike's accordion lessons hadn't made Mike a Frankie Yankovic!).

## Respect for Nature

Connie introduced his two sons Mike and Mark to deer hunting in Pope and Pike Counties prior to his retirement. He taught them all the secrets of the hunt, yet never shot a deer himself in almost 20 years. He enjoyed just being outdoors with his sons, and he taught them to respect and enjoy nature.

His sons firmly believe that he could have harvested deer many times, but felt sorry for the poor animals. Upon their arrival, we suspect he would shoo them away with his handkerchief, before returning to camp with stories like, "I saw some, but they were too far away...There were too many trees in the way to shoot," or "The darn vodka from the previous night around the campfire made me fall asleep in the woods while lying in wait."

## A Repository of History

Connie enjoyed an occasional glass of beer, and was always eager to have someone sit down with him to just talk. His knowledge of World War II politics and his post-war stories about Russia and Lithuania could keep folks listening for hours. He could also relate the hardships of living in a displaced person's camp with his wife Helgi prior to immigrating to the U.S. in 1950.

Yet, he never complained about those hardships. He only just spoke of how lucky he was to have himself and his immediate family in the best country in the world!

Connie died July 24, 2000, in Springfield.

*Photos courtesy of Mike Lelys.*

# Chapter 38
# Following the Golden Thread

A flaxen thread connects almost every Lithuanian-American to one of the most important folk ways of our immigrant ancestors: the "homespun" production of linen clothes, sheets, bedspreads and towels.

For most of us, the person who connects us to our flaxen past is a great- or even a great-great grandmother. For me, it was my paternal grandmother who spun the flaxen fibers she, herself, had cultivated into the thread that she then wove into warm linen clothes for her nine children. (The family also raised sheep for wool.)

If my grandmother Petronėlė Baksiene of Viduklė, Lithuania, was typical, her large wooden loom probably occupied a central location in the family's two-room fir log house not far from the ceramic stove.

I never met my Lithuanian grandmother. But World War II Lithuanian immigrant Paul Endzelis helped master weaver and author Kati Reeder Meek show me how my grandmother lived.

Three of Paul's lovely inked weaving designs.

During the 1990s, Paul translated entire Lithuanian source books and inked hundreds of patterned designs for Kati's book in English entitled, *Reflections from a Flaxen Past: For Love of Lithuanian Weaving* (available on *Amazon.com*).

Kati is an acquaintance of long-time Springfield Lithuanian-American Club member Barbara (Spence) Endzelis. That's how Barbara's father-in-law Paul became involved in bringing the story of Lithuanian linen (*linas*) to life.

Paul Endzelis as a student, 1930s.

## A Young Nation's Hope

But if linen has a story, so does Paul, the son of small farmers Boleslava and Vincentas Endzelis of Stempliai in the Silute region. Despite his father's death in a German POW camp during World War I, Paul's mother was successful enough with the family's hardscrabble farm to send Paul to secondary school. After that, Paul completed officer military training, three years of accelerated business college in Klaipeda, and advanced German language studies in Hamburg before working during the 1930s at the State Savings Bank in Kaunas.

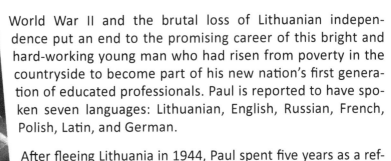

World War II and the brutal loss of Lithuanian independence put an end to the promising career of this bright and hard-working young man who had risen from poverty in the countryside to become part of his new nation's first generation of educated professionals. Paul is reported to have spoken seven languages: Lithuanian, English, Russian, French, Polish, Latin, and German.

After fleeing Lithuania in 1944, Paul spent five years as a refugee in Germany. He then immigrated with his teacher-wife Sophie (Brusokaite) of Suvolkija and their three-year-old son Arvydas (Hank) to Pittsburgh, where he found his first job as a laborer on a highway crew.

Young Sophie Endzelis, 1930s.

## Struggling Back into Business

Paul, Sophie and Hank eventually moved to Cicero, Ill., where Paul tried to kick-start his aborted business career by going to electronics technical school while Sophie worked in a factory. The family's next move was to Chicago's Lithuanian neighborhood in Marquette Park, where Sophie went to work in a Nabisco factory and Paul got a job at Budrik's Furniture in Bridgeport.

Finally, Paul found the right combination of resources—namely, a few colleagues from that store who joined with him to open their own TV, radio, and electronics sales and service store. That business operated for many years in Chicago's Bridgeport neighborhood.

After the couple retired and Sophie died, in 1984 Paul joined son Hank (an employee of the Illinois State Police Academy), wife Barbara and their two sons John and Joe Endzelis in Riverton for 14 years. He invested his meticulous attention to detail—and possibly, his attraction to tiny electrical circuitry—in hundreds of pages of intricate, geometric Lithuanian

Sophie and Paul, 1970s.

weaving designs when asked to assist Kati Reeder Meek. Several of Paul's drawings, along with his biography, appear in Kati's book.

In 1998, despite his advanced age and health concerns, Paul fulfilled every émigré's dream by actually returning to his homeland to live out his last years in the (again) newly free Lithuania. He died and was buried there in 2007, shortly before what would have been his 94th birthday.

*Dedicated to the memory of an extraordinary couple who made history their footnote, instead of becoming a footnote to history.*

Another of Paul's meticulously inked weaving designs.
*Photos courtesy of Barbara Endzelis.*

*Post-script: Kati Reeder Meek's book is hardcover and handsomely photographed. It has black-and-white historical photos of flax cultivation and weaving in the Lithuanian countryside prior to World War II, photos and descriptions of the Lithuanian national costume, and profiles of master weavers in the Lithuanian style from the U.S. and Canada.*

# Chapter 39
# Joe Koncius and Lithuanian Language School

Usually when you meet a person born in Illinois who speaks Lithuanian, it turns out that they grew up in Chicago and went to Lithuanian Saturday school in Marquette Park or Lemont. Few know there was once a small Lithuanian Saturday school in Springfield for children of the post-World War II immigrants, called displaced persons or "DPs."

Violeta Abramikas Abad of Ohio, formerly a child DP, tells me that the Uzgiris DP family hosted such a school in their Springfield home from 1949 through about 1957. This made sense, since the Uzgirises had three of the seven children attending the school—and the largest study table.

## Literacy in the Second Wave

After writing so much about the illiteracy that blighted the lives of first-wave, turn-of-the-century Lithuanian immigrants, I must underscore the dedication to education that was a hallmark of the second wave of Lithuanian immigrants after WWII. My DP father Vince also shared this value, and spoke about his girls attending college from our earliest years.

Dad grew up on a subsistence farm in the Lithuanian countryside between the wars. But he directly benefited from the mandate of newly independent Lithuania to provide the universal public education that the country's rural poor had been denied under centuries of feudalism and the Russian czars.

Nevertheless, as a country boy whose father had died when he was five, Dad was needed for hours of farm work every day. So he didn't get further than 1930s Lithuania's mandatory three years of reading, writing, and math. His reading subsequently was limited to a few books a year and a weekly or monthly newspaper perused by kerosene lamp after a long day's work.

## 'Brain Drain'

After immigrating, Dad prided himself on learning English well enough to read the *State Journal-Register* every day. In fact, he regarded our daily newspaper—any newspaper—as a kind of gift.

Other Lithuanians who ended up in the U.S. after 1948 were urban professionals with far more education who were able to pursue further education for themselves and their children even in the DP camps of war-ravaged Germany.

(In one of these camps organized by nationality, Dad once shared a room with a Lithuanian Supreme Court justice and an army general, to give you an idea of the "brain drain" from Lithuania at that time. Over and above the devastation of five years of war, the loss of so many craftsmen, tradesmen, and professionals to two Soviet reigns of terror, the Nazi Holocaust, and the 1944 massive flight westward, must have afflicted Lithuania for years.)

Joe with his "princess" granddaughters Sigita and Ina. Circa 1990.

## Education Disrupted by War

One remarkable second-waver, my father's friend **Joseph (Juozas) Koncius**, embodied the émigré quest for education like no one else. Joe was in the midst of his high school education in Silales, Lithuania, when WWII intervened. Somehow, he managed to complete his gymnasium studies as a displaced person in Eichstätt, Germany, in 1946.

Joe then went on to study philosophy and pedagogy at Eichstätt College. And, with other Lithuanian students in Eichstätt, he edited a chronicle called *Ukonas* before immigrating to Springfield in 1949.

In his young 20s, Joe was one of several single men living in apartments owned by the Lapinskis on or near East Washington Street. That's when he somehow met my still-single, 30-year-old émigré father Vince, and the two palled around in Dad's new Chevy sedan.

Already fluent in Lithuanian, French, German, and Russian, Joe doubtless impressed Dad with his dream of being admitted to a U.S. college to become a language teacher. But first he had to master still another language—English.

## Teaching His First Language Class

That didn't stop Joe from putting his German-acquired pedagogy skills to work for the first time by helping the Uzgiris family organize Lithuanian Saturday school. From about 1950 to 1957, Violeta remembers attending school at the Uzgiris home every Saturday morning from 9 a.m. to noon, along with Rimgaile (daughter of August) Paulionis, as well as young Egidijus, Sarunas, and O'Tilija Uzgiris.

Older Uzgiris brother Vytas taught, along with teachers Joe Koncius and Stase Sidlauskas (whose sons Audrys and Jonas also attended the school) and a single man, Mr. Spetyla. Violeta remembers studying the history of Lithuania along with Lithuanian grammar, reading and writing.

In the early 1950s, after serving as best man at my parents' wedding, Joe achieved his dream and left Springfield to be admitted to the University of Illinois at Champaign-Urbana. He graduated in 1956 with a master's degree in education and a certification to teach the French language. Already qualified in German, after further study Joe earned the necessary certification also to teach Russian.

Wedding day: my parents Vincas and Josephine (Kohlrus) Baksys, Sept. 20, 1952.

## Head of Foreign Languages Department

From 1956 to 1987, Joe Koncius made his career teaching French, German, and Russian at Riverside-Brookfield High School in the Chicago area, and heading the school's Foreign Languages Department.

Even after Joe's death in Lemont, Ill., on Sept. 10, 2014, his dedication to education continued with a request for memorial donations to Child's Gate to Learning, a charity supporting education in Lithuania. Joe also lived his lifelong Lithuanian patriotism in service to numerous Chicago-based Lithuanian-Amer-

Joe and wife Giedre, 1990s.

ican organizations, serving as secretary of the Lithuanian Foundation and media/publicity chair for the Lithuanian Opera.

In 1989 he spearheaded a relief fund to rebuild the Catholic church in his hometown of Kaltinenu, Lithuania, after it burned. He also participated in a dental charity called the Lithuanian Fund for Healthy Teeth. And from 1956, he was a member of the Lithuanian Newcomers (*Ateitininkai*) society, where he held the honorary position of *Kestutis* and various posts on the board of directors. Joe captured his own life experiences in a memoir entitled, *A Journey into a Secret Country.*

## A Legacy of Education

Undoubtedly, his most enduring legacy is his impact as a teacher on thousands of language students, beginning, I am honored to say, here in Springfield. Joe, his surviving wife Giedre Teresa (Kizlauskaite); daughters Maria Bereckis and Ruta Salkliene; grandchildren Benjamin, Hanna, Ina and Sigita; great-granddaughter Matija; and nephews Arunas Koncius and Alfonsas Vitkevicius, would surely be proud to know how some of Joe's first child DP students here in Springfield fulfilled their own educational potential.

Vytas Uzgiris graduated from the U of I and became a medical doctor; Sarunas Uzgiris also graduated from the U of I in mechanical engineering, went on to get his Ph.D. and become a university professor; Egidijus Uzgiris graduated from the U of I in engineering with highest academic honors, his name inscribed in the university's famous bronze tablet; and finally, O'Tilija, the youngest and only girl, graduated from

Joe, his wife Giedre, her mother Brone Kizlauskas (Kizlauskiene) and Koncius daughters (l to r) Ruta holding Sigita and Maria holding Ina. 1980s.

the U of I in Russian, which was greatly in demand during the Cold War. She earned her master's degree and started work as a translator for the Chicago Public Library.

*Family photos courtesy of Giedre Koncius.*

*Dedicated to the memory of my father's unforgettable friend, a gifted teacher who prevailed over great adversity to realize his dreams.*

# Chapter 40
# The Zemaitises and 'The Other Dream Team'

Hosting a showing of the rousing documentary film, *The Other Dream Team*, reminded me of an important Springfield connection with our 1980s-90s Lithuanian Olympic basketball heroes. Benedict and Vita Zemaitis of Chatham met Sarunas Marciulionis, Arvydas Sabonis (one of the greatest centers of all time), Rimas Kurtinaitis, and Voldemaras Chomicius after a 1987 exhibition game at the downtown Prairie Capital Convention Center.

The tour of Springfield they gave these young hoopsters resulted in follow-up meetings in other U.S. cities, as well as the Zemaitises' first return to their Soviet-controlled homeland since leaving as children in 1944.

Back in the 1980s era of Gorbachev, *glasnost* and *perestroika*, the four Lithuanian players formed the core of the U.S.S.R. national team (Marciulionis was named "Soviet Athlete of the Year"). However, according to the film, what they really wanted was to have the opportunity to play professionally in the U.S. and Europe, and of course, on a national team for their own country, Lithuania.

When Vita and Ben Zemaitis met the players in 1987, it was one year after Sabonis had been drafted, in absentia, by the Portland Trailblazers. Sabonis did not actually get to play for the Trailblazers for about another decade. His career was also shortened due to injuries he had sustained playing for years in the Soviet system.

Vita with Sarunas
Marciulionis in Lithuania.
Circa 1990.

The players' meeting with the Zemaitises in Springfield also occurred one year before our Lithuanian superstars led the U.S.S.R. team to its famous 1988 Olympic gold medal victory over the United States. In *The Other Dream Team* film, the players explain that their victory was motivated by a Soviet quid pro quo that if they brought the Soviets gold, they would finally be permitted to play abroad.

Fall 1988, Lawrence, Kans., from left: Arvydas Sabonis, Rimas Kurtinaitis, S. Marciulionis, Vita.

Marciulionis, Vita, Chomicius, Kurtinaitis, Ben in front of
Illinois State Capitol, Springfield, 1987.

## Lithuanian Players Tour Springfield

Also in the movie, the Lithuanian players describe being guarded by KGB agents whenever on international tour. Still, they often managed to get away from their U.S. hotels and meet with Lithuanian-Americans who picked them up in parking garages and spirited them away in car trunks, returning them later the same way.

Here in Springfield, Ben explains that he merely called the players' Russian coach at the hotel where the team was staying and asked permission to show the young men around Springfield and its Lincoln sites. Perhaps thanks to the new era of *glasnost*, permission was given.

Through their acquaintance with the Lithuanian players, the Zemaitises also met Donnie Nelson, who spearheaded the exit of Marciulionis from the U.S.S.R. to play for the Golden State Warriors in 1989. In 1992, Nelson also marched into the Barcelona Olympic Stadium with the first Lithuanian Olympic team to participate in the Summer Games in more than 50 years.

From left: Kurtinaitis, Marciulionis, Vita, and Donnie Nelson in Lawrence, Kans., 1988.

Earlier that summer, in a sports-meets-rock-'n-roll

twist, Nelson had helped Marciulionis secure funding and tee-shirt branding rights from the Grateful Dead for the famous tie-dyed Lithuanian Olympic basketball "Dream Team." (Nelson later became general manager of the Dallas Mavericks.) Do you have one of those famous tie-died tee-shirts with the "Slammin Skeleton" trademarked design by Greg Speirs?

"The Other Dream Team" tie-died commemorative tee.

Vita's parents Kazimiera (Daililde) and Joseph Zubkus, M.D. Undated.

## Who Was Vita?

I was so involved, stateside, with the Lithuanian "Singing Revolution" that the athlete-patriots who carried such strong hopes for their country became my heroes, as well. I only wish Vita could have lived to see such stirring history documented in *The Other Dream Team* film. But then again, she lived it.

Vita Zemaitis was born July 12, 1936, in Kaunas, Lithuania, the daughter of Dr. Joseph and Kazimiera (Dailide) Zubkus. She met Benedict R. Zemaitis while the two were both top athletes in the Chicago Park District summer athletics programs. The couple married in 1956, and had a son, Darius, who died in 1985.

Vita attended the University of Illinois and De Paul University in Chicago and subsequently worked for nearly 20 years as an accountant and bookkeeper. Ben worked for 30 years as an auditor, then chief internal auditor for the Illinois Department of Revenue after earning accounting degrees at the U of I and Chicago's Roosevelt University.

Vita in Kaunas, Lithuania, 1936.

His expertise in internal auditing controls and performance auditing allowed him to render key assistance to the auditor general of newly independent Lithuania in 1999 and 2000 at the request of then-Lithuanian President Valdas Adamkus. (Zemaitis and Adamkus actually had known each other as young DPs and students in Chicago.) Ben's service resulted in a special recognition award and medal on Jan. 16, 2004 from Lithuania's auditor general.

Vita and brother Sigitas, circa 1942.

Throughout their married life, Ben and Vita shared not only a profession in numbers, but also continuing involvement in sports and Lithuanian causes and groups. She was a member of the U.S Tennis Association for a number of years and played in local and state tournaments. Vita also served as treasurer of Springfield's Lithuanian-American Club for several terms and taught the Lithuanian language at Lincoln Land Community College.

She was also an avid gardener, a cat lover, and a wonderful cook and hostess. As a frequent contributor to the *State Journal-Register,* she had at least 100 "Letters to Editor" published over the last twenty years of her life.

A letter written after she became terminally ill, and published on Dec. 8, 2009, shortly before her death, recalled Vita's childhood and immigration to the United States:

*...Back when World War II started, it also started for me.*

*There was this beautiful, large fragrant linden tree in full bloom in my mother's country home in Lithuania. Right under the tree, I was the proud owner of a sandbox where barefoot, in shorts, I built my sand castles and talked to the chickens as they passed by.*

*All of a sudden (in 1944), my mother came running, grabbed me in her arms and said there was shooting nearby. There was no time to dress, no time to put on shoes. Our car had been confiscated by the Germans; there was only an old wagon with a couple of old horses. She threw me in the wagon with a couple of blankets and off we went; my father and my brother also were surprised by our hurried departure. The Germans were being pushed back by the Russians and there was fighting everywhere.*

*We crossed the border into German-held territory. I was still barefoot, wrapped in a blanket, and soon became very sick. My fever lasted for days, but my father was a doctor and managed to keep me alive.*

*We rode through different villages and cities. Some cities were in smoldering ruins and I remember the stench of burning bodies. Allied bombing brought hope that this conflict would end and soon the Americans and British would be in control.*

Vita and brother in Lithuanian donkey cart, circa 1940.

*Many refugees ended up in displaced persons camps administered by the UNRA and the Red Cross. We received boxes of food and other essentials (powdered milk, flour and sugar). We also received peanut butter. I thought that was the best thing I ever ate.*

Vita often accompanied her physician father on house calls in his 1938 Buick.

Lithuanians who didn't flee often ended up in Siberia. Vita's uncle and aunt Jonas and Koste Zubkus in Siberia with unidentified man. 1940s.

*Eventually, we were allowed to immigrate to the U.S.A.*

*It took two weeks on violent seas and I was sick again. During the storms, several people died. Finally, we reached the shores of the U.S., but they had to carry me in. I knew that I would be learning a new language again (after learning German). Father did not think that was a problem. He spoke Lithuanian, Russian, German and English, and as a medical doctor, had to know Latin. (Vita's father died of a heart attack from overwork in Chicago hospitals not long after the family settled there. A collection of his medical books has been donated to his hometown library in Lithuania, to honor him.)*

*Here I go again, I thought. At least they have peanut butter and there won't be any fighting.*

*Vita Zemaitis*

*Family photos courtesy of Ben Zemaitis.*

*In memory of my friend Vita (Zubkus) Zemaitis (July 12, 1936—Dec. 14, 2009).*

# Chapter 41
# Behind the Iron Curtain

Young Lithuanian-Americans demonstrate publicly for Lithuanian freedom. *Collection of Mary (Chernis) Urbanckas.*

I recently came across this striking and significant reminder of local Lithuanian Cold War activism against the U.S.S.R's occupation of Lithuania. "Lithuania Behind the Iron Curtain" was a float that took part in a downtown Springfield parade, possibly on Columbus Day or Veterans Day, circa 1955.

In this photo, Violeta (Abramikas) Abad, then in high school, stands at rear in national costume (with amber necklace and an unmarried girl's headdress) to represent the captive nation of Lithuania. It's the same costume Violeta's mother Stephanie wore on her wedding day before the family was forced to flee Lithuania. The costume continues to live on as part of the Abramikas-Abad family heritage.

It was worn by Violeta's granddaughter Catalina, when she was just 12 years old, for a school report on how her Lithuanian great-grandparents and her grandmother immigrated to the United States.

From left: Regina, Stephanie,
Violeta and Walter Abramikas, circa 1980.
*Courtesy of Regina (Abramikas) Buedel.*

## Girls in White

The girls in white with Violeta on the float represent *Vaidolutes*, vestal virgins guarding the eternal flame of Lithuania's national spirit and independence. The flame is represented by a symbolic campfire made of sticks in the center of the float.

The girl in white sitting right in front and wearing glasses is Romualda (Sidlauskas) Capranica. Behind her is Bernadine (Staken) Mikels. Other girls on the float include: Pat (Urbanckas) Mathews, and across from her to Violeta's right, Pat's late sister Donna (Urbanckas) Frost. In front of Donna is Otilija Uzgiris, and some think the girl in front of Otilija is the late Marilyn (Urbanckas) Stark.

Tree branches decorating the back of the float signify Lithuania's many forests. Red, green, and yellow crepe streamers around the sides of the float represented the colors of the Lithuanian flag.

There was probably a sign on the front of the float identifying the sponsoring Lithuanian Catholic youth organization, the *Ateitininkai*, which is still in existence today. World War II refugee Mrs. Stase Sidlauskas was reportedly the leader of the Springfield chapter.

# Chapter 42
# Our Founding Mother:
# The Julia Wisnosky Story

Julia (Stockus) Wisnosky
at 16, 1933.

When I first received this photo of Julia Wisnosky (Vysni-auskas) I thought, "This must have been the most beautiful Lithuanian-American girl in Springfield." Granted, that would have been some contest back in the 1920s and '30s, based on all the photos I've seen.

What makes Julia really interesting, however, is how her leadership in various Lithuanian causes helped her fulfill an innate drive for a role in the wider world outside of home and family—the traditional domains for women of her time. One of the achievements of which you'll soon read is how Julia acted as the catalyst in 1988 for the founding of Springfield's still surviving Lithuanian-American Club.

Job one for a young girl of any era, of course, is beauty. And we are reminded of that by this photo. Yet knowing what I know of Julia's early life, I find myself transported back in time to her two-room childhood home without indoor plumbing across from the state fairgrounds on Peoria Road. And there, behind the gilded image, stands a disappointed young girl who has had to end her education while still in Ridgely Elementary School so she can support her immigrant family by taking in laundry.

How will she fulfill her dream of moving beyond the hard life of her parents? How will she even keep up with the other girls and boys she knows from school? According to daughter Janice (Wisnosky) Kansy, missing high school is such a blow that, even after catching up with night classes, it will always be Julia's closely-guarded secret.

Julia behind the counter
at the Woolworth's soda fountain downtown,
Fifth and Monroe streets, 1930s.

## A Challenging Start

Julia was born in 1917 in Springfield, the daughter of Lithuanian coal miner Anton (Antanas) Stockus and his wife Verna (Backovitch). Her childhood was difficult in many ways: Parents who drank too much. Appendicitis. A lightning strike on her home in which she was cut (but not on the face) by flying glass. And who knows how many other dangers to the safety and self-esteem of a young girl lurked in her rough immigrant neighborhood—along with the warm embrace of grandparents, aunts, uncles and cousins right next door and across the alley.

Maybe all the hardship and roughness around the edges—outhouses and chickens in the backyard, hand-made material goods, public drunkenness and fights—are precisely what explain that veritable glamour shot of a 16-year-old girl with a far from glamorous life.

George Wisnosky and Julia Stockus wedding, 1930s.

## From Childless to Five Children

Introduced by a cousin, at around age 20 Julia married George Wisnosky, Jr., (brother of "Gus," Ann, and Joe, who died of leukemia at 18). Their wedding took place at St. Vincent de Paul (Lithuanian) Catholic Church. Julia's father-in-law, George, Sr., was a founder of St. Vincent's, and Lithuanian was the principal language in his home. Thus, by relating to her in-laws, particularly her mother-in-law, Julia learned her life's best Lithuanian, according to Janice.

During her first 11 years of marriage, Julia did not conceive, and was told she probably could not. So she and George adopted a daughter, three-month-old Georgeann, born in Pana. Just after World War II, they sponsored a "DP" family, the Sidlauskases, housing the couple with two boys in an apartment they owned, probably on Lowell Avenue.

Hearing from the Sidlauskases about two distantly-related orphan children, sister and brother Romualda and Vytautas ("Vito") Sidlauskas, who were still living in a DP camp in Germany, Julia and George also arranged to take in Romualda and Vito. And, as you might guess, in almost no time, Julia miraculously conceived her first biological child, Janice. In fact, Julia was pregnant with Janice the day she and George took little Georgeann to the Springfield train station to pick up the Sidlauskas children.

Soon after that, Julia also had a son, Mark—in the space of a few short years, going straight from a sentence of lifelong childlessness to a houseful of (five) children.

## Working in Town and on the Farm

For most of their married life, Julia and her postal worker husband moved often. Janice remembers the family's longest stint in one place: nine years owning and working a farm off Route 54 in Barkley (Sherman postal address). Before marrying, her dad George had wanted to be a doctor, but had had to quit the University of Illinois after two years to work off family medical bills.

On the farm, Janice reports that George and Julia would alternate working in town while the other worked the farm, caring for the animals: a horse and a goat, but mostly pigs and cows that were sold for slaughter. While it is almost certain that Julia preferred working in an office, she obviously retained the guts and versatility from her youth to do manual labor when necessary. After George was disabled by arthritis, Julia worked full-time as a secretary at Grant Middle School.

Now a part-time teacher of chemistry and biology at a community college north of Seattle, Janice recalls how firmly both her parents clung to their ideal of higher education. For her father George, this was manifested by a desire for his kids to earn degrees from the U of I, where his dream of becoming a doctor had been cut short so many years ago.

## Keeping up Appearances

Janice also recalls: "My mom was quite a seamstress. She made all of our Easter clothes, even my brother's suit. She was very into the home, re-finishing furniture and decorating, and she loved clothes. She really cared how she looked." Here I think back to Julia's parents, whose workaday immigrant reality of hard, manual labor and many daily indignities was redeemed by their Sunday fashions.

And I get two completely opposite pictures of Julia in my mind: one in muddy clothes working the farm in Barkley, and the other, walk-

A talented and industrious seamstress.

ing in high-fashion "Easter parade" with her children. Maybe it was precisely this "down-in-the-mud" part of her life—any life—that made dressing up especially meaningful and necessary, as a kind of antidote. (Ironically, Americans stopped dressing up to be seen at church, in movies, shopping, etc., and became permanently "casual" when their lives became cleaner, wealthier, easier— and they no longer had so much about themselves to prove.)

Easter Parade. Top row from left: foster children Vito and Romualda Sidlauskas with Julia. Bottom from left: Julia's son Mark, daughters Janice and Georgeann, 1950s.

## Happy Times at St. Vincent's

"My folks never had a babysitter," Janice recalls. "They never went out, just once on New Year's Eve, to a big party at someone's house." These parties were hosted in the basements of friends from St. Vincent de Paul's, usually by Ann (Wisnosky) Urbanck-as, George's sister, or his brother "Gus," and their spouses Al and Ann, respective-ly. Peter and Bernice Kurila and John and Adele Arnish also hosted some of the basement parties.

New Year's Eve basement party. Undated.

The St. Vincent's friends and relatives were a tight group who shared the ups and downs of life and many happy social times. "The church used to have an annual spring bazaar that they all worked at. There was also a tradition that on Easter Sunday, there would be a progressive dinner starting with coffee and rolls at Fr. Yunker's house after Mass. Then everybody would go from house to house to eat different foods and visit for half the day."

## Lithuanian Club Founder

Traditional Lithuanian *Kucios* dinner at the Wisnosky home, featuring evergreen branches under the tablecloth and Christmas wafers. Original glossy by the *State Journal-Register.*

Two of Julia's proudest achievements outside the home are both mentioned in her obituary, dated August 11, 2004. The first was her rise to director of the audio/visual department at Scottsdale Community College in Arizona, where she and George initially retired. Her second achievement came after retiring from that college job in 1980 and moving back to Springfield.

Once here, it appears Julia embraced a new challenge: helping to found a new Lithuanian-American club as a social and cultural outlet for those who had been members of the then-defunct St. Vincent de Paul Church.

When St. Vincent's was closed and demolished by the diocese over parishioners' protests, those who still wanted to continue as practicing Catholics had had no choice but to move on to other parishes. But they still kept their ethnic social ties from their St. Vincent's days. That's how enough of a core ethnic group remained, 16 years after the church's demise, to launch the new club.

(The advent of the club also coincided with the beginning of a dramatic "Singing Revolution" in Lithuania that spurred an upsurge in Lithuanian ethnic identity and activism all over the world. And soon enough, Springfield's new club was actively supporting that non-violent movement for Lithuania's independence from the Soviet Union.)

## Final Service to the Cause

According to the late Ann (Pazemetsky) Traeger, it was Julia who phoned Tom Mack, local McDonald's franchisee, with the idea for a new club. Shortly thereafer, in the summer of 1988, Julia, Tom, Julia's daughter Georgeann, Joe Turasky of Y-T Packing, Peter Urbanckas, Ann Traeger, George and Helen Rackauskas, and Fritzi Cartwright met in Tom's Sixth Street office, and the club was founded. The original slate of officers drew from the ranks of these founders, including President Tom Mack and Vice President Julia Wisnosky.

The club's first recorded meeting was Sept. 20, 1988, also in Tom Mack's office. By that time, 425 letters had been sent out to local Lithuanian-Americans, and 165 had already responded and become dues-paying (charter) members.

The new club's first social event was a fall dinner-dance scheduled for St. John Vianney Church Hall in Sherman Saturday, Oct. 22, 1988. Forty tables were set up with the Lithuanian tri-color, and the proposed program included an open bar, an opening prayer by the Rev. Charles E. Olshevsky, and an address by honorary member and then-U.S. Rep. Dick Durbin. Joe and Monty Yanor helped organize the event.

Within its first year, the club drew 500 dues-paying members. And its tradition of a fall dinner-dance was so successful that the dance with live music continued until around 2005.

"I remember buying Mom a corsage to wear to that first Lithuanian-American Club dinner-dance," says Janice, who did not share her mom's last, big act. As a molecular biologist, for decades Janice held posts at various universities and research labs out of state. But she remembers how important the club was to her mom and other family members.

Over the years as her health permitted, Julia faithfully served the club in many roles, along with her daughter Georgeann and foster daughter Romualda (Sidlauskas) Capranica.

*Photos courtesy of Janice (Wisnosky) Kansy.*

# Chapter 43
# Club Lobbies for Lithuanian Independence

The Baltic "Singing Revolutions" (1987-91) had a galvanizing effect on local Lithuanian-Americans. After 439 joined in 1988 to form Springfield's new Lithuanian-American Club, the group's officers and members often lobbied in the court of public opinion for Lithuania's independence.

They were especially active after Lithuania declared its restoration of sovereignty on March 11, 1990, which resulted in a punishing economic blockage by the Soviet Union that went on for many months. According to a *State Journal-Register* article dated April 3, 1990, club president Tom Mack, on behalf of 550 members, sent a letter to President George H.W. Bush stating the club's position:

*"Gorbachev's contention that Lithuania is a Republic of the U.S.S.R., and therefore must follow legal procedures in order to declare its independence, cannot be based on the illegal and forced annexation of 1940.*

*"Lithuania did not vote nor choose to join the U.S.S.R, and therefore is under no legal or political obligation to remain under the control of the U.S.S.R," the Club's letter declared.*

## Demonstrating with Rep. Dick Durbin

The *SJ-R* article continued: "The local Lithuanian-American Club is urging all people of Lithuanian descent and their friends to call or write to President George Bush to strongly reaffirm the United States' 1922 formal recognition of Lithuania as a free and independent nation. They're encouraging people to write or phone their senators and congressmen to voice support for U.S. Rep. Dick Durbin's House Concurrent Resolution 289."

One month later in May 1990, hundreds, including Lithuanian-American Durbin (soon to be Senator Durbin), my father and sisters participated in a demonstration organized by the club on the steps of the Cathedral downtown.

Club leaders Julia Wisnosky, Tom Mack and Regina (Abramikas) Buedel were photographed for the newspaper story. Other officers named in the article were: Joe Turasky, vice-president; Mary Chepulis, secretary; and Monty Yanor, treasurer, along with board members Frances Candioto, Fritzi Cartwright, Frank Tureskis, Vera Stasukinas, Rita Kupris, and Danute (Kuprenas) Durbin.

# Chapter 44
## 'Singing Revolution'

After 47 years of Soviet occupation, Lithuanians seized the opening created by *glasnost* and *perestroika* under Soviet President Mikhail Gorbachev in 1987 to agitate for the restoration of their personal and national rights. The first non-Soviet controlled cultural and political groups were formed, launching the so-called "Singing Revolution" that took its name from peaceful, mass demonstrations that involved the singing of Lithuanian folk songs.

Other Lithuanian cultural and religious values were also strongly asserted against Soviet authority, resulting in the restoration of the Lithuanian national flag and the return of the National Cathedral in Vilnius, which had been made into a museum.

The Baltic Way at Šeškinės Hill. *Photo by Gediminas Krunglevičius. Wikimedia Commons.*

One of the most famous and seminal mass actions of national resistance occurred when an estimated two million Lithuanians, Latvians and Estonians came out of their homes to form a human chain from Vilnius to Tallinn in "The Baltic Way" event (*pictured above*) on Aug. 23, 1989. This unprecedented, peaceful protest commemorated the 50th anniversary of the 1939 secret signing of the Molotov-Ribbentrop Pact by which Nazi Germany and the U.S.S.R. divided Poland and the Baltics between themselves at the opening of World War II.

For four exciting years (1987 to 1991), the eyes of the world and the news media were on Lithuania and its equally tiny Baltic neighbors who were often depicted as threats to Gorbachev and his efforts to reform the Soviet Union in order to save it. Baltic-Americans saw these revolutions differently, as inspired David vs. Goliath struggles for freedom by our long-oppressed relatives and countrymen overseas.

Vytautas Landsbergis, the first head of state of Lithuania after its declaration of independence from the Soviet Union on March 11, 1990, four months after the fall of the Berlin Wall. *Photo by Andreas Strasbourg, 2009.*

## Families Reunited After 45 Years

A joyful upsurge of national feeling occurred in Springfield and across the U.S., as Lithuanian-Americans were able to reclaim their ethnic identity with pride. Suddenly, a heritage that many had been taught to cherish within the private realms of church and family was again publicly relevant and inspiring to millions around the world who valued freedom and human rights.

This re-identification with our parents' and grandparents' homeland was re-inforced by the new freedom to communicate and visit with long-lost Lithuanian relatives. After a painful separation that had lasted for 45 years, one week in July 1989 I helped my immigrant father reunite with a sister he had not seen since 1944.

## Bringing Down the 'Evil Empire'

Yet, even for those without a direct family connection, here was an opportunity to stand on the right side of history, by the side of a small nation desperately struggling to regain its independence by peacefully leveraging the power of truth—and world opinion—against the Soviet superpower.

After the U.S.S.R recognized Lithuanian sovereignty in August 1991, many historians considered the return of Lithuania to the map one of the most improbable political victories of the twentieth century. Along with the Solidarity movement in Poland and the Velvet Revolution in Czechoslovakia, the Baltic countries' peaceful, committed struggle for independence was a key factor in the fall of the Soviet Empire and the liberation of the entire Soviet Bloc.

# Chapter 45
# Witness to History:
# Remembering January 1991

*By Irena Ivoskute Sorrells*

Flag vs. tank, Jan. 13, 1991.  http://www.kam.lt/images.
*Wikimedia Commons.*

When I was asked to write about the events of Jan. 13, 1991, I enthusiastically agreed. Today, as I try to put down thoughts on the blank screen of my computer, I understand that an easily given promise is not so easily fulfilled. Just thinking about those tragic events in Lithuania fills me with so much emotion, even after 24 years.

The words I reach for to express myself seem entirely inadequate, even artificial in the face of what happened. I remember not only my own feelings, but also the way they conflicted with the feelings of my family (especially my mom): uncertainty with faith; hesitation with determination.

My son Julius was just a year and a half old, and my mom, who was helping my brother, my sister and I raise our young children, adamantly opposed me leaving home that cold night with Soviet forces threatening the city, especially the U.S.S.R.'s elite Alpha "anti-terrorist" unit. I couldn't allow myself to tell her where I was planning to go—back to my old apartment across from the Radio and TV Committee building on Konarskio Street, one of the likeliest targets of Soviet military action. (I wonder how many other young adults and even teenagers did not tell their parents and grandparents the truth about where they were going that night.)

## Undermining Independence with Unrest

The Lithuanian government had resigned on January 8, and on January 11, the Soviet Army had invaded and taken control of the Vilnius Publishing House. People were saying that the Parliament (then called the Supreme Council) building would be next—that it was only a matter of days or maybe even hours. Lithuania's independence, declared less than a year earlier on March 11, 1990, had endured a long economic blockade by the U.S.S.R. against critical food and energy supplies. But that independence now truly hung by a thread.

A lot of people were upset that the Lithuanian government had increased food prices 300 percent a couple of months earlier due to the Soviet blockade. Inflation was raging out of control and common people were under tremendous pressure. That made it a good time for our enemies to believe that the population would not resist the now-imminent Soviet military takeover aimed at putting an end to Lithuanian independence.

More precisely, it seemed a good time for the pro-Soviet faction of the Lithuanian Communist Party, supported by Moscow, to try to "prove" to Mikhail Gorbachev, the Soviet President, that the ideal moment had arrived to take back control of the country from the Lithuanian independence movement. How wrong they were!

## People Power vs. Tanks

Still, my mother was not wrong to fear for my life as she pressed me not to leave her home that night. If she had known where I planned to go, it would have been even worse. As a teenager, at the very end of World War II, she had been severely injured in a grenade explosion that left her in a coma for three days. So she knew the worst can happen. But despite her fears, I was resolved to go to my old street and stand with the people there trying to defend the Radio and TV Committee building the only way they could—by forming a human barricade.

It was the same in front of all our major government and media buildings, including the Parliament and the most famous of all modern Vilnius landmarks, the TV Tower: unarmed people with nothing but their patriotism and their unity and their hope, standing together to somehow defend their country against Soviet soldiers and tanks. Nobody knew exactly how they could prevail against tanks and guns. Perhaps that was the essence of their courage—that the answer to the question was not as important as the need and the will to prevail.

## An Indescribable Spirit

On my way to Konarskio Street, I passed a sound truck with a pre-recorded message blaring that the National Committee for Salvation, consisting of enemies of Lithuania's independence, was now in control of the government. But that propaganda did not work—it didn't stop people from massing around key buildings to defend them. We were praying, singing, talking, or simply standing and waiting – peacefully. I think one way we kept up our courage was by believing that Soviet soldiers would not really start shooting unarmed civilians, especially in the presence of so much foreign media.

Many of us living near the Committee building ran back and forth to our apartments with food, hot water and tea or coffee to help the rest of the people in the street keep warm. I did this myself more than a dozen times that night. The threat of violence against us was so close, but as we all stood together, supporting and helping each other, there was no fear. The spirit of that night and those people, my people, is unforgettable and almost indescribable, even after all of these years.

Around midnight, I was drawn away from the scene because I could not reach my mom by phone and I was afraid that something might have happened to her and my young son

Funeral of the 14 patriots, National Cathedral, Vilnius, January 1991. http://www.kam.lt/images. *Wikimedia Commons.*

in another part of the city. And that is how I missed the attack on the Radio and TV Committee building that happened around 2 a.m. January 13th.

## Too Many Media, Too Many Willing to Die

I was so angry at myself for leaving behind the brave people standing guard. None of us slept that night as the shocking news poured in about the tanks running right over people at another location–the Vilnius TV Tower, along

Crosses of memory at the Vilnius TV tower.
*Photo by Marcin Białek, 2008. Wikimedia Commons.*

with the last images from the Committee building of a a Soviet soldier running toward the camera before the screen went black.

In the aftermath of all the attacks the night of January 12-13, 14 lay dead and about 700 injured, 140 of them, critically—many shot multiple times or crushed under tank treads. *(Three young women were run over by a tank while kneeling to pray, two of them injured critically, one of them killed.)*

At my old apartment building, people had to replace all the street-facing windows shattered by tanks firing blank rounds that deafened many of the Committee building protectors permanently.

But this violence against the unarmed failed. Later that morning of January 13, 50,000 people gathered around Parliament to defend their government with their lives. People built barricades and Soviet military trucks and tanks moved into the area, but the attack never happened. Why not? Too many media from around the world covering the events, and too many people ready to die.

*Dedicated to all those who bravely stood and raised their voices to save their country; especially to those who gave their lives or their health. May you live forever in a grateful nation's memory.*

# Chapter 46
# Three-Day Lithuanian Wedding:
# Eva Kasawich and Victor Alane

St. Vincent de Paul Church—Springfield, IL—September 25, 1927

What made traditional Lithuanian wedding parties so great? I would say the beer, food, music, dancing—and above all—the time family and friends devoted to the event. Whether everybody (not just the miners) left after night #1, went home and rested through the day, only to reconvene for nights #2 and #3, I'm not sure. I hope I learn the answer some day.

But we do have some lively and telling facts about the September 1927 wedding of Eva Kasawich and Victor Alane from the couple's descendants Elaine Alane, her husband Dick, and Elaine's in-laws Vic and Clarice Alane.

The date was Sept. 25-27, 1927. The location was the East Reynolds Street home of just-deceased Lithuanian-born coal miner Paul Kasawich (1872-1926) and his Lithuanian-born widow Anna Leschinsky, mother of bride **Eva Kasawich.** The groom was **Victor Alane** (Lith. Alaunis), son of Petronele Spendzninas and Lithuanian-born Joseph Alane (1876-1907), who had died in the Pennsylvania coal mines at age 31.

L to r: back row: Anna and mother Anna Kasawich, front row: Paul and Eva Kasawich. Circa 1916.

## How They Afforded It

Eva Kasawich became a bride on a Sunday, when she was just 19 years old. Her coal-miner father had died the previous year. So how did her widowed immigrant mother put on a "Roaring '20s" party that went on for three days?

It wasn't *Great Gatsby* extravagance by a long shot. But it was *Gatsby* fashion. Eva's lovely Charleston wedding gown was sewn by a local woman named Tillie, according to her daughter-in-law Elaine. As far as the food, it probably helped that the mother of the bride operated a corner grocery at 1900 E. Reynolds, right next to the family home.

Eva in her Charleston wedding gown. The bridesmaids' dresses were pink. Probably so, too, were the bride's roses.

The company that supplied bread to the Kasawich grocery store donated all of the bread for the reception. And all the rest of the food, except for the wedding cake, was prepared at the bride's home by her mother and older sister (both named Anna) and teams of neighborhood women. According to Elaine, it took them two days in the backyard just to butcher and clean all the chickens.

## The Wrong Cake

A huge banquet table set up in the basement was loaded with chicken, kielbasa, bread and traditional Lithuanian wedding fare, including (probably *kugelis*) and many homemade sweets. When the wedding cake was delivered, the baker had made a mistake and sent a very small cake. Eva cried and cried. A while later, a new, beautiful and very large cake arrived as a replacement.

The wedding party. Notice Kasawich home in left background and Model Ts in right background.

When the bridegroom arrived at the reception with his bride, some of the guests blocked the door and wouldn't let them in until the groom paid them. (*I don't have any more details about this custom.*)

In the living room, there were three musicians: a concertina player, a fiddler (and Eva later couldn't recall what the third instrument was). The carpet was rolled back and there was dancing. A lot of polka music was played. The bridegroom, Victor Alane, loved to polka and danced any chance he got, even after he was old and his knees were arthritic.

Homemade beer was served (we can assume, barrels of it, over three days). It was made in the attic of Eva's home by her mother Anna. Though Prohibition was in full swing, some whiskey called Old Mule also was served.

Adam Pazemetsky with clarinet, Mr. Karalitis with fiddle, and Mr. Petrovitch seated, with concertina, circa 1920. *Courtesy of Ann (Pazemetsky) Traeger.*

The wedding party strikes a pose.

## Cracking Piles of Plates

Eva and Victor's three sons were not yet born, so our only eye-witness description of their three-day wedding comes from Lithuanian-American coal miner Larry Mantowich (1911-1994). He remembered the bride and groom sitting at a table piled with cash gifts, concertinas playing, and throngs of friends and neighbors dancing and eating.

Mantowich reported that single "boarder" miners without their own families or any idea of a proper wedding gift made ostentatious shows of their generosity by tossing $10 and $20 bills on the gift table. (Ten dollars was a good two days' pay for loading 10 tons of coal.)

He also reported that after the first night of the party, the miners went to work in the morning, came home, got cleaned up and returned to the party for day two, and repeated this process for day three.

Eva Kasawich, Charleston-style wedding gown, 1927.

Also according to Mantowich, dozens of plates were bought and stacked high for an interesting tradition. If the bride or groom managed to crack a plate with a silver dollar, that dollar was theirs to keep. Apparently, they could keep on trying different plates until they succeeded. The couple must have worked hard at it, because Elaine says that when bridegroom Victor left the third day of the reception, the huge bag of silver dollars he carried off to the bank was so heavy he could barely lift it.

Clarice and Vic Alane wedding, 1950.

## The Next Generation

After his 1927 wedding, Victor delivered ice and worked as an electrician for Allis-Chalmers. He also was very handy and helped many of his Lithuanian neighbors with little fix-up jobs around their homes. Victor and Eva's son Vic went to Saint Peter & Paul grade school and Cathedral Boys High School (later Griffin High School). He worked in the Pillsbury Mills traffic department for four years, then served in the Illinois National Guard for six years, the last two in Europe.

DAVE DURAKO (accordion), VIC ALANE (trumpet, vibra-harp), and MEREDITH SAXER (bass), JOE RICHIUSA (drums).

Vic Alane & the Keynotes. Vic on right edge.

In 1954, Vic was hired by the transportation department of Allis-Chalmers. The company eventually transferred him to West Allis, Wis., then Milwaukee. Before moving to Wisconsin, Vic led the local Springfield band, Vic Alane & the Keynotes, playing trumpet and vibra-harp. He and his quartet entertained at many of Springfield's premier venues, including the Island Bay Yacht Club and the Illini Country Club.

After Vic was let go by Allis-Chalmers in 1970, a business he had conceived in his parents' basement helped provide a new living. He and his brother Dick ended up working in the new company, Jet Permit, Ltd., helping long-haul truckers obtain state highway permits. Today Vic also owns campground Nature's Villa in Helenville, Wis.

Corner grocery store / tavern of Anna (Leschinsky) Kasawich, circa 1990.

At Jet Permit for 40 years, Dick Alane took permits and later was comptroller. A talented athlete like his father, Dick played football, baseball and basketball at Griffin High School (mentioned in Chapter 17) and served in the U.S. Navy.

## Scene of the Wedding: 65 Years Later

The above photo is reportedly from the early 1990s. According to Elaine Alane, the larger home two doors down on the left of the corner tavern/store building is where the 1927 wedding reception took place. The smaller building just to the left of the store was the Kasawich family's original home and was used in later years by other relatives working to buy a house of their own.

The little house barely visible in the background, to the right of the store, also belonged to the Kasawiches; Eva's older sister, Anna, lived there after her husband died young. While Eva was having and raising her sons with Victor, Eva's mother Anna and older sister Anna continued to run the store for many years.

*Photos courtesy of Elaine Alane and Ann (Pazemetsky) Traeger.*

*Post-script: The Mantowich oral history, in three volumes constituting almost 400 pages, was recorded by Sangamon State University back in the 1970s. Read his Lithuanian wedding and wake memories on pages 124-129. In other parts of the transcript, you can read about the making of home sausage and blood soup, moon-shining, politics, and other topics.*

# Chapter 47
# Weddings

For most of the twentieth century, marriage was honored as a lifelong commitment, the wellspring of the family, and the bedrock of communities. As a result, wedding receptions were occasions of great social import and notable financial extravagance.

When I look at the oldest photos here, I think, what a singular outpouring of love, sweat, and joy a daughter's wedding must have been to a poor mining family. However, the traditional three days of feasting and celebration probably followed these ceremonies only up through the 1920s, giving way to shorter, but no less spirited receptions in the face of the Great Depression. By the 1930s and '40s, immigrant wedding customs also were yielding to American norms.

Personally, I think of parents creating these truly grand occasions to assert the spiritual vibrancy of their families and the larger meaning of their lives. Open to the extended family and much of the neighborhood, the traditional Lithuanian wedding reception was the greatest, ever, (socially sanctioned) opportunity to throw off worry and penury, kick up one's heels and indulge.

See if you can look beyond the solemnity of these formal photos to enjoy their timeless fashion statements—and picture the party of all parties that was just about to begin.

Stanley Stankavich and Frances Missavich wedding, 1911. *Courtesy of Fritzi (Stankavich) Cartwright.*

Likely the Peter Bernotas and Anna Klimaitis
wedding, 1916. *Courtesy of Susan (Bernotas) Potter.*

John Treinis and Tillie (Theophilia) Rinkavich wedding couple on the right; John's
cousin "Big John" Treinis of Chicago and his wife on the left, 1912.
*Courtesy of Eleanora (Treinis) Yuskavich.*

Wedding of the parents of Julia (Stockus) Wisnosky. Undated. *Courtesy of Janice Kansy.*

Michael Makarauskas and Adella Klimaitis wedding, 1933. Brother John Makarauskas standing directly behind the seated groom with his wife or wife-to-be, Mary Gidus, on his right. Michael died in a car-train accident in 1936. *Courtesy of Dorothy Makarauskas.*

George Wisnosky and Julia Stockus wedding, 1937. *Collection of Al Urbanckas, D.D.S.*

Ann Wisnosky becoming Ann Urbanckas, 1934. *Courtesy of Al Urbanckas, D.D.S.*

Alfred Urbanckas and Ann Wisnosky wedding, 1934. "Gus" Wisnosky and Ann Tisckos on either side of the bride and groom. Others in photo: Mary Chernis, Jeanne Klickna, Helen Marchulones, Peter Urbanckas, Adolph Tisckos and George Wisnosky. *Courtesy of Al Urbanckas, D.D.S.*

Peter Urbanckas and Mary Chernis wedding, 1939. *Collection of Al Urbanckas, D.D.S.*

Peter and Mary (Chernis) Urbanckas exit St. Vincent de Paul Church, 1939. *Collection of Al Urbanckas, D.D.S.*

Joseph Yanor and Monica ("Monty") Susinskas wedding, 1946. With the couple: Bill and Josephine (Yanor) Stankavich and flower girl Georgeann Carver. Monty was the first woman in Illinois to hold a hunter safety instructor license and also worked as a designer for Chrysler Corp. in Detroit. *Courtesy of Georgeann (Carver) Madison.*

Four Baksys siblings, circa 1952: From left, Vincas with his wife Josephine, (bride) Joana with her new husband Antanas Pumputis, Bronius (Bruno) with friend and Jonas with wife Grazina.

Mick Madison and Georgeann Carver wedding, 1962.
*Courtesy of Georgeann (Carver) Madison.*

# Chapter 48
# Mother's Day Pilgrimage

Memorial mass at Franciscan convent Adoration Chapel, Riverton, 2014.

Six Minnesota siblings with deep roots in Springfield traveled here to bury their mother's ashes at the grave of her own parents, thus honoring two generations of their Lithuanian-American family. John (Steve), Jim, Dave and Terri White, and their sisters Mary Doberstein and Kathy DeGrote, all traveled to Springfield to attend a memorial mass for their mom Christina Virginia (Cooper) White May 9, 2014 at the St. Clare of Assisi Adoration Chapel at the St. Francis Convent near Riverton.

Ginny (Cooper) White died in 2012 at age 92 in Anoka, Minn., where she had lived with her dentist husband for many years. Known to her Minnesota friends as "Chris," she was born in 1919 in Springfield to Anthony and Catherine (Gillette) Cooper and had grown up here. Ginny's own mother Catherine had been born in Cantrall in 1898 to Lithuanian immigrants Joseph Gilletties and Anna Marie (Smylus) Stuches.

Baby Christina Virginia ("Ginny") with her mother Catherine (Gillette) Cooper, circa 1920.

## Disowned by Wealthy Family

As the story goes, Anna (Ona) Stuches was disinherited by her wealthy family near Kaunas when she fell in love with her future husband, Joseph Gilletties, the family's carriage driver. Thus, she became one of the few Lithuanian women forced into immigration and the harsh coal-mining life not by the poverty of her birth, but by the poverty of the man she loved.

Anna and Joseph were married in Liverpool, England, in 1892, and their first child was born that same year. They immigrated to the U.S. in 1893, first to Kansas City, then the Springfield area. The couple's union produced an amazing eight daughters and four sons who lived to adulthood, in addition to three boys who died in infancy.

According to Anna's great-granddaughters Terri, Kathy and Mary, Anna preserved a little of her high birth and refinement even as a struggling immigrant by making sure her 12 surviving children had impeccable table manners and all played a musical

"Ginny" Cooper as flower girl at Kasawich-Alane wedding, 1927.

instrument. In fact, the Stuches-Gillette children, including Catherine Cooper, comprised something of a family band who filled their own home with music on holidays and other special occasions.

Catherine (Gillette) Cooper

Catherine Gillette married Anthony Cooper (Lith. Antanas Pikcilingis), born in Sapiskis, Lithuania, in 1886, who had immigrated to the U.S. in 1905. Anthony worked as a liquor distributor, and Catherine as a skilled floral designer (an echo of her mother's patrician past?) for Winch and Heimbracher Floral Designs of Springfield, often traveling to Chicago for special projects.

## Backbone of St. Vincent de Paul's

Antanas (Anthony) Cooper, circa 1927.

Among her local honors were decorating former President Herbert Hoover's train when it stopped in Springfield, and once pinning an orchid on visiting First Lady Eleanor Roosevelt. According to an undated newspaper clipping, while with the S.Y. Bloom Flower Shop in Chicago, Catherine Cooper invented the bridal wrist bouquet and decorated the Ambassador East Hotel room of President Dwight D. Eisenhower.

As you have read in my 'Knights' of Music, Baseball, Politics chapter, Catherine and Anthony Cooper were the backbone of St. Vincent de Paul (Lithuanian) Catholic Church and the local Knights of Lithuania for decades. This included K of L leadership and recruiting roles for Anthony, as well as singing roles for both spouses in the group's choir and operettas.

The Coopers had one daughter, Christina Virginia ("Ginny"), who grew up on East Phillips Street and reportedly always was dressed to the nines due to her status as a cherished only child—and the extra income from her mother's floral employment. (While growing up in Minnesota, the Cooper-White children remember frequently being brought back to Springfield by their mother Ginny to visit her parents on East Phillips.)

"Ginny" Cooper and John White wedding, 1946.

## A Dutiful Daughter

Ginny attended St. Peter & Paul Grade School, class of '33, and was the first to receive a diploma in the first graduating class at Lanphier High School in 1937. She received a "full ride" college scholarship to St. Mary's College (sister school to Notre Dame), but felt obliged to be a dutiful daughter and stay in Springfield when her mother, who was working in Chicago at the time, asked Ginny to stay home and take care of her father.

Later (1945), Ginny graduated from St. John's College of Nursing in Springfield. She married John F. White, D.D.S., in 1946 and raised seven children in Pipestone, St. Peter and Anoka, Minn. Since a four-year college degree remained very important to her all her life, after raising her children and ensuring their education, in 1981 Ginny finally realized her dream and earned a B.S. from the College of St. Francis.

She was past president of the Minnesota Southern District Women's Dental Auxiliary, and her husband and son William preceded her in death.

I was touched by the Cooper-White children's loving pilgrimage back to Springfield to bury their mother's ashes—and also by their mother's fervent wish to be returned to her native Springfield to be close to her parents. Ginny's father Anthony was an immigrant, and I have found in my own life that a bond to an immigrant father or mother can be one of the most unbreakable in life.

"Ginny" Cooper White, circa 1950.

As for the Cooper-White children, what a special way to celebrate Mother's Day, honoring their mother and their shared memories of her. How pleased she would have been to see her children all together, as a family, in her own hometown.

Cooper-White kids and their spouses. From left: Jim, Mary, Krista, John (Steve), Roberta, Kathy, Terri, Michael, and David at Calvary Cemetery, May 9, 2014.

The Cooper-White children, circa 1970.

*Photos courtesy of Terri White.*

*Post-script: The Anthony and Catherine Cooper grave in Calvary Cemetery, where their daughter Ginny's ashes were buried, is within 25 yards of stones bearing many other local Lithuanian family names: Bernotas, Kazokaitis, Yakst, Pazemetsky, Grigas, Gedman, Butkus, Bumpus, Usas, Jurkonis, Stanka-vich, and Klutnick.*

# Chapter 49
# The Blended Immigrant Family

Lithuanian coal-mining families in Springfield at the turn of the 20th Century had many hardships—and virtues—in common. Hard work, faith and determination were necessary just to survive. As for the hardships...In addition to the loss of infants and children that many parents suffered, children often endured the loss of a parent. Fathers died or were disabled in the mines. And more often than today, overworked young mothers died, too.

After being widowed, spouses often re-married, creating a good number of blended families long before divorce was respectable or common. In fact, over the course of my research, I was surprised to see how many immigrants, men and women, were married two and three times, and the number of children in the same family with different surnames—including step-step children brought along by a new wife from her previous husband's marriage to a previous wife.

Eleanora Treinis with her mom, Theophilia.

Eleanora Treinis, 1920s.

## Losing a Mother at Six

One of the oldest members of our Lithuanian-American community, Eleanora (Treinis) Yuskavich, lost her mother, Tillie (Theophilia Rinkienve or Rinkavich), when Eleanora was just six to endocarditis (infection of a heart valve). Born in Lithuania, Tillie had arrived in Springfield around 1911 and was working as a laundress and boarding at the downtown St. Nicholas Hotel when she met John Treinis, a coal miner, also born in Lithuania, who came to the U.S. in 1908.

After the couple married in 1912, Tillie continued working as a maid at the Leland Hotel, probably among other jobs. Not until 10 years after Tillie's death did her widower John Treinis get re-married to Lithuanian immigrant Nancy Kensman, daughter of Antanas and Anna (Begaila) Kensman (Cachmiscus). As for Nancy, she previously had been married to a man named Nevada (Nevardoskus or Nevidauski), giving Eleanora a stepbrother (John). What's more, after Mr. Nevada, Nancy had been married to Ignatius Zakar, giving Eleanor a step-sister (Cecelia) and another step-brother (Joseph) who had been born to Mr. Zakar by a previous wife.

John Treinis, circa 1920.

## Taking a Third Husband

This was an impressive amount of family "blending," perhaps even for the time. However, unlike today when re-marriages seem to occur quickly, while children are still young, resulting in step-siblings living together, it's clear that widower John Treinis postponed re-marriage until Eleanora was mostly grown. Basic economics, the number of children who needed to be parented, and the support of other relatives probably determined how soon a widower needed to re-marry. For widows, a quick re-marriage was often imperative to restore a male bread-winner to the household.

Eleanora remembers her

Eleanora Treinis, 14, in the wedding party where she met her future husband, circa 1932.

stepmom Nancy from her later teens, when she and her father lived in rooms above a tavern around 16th and Carpenter that Nancy owned (probably inherited from deceased spouse Nevada or Zakar). Years later, Eleanora made step-brother John Nevada, a World War II veteran, godfather to one of her daughters.

John P. Yuskavich, Jr., with his mother Stella (Kuizin) and father John P., circa 1920.

240

What we know about Eleanora's father John Treinis is that he registered for the draft for World War I. He worked at the local Tuxhorn Mine and owned several of his own grocery stores, one at 1601 E. Converse and another at North Grand Avenue and Milton.

Daughter Eleanora always helped her dad in his stores, and she lived with him in quarters behind the storefront. One night after closing, during the heart of the Depression when Eleanora was just 13, she and her dad were robbed at gunpoint. Fortunately, neither was hurt.

Eleanora Treinis and John P. Yuskavich, Jr., wedding, 1939.

Eleanora met her future husband, John Phillip Yuskavich, Jr., at a wedding when she was just 14. They married in 1939 at St. Vincent de Paul (Lithuanian) Catholic Church. John was the son of Lithuanian immigrants John P., Sr., and Stella (Kuizin) Yuskavich. Not long after John, Jr., and Eleanora married, he and his brother Anthony served in World War II.

Little John and Tony Yuskavich, 1920s.

# Working Around the Clock

Little Tony and George Yuskavich with puppy, flowers, 1920s.

Over the years, John and Eleanora worked hard to support their own family of two girls. Eleanora was an elevator operator at the Hotel Abraham Lincoln, first at the back of the hotel, then, by promotion, in the main front elevator. She was also a packer at Pillsbury Mills, and later, a full-time homemaker for John and daughters Pat (Towner) and Mary Ann (Wycoff).

John's work history was particularly enterprising. After leaving school to mine coal, he worked at the Springfield International Shoe Factory, then in a steel mill in Indiana and in the Depression-era Civilian Conservation Corps, and later as a bus driver for the Springfield Mass Transit District. Finally, like several other Lithuanian-Americans, he got on at the U.S. Post Office, where he started as a mechanic in the Springfield garage, later rising to supervisor of the garage and drivers.

Here's the really enterprising part: While working for the Post Office during the day, John managed two gas stations at night, and also owned a truck for which he hired drivers to pick up the *Illinois State Journal* and *Register* newspapers each day at 2 a.m. and 2 p.m. (respectively) and drop off bundles to scores of newspaper boys for home delivery.

George Yuskavich portrait, 18 years old, circa 1940.

In addition to her two daughters, Eleanora (Treinis) Yuskavich has grandsons Jason and Matthew Towner and granddaughter Robin Watts, as well as great-grandchildren Jordan and Jade Watts and Jonathan Towner. Robin Watts' husband Jim recently started his own business, Watts Electric.

(John and Tony Yuskavich's youngest brother George and his wife Catherine had daughters Barb Devine and Kathy Plough.)

*Photos courtesy of Pat (Yuskavich) Towner and Barb (Yuskavich) Devine.*

# Chapter 50
# Comedy Dance Man Joey Mack

I write a lot about coal miners on this blog, but perhaps the most famous Lithuanian-American in Springfield in the 1940s was in show business: Joey Yanaitis (Lith. Janaitis or Jonaitis) Mack. Famous in Boston, Rockford, Ill., Cleveland, Augusta, Ga., and dozens of places in between, from the late 1930s through the 1940s, Joey was the male half of the traveling married vaudeville dance team of Betty Jo (Yanda Connors) and Joey Mack (billed as Jo and Joey Mack).

Joey and his wife Betty Jo began to make their significant contribution to live entertainment in Springfield back when members of civic groups routinely staffed their own musical programs (including minstrel shows) by dancing and acting out comedy sketches in costume and playing live music based on themes from vaudeville and the silver screen. In addition to helping groups like the Rotary, Elks, etc., with choreography, staging and performers,

COMEDY TEAM VISITS HERE

MR. AND MRS. JOEY MACK.

Mr. and Mrs. Joey Mack of the professional comedy team, Jo and Joey Mack, have returned east after spending a few days with Mrs. Mack's parents, Mr. and Mrs. William Connors, 2513 South Ninth street. Having recently completed a six months tour of army camps and navy bases entertaining the servicemen under auspices of the U.S.O. camp shows, they are beginning their winter season in eastern theatres. Mrs. Mack was the former Betty Jo Yanda, of Springfield.

*State Journal-Register* article, early 1940s.

the Macks mounted their own small troop of dancers and actors who did this professionally at local luncheon and dinner banquets, reportedly raising the form to elaborate and inventive heights.

*(See what ended with the advent of television? Although, for a time at the dawn of television, when much programming was local, Joey Mack also performed on a program called "Pegwill Circus.")*

The Macks settled in Springfield, Betty Jo's hometown, in 1945, as their USO and vaudeville careers were winding down, and Betty Jo gave birth to the couple's son, Jerry. Soon they opened the Mack Professional School of Dance. The school first seems to have been located in the old Kerasotes Building downtown—where the school of Betty Jo's instructor, Mildred Caskey, was located—then at Spring Street and South Grand Avenue.

(I visited the Mack dance studio on South Grand with my mother in 1966, just two years before it closed in 1968. The wonderful Mary Judith Kraus, who taught me on scholarship for seven years, was one of several Springfield-area dance teachers who first studied or taught at the Mack school, including Jan Regan Burghart of Jan's Dance Studio in Chatham.)

## Adopted into the Mack Brothers Act

Joey's obit from 1995 reports that he was born in 1909 in Amsterdam, N.Y., of Lithuanian immigrant Anthony Yanaitis and Sally (Snow) Yanaitis. His early days are shrouded in mystery, though Joey reported in a 1981 *Peoria Journal-Star* story that he was 13 in upstate New York when Bobby Mack and his son Harold "took him in and gave him their name."

It's unclear exactly when, but Joey joined a comedy and acrobatic vaudeville act called The Mack Brothers, and proceeded to perform not just at New York City's biggest live-entertainment theatres, the Paramount, Palace, Hippodrome and Capitol, but also in London, France, Italy, and Germany.

His 1981 newspaper interview reports that in his heyday, Joey shared stage billings with Judy Garland, Jack Benny, Chico Marx, Bette Davis, Buster Keaton, and Johnny Weismuller, and a larger group of leading lights known mainly on the vaudeville stage, not from movies. Joey even reportedly appeared in a dance routine in a movie called *Three Sailors on a Holiday*.

Other clippings I found in my research hinted at a gig with Alvin Feig as part of a Cleveland, Ohio "song and dance team" that included a jazz band—and before that, a stint with Wesley Barry's "movie and stage act." The fact that Joey played the violin, sometimes on the floor of the Illinois Senate in his last stint as the Senate's sergeant-at-arms, and that his obit states he was a long-time member of the American Federation of Musicians, seem to support the Cleveland connection.

## A Boxing Connection?

One of my most interesting finds was a clipping referring to an International Amateur Boxing Tournament at the Chicago Stadium in Rockford in 1929, where a Joey Mack of New York defeated Ray Trumblie in a four-round middleweight bout by judges' decision. If this was the same Joey Mack, it points to a fluid career for a "hoofer" with both musical and athletic gifts from the Roaring '20s through the Great Depression, when survival, itself, for the son of impoverished immigrants, was an entrepreneurial–if not acrobatic–exercise.

In the days when running away to the circus was not a fictional career path, it's possible that young Joey Yanaitis was already tumbling/playing music/boxing/acting by the age of 13, when he met the Macks.

Even a brief background in boxing would have given Joey something in common with his future wife, Betty Jo Yanda Connors. Betty Jo was a professional dancer ("chorus girl") when the couple met while traveling separately on the vaudeville circuit in 1939.

She was also the step-granddaughter of famous Springfield featherweight fighter, boxing promoter and Empire Hotel and Theatre owner Johnny Connors of North Fifth Street. (The architecturally interesting Connors house in Enos Park is currently being rehabbed after a fire in 2013).

## Showbiz in Her Blood

Betty Jo's career as a beautiful chorus girl was no accident; it was in the blood. According to newspaper reports, her maternal grandfather, Aidan Moses McCann, had won several prizes in local dance contests. Betty Jo's mother Jerry McCann (Yanda) Connors, born in 1899, was a bathing beauty who appeared in *Yankee Doodle in Berlin*, a 1919 World War I silent comedy/propaganda film produced by Mack Sennett.

Jerry toured for three years promoting that film and others–one starring Gloria Swanson. So there's not much doubt where Betty Jo got the stage bug.

Jo and Joey Mack also had something else in common. Joey's mother, whose re-married last name was Punibajas (sp?), ended up living in Springfield, though I'm unsure whether this was before or after son Joey moved here.

## 'Knockabout Funsters'

Billed as "novelty entertainers," a "madcap dance team," "comedy knockabout dancers," and "knockabout funsters," Jo and Joey combined Betty Jo's refined dance skills–some of them acquired at the famous Martha Graham School in New York–with Joey's vaudevillian comedy acrobatics and pantomime.

THIS IS DANCE-O-RAMA"

TWELFTH ANNUAL REVUE
Staged by Jo and Joey Mack

SPRINGFIELD HIGH SCHOOL AUDITORIUM
JUNE 5, 1958          8:00 P. M.

Jo and Joey Mack School of Dance annual recital program, Springfield High School Auditorium, 1958. Sangamon Valley Collection, Lincoln Library.

On the live-theatre vaudeville circuit, the couple's act often followed a "warm-up" burlesque show–exotic ladies of all descriptions. After the burlesque was over, band and singing acts and other comedy and dance routines like Jo and Joey Mack's closed out the evening.

One report says that the act blended Betty Jo's dancing with Joey falling down in various hilarious ways. Another clipping refers to Joey's comedic pantomime of a woman getting dressed in the morning. Joey considered his comic impressions and mannerisms a core component of his tradecraft.

Unfortunately, none of us will ever see any of Jo and Joey's storied routines. It's even more regrettable, still, that not a single glossy publicity photo of the couple in their heyday survives anywhere that I searched.

## Mack Enterprises

At the peak of their Springfield careers in 1956 (the couple later divorced), "Mack Enterprises" included Springfield, Taylorville, and Southern View dance studios, a dance accessory store, and a costume manufacturing business, as well as the professional troupe I mentioned at the beginning of the chapter. With hundreds of students, finding the appropriate slot(s) for every student in the annual recital (and pleasing every parent) must have been a nightmare.

While running their dance school, Betty Jo also worked as a women's physical education instructor at Springfield College, Joey made and repaired violins and wrote comedy scripts for old show business friends, and the couple occasionally performed a traveling act that included their young son, Jerry. I can't imagine juggling that much, but Jo and Joey were from a different time, and they were nothing if not "fleet of feet."

# Chapter 51
# A Grandmother's Spiritual Legacy

One of the most accomplished and interesting people I have met through this blog is Maria (Fry) Race, a fourth-generation Lithuanian-American who is an energy company executive and lives in Elmhurst, Ill.

Maria grew up in the Laketown neighborhood, the older of two daughters of Frederick and Jeanette (Gooch) Fry. Her maternal grandmother, Agnes (Tonila) Gooch, grew up on Reynolds Street, one of nine children of John George and Agatha (Mankus) Tonila, who emigrated separately from Lithuania around 1900.

Agatha's father Sylvester Mankus (1836-1926) had emigrated sometime before that. Agatha also had a brother, Charles, and a sister, Mary, who married Simon ("Sam") Lapinski, Sr., and helped him operate Lapinski's tavern near 10th and Washington streets.

Immigrant Agatha (Mankus) Tonila (seated, right) with four of her girls. Daughter Agnes with hands on her mother's shoulders.

John George (Jonas Jurgis) Tonila was a coal miner and Agatha was a homemaker and mother to the couple's nine children born in this order: Helen, Marie, Edward, Minnie, John, Adella, Anne (Patsy), Agnes (Maria's maternal grandmother), and Mildred.

Johnny Tonila grave, Calvary Cemetery.

One of the Tonila sons, John (Johnny) Tonila, (Maria's great uncle and a Golden Gloves champ, according to family lore) gave his life in the World War battle of Monte Cassino near Rome, Italy, in May 1944. Along with other Lithuanian-American war dead, he was memorialized on a plaque in Springfield's St. Vincent de Paul Church.

## Laundry and Rosary

John George and Agatha's daughter Agnes, Maria's maternal grandmother, was "a quiet and spiritual woman." Like most of her siblings, she had an eighth-grade education. According to Maria, "she worked at laundries doing the hard, manual women's labor of the day, finally at St. John's hospital. I always found it novel that she didn't have fingerprints—they were burned off by the hot sheets she handled on the job."

Like many Lithuanian-Americans, Agnes went to St. Vincent de Paul's, and after it was closed on Jan. 1, 1972, she never went back to church. Instead, Agnes continued her daily rosary and taught Maria the rosary, as well.

Agnes Tonila, undated.

"Grandma Agnes always bought me new shoes for school and clothes for Christmas because she remembered getting hand-me-downs all the time as one of the youngest in her large family and never having new things for herself. She idolized her big brother Johnny who had died in the war, and always talked about him. Her sister, my Great Aunt Adella (Tonila) Barger, a beautiful woman, also died too young after a tooth abscess caused a brain infection," Maria says.

Adella Tonila, undated.

Engagement photo: Agnes Tonila and Howard Gooch, 1940s.

## First to Attend College

Agnes married Howard Gooch, from a German family. Their daughter Jeanette married Frederick Fry at St. Vincent de Paul's and later baptized Maria and her sister there. "My younger sister Stefanie and I were the first in our family to go to college," Maria recalls, "and my mother pushed us both hard to be successful because she wished she had gotten the chance to go."

Stefanie had straight "A"s at the University of Illinois in Champaign (Bronze Plaque 1987) and went to U of I Chicago Circle for an M.D. (Today Stefanie saves lives as a cardiologist in Boise, Idaho.)

Maria pursued a double major in art and physics at Parkland Community College, then earned a B.S. in physics at the U of I Champaign, followed by a master's in environmental technology at the New York Institute of Technology.

Her spirituality conflicted with the defense work that would have been the easiest application for her physics degree. So she moved into the environmental field, initially working at an energy conglomerate in hazardous waste policy and compliance. Today her executive responsibilities are also on the business side and involve frequent travel.

## A Religious Journey

Over the years, Maria explored many religions: Judaism, Buddhism, and Unitarianism. But she says, "I have gone back to my Catholic roots, as the ancient voices called me from my ancestors on both the Lithuanian and Irish sides of the family."

In 2013, she started painting icons, which has become a passion. She is also an oblate at Monastery of the Holy Cross in the Chicago Bridgeport neighborhood, where there once was a Lithuanian church.

Maria explains, "This means that I follow liturgy of the hours and St. Benedict's Rule as closely as I can as a lay person living in the world. I regularly go to the monastery for classes. I am particularly devoted to St. Hildegard of Bingen, and have been to visit her relics. She was an artist and scientist and I feel she guides my life."

Maria's painted Christ icon.

## Helping Post-Soviet Lithuania

Starting in the mid-1990s, while Lithuania was re-establishing itself and struggling to survive economically, Maria began donating money to the medical relief charity Lithuanian Mercy Lift. She subsequently began helping Mercy Lift president Ausrine Karaitis locate discarded, but still sterile and usable medical equipment in the University of Illinois at Chicago labs, where both women were working. In 2011, just after Mercy Lift disbanded, Maria accompanied Ausrine to visit some of the Lithuanian hospitals and nursing homes they had helped.

During that trip with her husband Tim, who also has Lithuanian roots, Maria got to visit with former Lithuanian President Valdas Adamkus and his wife Alma. (Adamkus was a Lithuanian-born

Maria and Tim Race with former Lithuanian President Valdas Adamkus and his wife Alma, 2011.

U.S. citizen and Chicago-based regional EPA administrator before being elected to Lithuania's presidency.)

While in Lithuania, Maria also took a rosary that had been at her grandmother Agnes's grave at Calvary Cemetery and placed it at the famous Hill of Crosses in Siauliai. "It was hard to leave it there because it was something precious from my grandmother, and I had had it for a long time, but it felt right."

Agnes Tonila's rosary, black & white beads, center, among so many others at the Hill of Crosses, Siauliai. 2011.

*Photos courtesy of Maria (Fry) Race.*

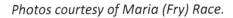

# Chapter 52
# The Galman Family Band

Young David Black plays tenor sax with his grandpa John Galman on concertina, 1979.

Those of us who grew up watching *The Lawrence Welk Show* with our ethnic parents and grandparents remember their enjoyment of the accordion and polka music, even as we embraced the "Rock 'n Roll" of our own generation. Back in the 1950s and '60s, more than one young Elvis or Beatle wannabe had to take accordion instead of guitar lessons at the behest of parents still part of a musical tradition going back to the old country.

Whether your immigrant forebears were from Lithuania, Hungary, or Poland, traditional music—at least as it survived in Springfield—seemed to be defined by the concertina or squeeze box and lively, danceable tunes.

One of the few valuables my mother Josephine (Kohlrus) Baksys acquired while growing up in her own immigrant family (both her parents and several siblings were born in Veszprem County, Hungary) was a huge accordion, on which she sometimes played the gypsy song "Dark Eyes."

# Close Encounters with the Accordion

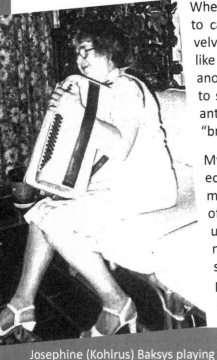

When we were big enough, we girls were allowed to carefully take the huge instrument out of its velvet-lined case and try to pick out a tune. It was like playing the piano—if you had to hold that piano in your arms and play it without being able to see any of the keys, while also pumping a giant bellows. Just making that full-size accordion "breathe" was hard work.

My close encounters with the accordion are echoed even more sweetly and strongly in the memories of David Black, a Lithuanian-American of the Galman (Lith. Galminas) clan who grew up in Springfield but now lives in North Carolina. David has been a musician most of his life, starting with alto sax in Fairview Grade School, progressing to tenor sax in the stage band at Lanphier High School and the jazz band at Lincoln Land Community College.

Josephine (Kohlrus) Baksys playing son-in-law Jay Wheeler's accordion, 1984, Courtland, Calif. *Courtesy of Cindy Baksys.*

Later, David, who also plays electric and acoustic bass, did weekend gigs with jazz and R&B bands in Silicon Valley, where he worked in high tech after earning pre-engineering (LLCC) and computer science (U of I Champaign) degrees. Exposed to both the music of his times and the concertina-polka passions of his maternal grandfather John Galman, David definitely grew up knowing music has no boundaries.

## Lithuanian Roots

The Galman story goes back to Lithuanian immigrants Jonas and Eva (Shouygaska or Swieguski) Galminas, who immigrated to the U.S. in 1905. Jonas, who changed his name to John Galman, was a coal miner who became a naturalized U.S. citizen in 1931 at age 53. He and wife Eva raised sons Antanas (Antone), Adolph, John (Jr.) and Charles Galman at the family home at 1728 E. Moffatt St.

Jonas Galminas (John Galman, Sr.) Certificate of U.S. Citizenship, 1931.

# The Original Galman 'Music Man'

David's grandfather John, Jr. (1909-1998), was the "music man" of his extended family who loved, collected and played concertinas: small, accordion-like instruments. According to David, "Grandpa John played the concertina very well, and he used to play polkas with me on tenor saxophone.

"He would drive to Chicago and buy these marvelous, large concertinas of a type called Chemnitzer, named after the area of Germany where they were invented." For a time Grandpa John also played concertina for the customers at Lithuanian-owned Pokora's Tavern on South Grand Avenue East.

John is also remembered for working as a master plasterer and at the Illinois department of signs before joining Pillsbury Mills, where he worked as a custodian for many years. Relatives also report that when he was teenager during Prohibition, John made bulk sugar deliveries or "runs" to the still in the basement of The Mill tavern at 15th and Matheny.

David Black as a little boy with his grandpa John Galman, circa 1965.

Growing up on Fairfield Drive, David still remembers watching his grandfather walk home from Pillsbury along the C&IM tracks with a cotton sack of donuts slung over his shoulder. David explains: "707 N. 19th, where he and my grandmother Clema lived, was a block south of the C&IM switchyard.

"Grandpa must have worked near or knew someone in the Pillsbury test kitchen, where they baked all kinds of stuff. That's how he got the powdered donuts and angel food cakes to bring home and share with us." Grandpa John was also a good home cook who had about a fifth of his garden in dill weed and garlic, and who enjoyed making dishes with shrimp, as well as turtle and rabbit soup.

When he was about five, Grandpa John took David fishing at Lake Springfield, where he caught a 4.5 pound catfish—huge for such a little boy. "It was funny," David recalls. "Even though all Grandpa ever used was a cane pole and bobber, he always caught about three times as many fish as I did."

## Hanging Out at Alby's, the Lazy Lou

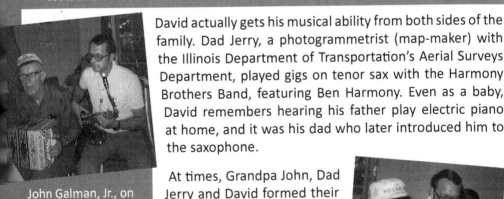

Grandpa John, his wife Clema and their children (sons David and John III and daughter Marilyn) associated with other Lithuanian-Americans in the neighborhood, especially the Albert Stasukinas family that owned Alby's tavern. David Galman (David Black's uncle) was so close to Albert's son John Stasukinas that he was nicknamed "Stutz." The Galmans also socialized at the Lithuanian-American tavern just around the corner at 1737 E. Moffatt: the Lazy Lou, which was owned by Frank W. and Mary (Gerula) Grinn.

*Grandpa John, bottom left, with sons David, upper left, and John (III)—and daughter Marilyn.*

David's mom Marilyn Galman graduated from Lanphier in 1959. "I remember her telling me she was a Lanphier track queen, and after graduating, she also did a few modeling jobs. She was a pretty woman with an irresistible smile," he recalls. After high school, Marilyn worked for the Illinois Department of Vocational Rehabilitation until marrying Jerry Paul Black in 1962. Three sons followed: David, Dan, and Tim.

## Music from Both Sides

David actually gets his musical ability from both sides of the family. Dad Jerry, a photogrammetrist (map-maker) with the Illinois Department of Transportation's Aerial Surveys Department, played gigs on tenor sax with the Harmony Brothers Band, featuring Ben Harmony. Even as a baby, David remembers hearing his father play electric piano at home, and it was his dad who later introduced him to the saxophone.

*John Galman, Jr., on concertina and son-in-law Jerry Black on tenor sax, 1979.*

At times, Grandpa John, Dad Jerry and David formed their own family band. This lovely photo series from 1979 captures a jam session when David and his dad took turns accompanying Grandpa John on the tenor sax as John taught them polka classics on "his wondrous Stradivarius concertina."

*Galman family photos courtesy of David Black.*

Grandpa John (in his Pillsbury ha on concertina, with Jerry on teno sax and David in background, 19

# Chapter 53
# Stankaitis Garden of Earthly Delights

Lithuanian immigrants at the turn of the twentieth century were mostly "people of the land." No single phrase better captures the totality of their lives as subsistence farmers and farm workers before they were driven into new lands and new occupations, mostly industrial.

This phrase also describes a thousand-year-old spiritual and practical tradition whereby the land from which Lithuanians drew their existence not only belonged to them, but they to it.

How did this deep-rooted identity survive immigrants' drastic uprooting? One answer can be found in the abundant gardens that many Lithuanians cultivated all over Springfield well through the 1950s: a thriving form of agriculture that dwarfs our modern concept of "growing local" and "urban farming."

Bertha (Wallick) Stankaitis, age 18, circa 1906.

## A Gift from Her Son

One local Lithuanian garden was particularly memorable for its scale and diversity: that of Bertha (Wallick) Stankaitis, born in Lithuania in 1886. Loving granddaughters Barb (Stankitis) Pelan and Marita (Stankitis) Brake still recall with bliss their Grandma Stankaitis's "Garden of Earthly Delights," which covered 2.5 city lots on South 17th Street from about 1931 to 1980.

Barb and Marita report that their father, John Stankitis, bought the house and adjacent lots for his mother Bertha when he was about 20 years old and his mother was about 40. (This was around the height of the Great Depression. So, like the gardens tended by immigrant families all over Springfield, Bertha's mini-farm undoubtedly provided "free" food during jobless and cash-poor times.)

Grandmother Stankaitis proceeded to garden her 2.5 lots for hours every spring and summer day for the next 50 years, often in a long cotton

Grandma Stankaitis with her flowers, circa 1980.

dress with deep pockets covered by an apron, her hair coiled in a bun at the nape of her neck. (She had probably gardened at other addresses before moving to South 17th Street.)

## Living from the Land

Grandma's "Garden of Earthly Delights" had everything in abundance: vegetables such as red and white radishes, spring onions, leaf lettuce, carrots, cabbage, beets, potatoes, tomatoes, corn, green beans and cucumbers. Cherry, apple, pear, peach and apricot trees. Livestock such as chickens and rabbits.

Granddaughter Barb remembers Grandmother Stankaitis killing and preparing chickens for Sunday dinner, and making egg noodles from the eggs Barb collected as a child while taking great care not to rile the resident rooster.

At the back of the garden were blackberry and raspberry bushes and rows of ripe, red strawberries. A grape arbor produced plump purple grapes for jelly. All of the fruits and vegetables that could be preserved or canned were, making for a very busy harvest season.

## 'Flower Girls'

Marita (Stankitis) Brake amid apple blossoms, like her grandmother's, undated.

I can't imagine what it must have been like to grow up so close to the earth in the glow of such a gardener extraordinaire. Barb and Marita describe it as a life-shaping experience that nurtured in them a special kind of imagination and creativity. Marita grew up to become a published writer and composer of folk music who performed at Carnegie Hall and the 1997 Clinton inaugural.

Barb wrote on her blog, *Prairie Ponderings:* "When I was a young child, I would wake up in the morning and look out the second floor window to the golden glow over my Lithuanian grandmother's garden. It was like a Monet painting and seemed surreal in its beauty. I was mesmerized..."

Perhaps the most special part of the garden were the flowers: bridal wreath, hollyhocks, four-o-clocks, zinnias, daisies, orange tiger lilies, purple irises. The roses that were especially beloved by Grandmother Stankaitis reined in pink, red and white in their "own private spot."

Barb recalls making dolls of all different colors from the hollyhocks, and Marita remembers "playing bride" in the white blossoms of snowball hydrangeas.

After Grandmother Stankaitis died around 1980, her son John—Barb and Marita's father—transferred his mother's beloved roses to his own yard on Bennington Drive and tended them in loving tribute for the rest of his life.

*Photos courtesy of Marita (Stankitis) Brake.*

# Chapter 54
# Gedman Family Mystery

The Gedman family took an unusually circuitous route to Springfield. Along the way, a mystery emerged: two local Gedman families who apparently don't know each other, but whose ancestors physically resemble each other, suggesting they are closely related.

Kaitonis Gedman (Lith. Kajetonas Gedmanis or Gedminis?) was born in Kvedarna, Lithuania, in 1859. When he emigrated to work in the coal mines of Bentlyville, Penn., he left behind his second wife, Petronėlė Kupšaitė, born in Kvedarna in 1864, and one child from each of his two marriages.

A strapping Lithuanian man: Kaitonis (Kajetonas) Gedman, circa 1900.

In 1903 tragedy struck again when second wife Petronėlė also died, forcing Kaitonis to send back to Lithuania for his daughter, Anna, who had been born in 1882 of his first wife, and his son with Petronėlė (named Joseph), to join him in Pennsylvania.

Kaitonis, passport photo, undated.

Based on his two marriages and the widely spaced births of his two children, he probably went back and forth between the U.S. and Lithuania several times.

## The Coalton Connection

Joseph C. Gedman, who had been born in Kaunas in 1895, came to the U.S. when he was just eight with his half-sister Anna Gedman (later Pinkes), who was 21. Joseph had less than a year of schooling when he followed his father into the mines and later, ordnance plants.

Joseph Gedman, 1940s.

He worked first in Pennsylvania, then struck out on his own in Coalton, Okla., where he returned to live and work after fighting in World War I. Interestingly, Joseph secured his U.S. citizenship via honorable discharge from his military service.

Half-sister Anna (Gedman) Pinkes apparently stayed close after seeing him through the childhood loss of his mother. She had all of her five or six children in Coalton before preceding Joseph to Springfield.

## From Coalton to Springfield

Joseph married Helen Beneky, the 20-year-old Springfield daughter of Lithuanian-born Anthony and Barbara (Wisnoski) Beneky. The couple apparently were introduced by Helen's cousin, Jack Harmon, whom Joseph had met while Jack was working in Coalton.

We don't know what the Joseph and Helen multistate courtship was like, but we do know that the couple married in 1921 at Helen's "native" church, St. Vincent de Paul's in Springfield. After living for a time in Coalton, where their only child, James L. Gedman, was born later in 1921, Joseph and Helen moved to 2110 Peoria Rd. near the Illinois State Fairgrounds, in close proximity to many other Lithuanian immigrant families, like the Klicknas and Yanor-Stankaviches.

## The Gedman-Beneky Alliance

In 1937, Joseph's niece Ann, from his much older half-sister Anna (Gedman) Pinkes, married his wife Helen's brother, Louis Beneky (weaving the Gedman and Beneky families even more tightly together). Ann and Louie lived at 1531 E. Converse their entire married life, and later took care of Ann's immigrant mother Anna Pinkes in their home.

Patricia (Chepulis) Wade remembers old Mrs. Pinkes visiting her own grandmother, Mary (Lelesius) Chepulis (1884–1961), after Mary had a stroke. Patricia also remembers visiting Anna and Louie Beneky's house in the 1950s and Louie working for her father Joe and uncle Bill Chepulis at Champion Garage.

## Streetcar Accident

According to Betty Gedman (Joseph and Helen's granddaughter), as a young girl, Helen Beneky slipped getting off the streetcar (inter-urban) that used to run down Peoria Road, and lost all but two of the fingers on her right hand. Yet she went on to have perfect handwriting (schools forced everyone to be right-handed back then)--and to work at the International Shoe Factory for many years, "outworking many of the men there."

Helen (Beneky) Gedman also played an important role in the 1932-36 "Mine Wars" as a board member of the Illinois Women's Auxiliary of the Progressive Miners of America, representing Springfield. Helen died in 1947 at the age of just 46, only five years after the death of paterfamilias Kaitonis in 1942 at age 83.

Kaitonis had finally arrived in Springfield by 1925, following his daughter Anna and son Joseph. (Joseph died in Springfield in 1990 at age 95.) Interestingly, the Gedman family also stayed close after death. Immigrant Joseph's half-sister Anna Pinkes, who died in 1969 at age 87, is buried in the Gedman family plot with Joseph and father Kaitonis.

James and Loretta (Gietl) Gedman, 1950s.

## Next Generations

Joseph and Helen's son James, who served in World War II, worked as a lineman and mechanic for Illinois Bell Telephone. He married Loretta Rose Gietl in 1950, and they raised three children at 1703 E. Matheny: twins Helen Gedman (Coleman) and Betty Gedman—and son Joe. Helen died in 1980 at 29, but had a son, John, and daughter, Erin. Joe, of Belleville, is retired from the U.S. Air Force and has two children.

Betty Gedman, the informant for this piece, is an R.N. and perioperative nurse manager in West Virginia. Her husband John Wiley is of Connecticut Lithuanian heritage on his mother's side (Neverdousky).

Betty Gedman with husband John Wiley.

## Mysterious Resemblance

Now here comes the mystery: Does anyone know the connection, if any, between Kaitonis, Joseph and James Gedman's family and a Charles Gedman of Springfield who married Emma Valentine (also spelled Valtioneys, Valentina-ocius) and in 1902 had daughter Julia, who married Peter Lukitis?

Julia (Gedman) Lukitis was a devoted parishioner of St. Vincent de Paul's, worked for many years as a cashier at The Hub Clothier, and had a daughter, Rita Mae Marley of Decatur, and two granddaughters.

You can see the "Gedman look" in her photo below, second from right, back row.

Mrs. Julia Casper (Swinkunas) ── ── ── ── ── Inglewood, California
Mrs. Marge Ehringer (Casper) ── ── ── ── ── East Lansing, Michigan
Mrs. Anna Frisch (Gudausky) ── ── ── ── ── New York, New York
Mrs. Della Gerke (Wayne) ── ── ── ── ── ── ── Chicago, Illinois
Mrs. Josephine Thompkins (Sugent) ── ── ── ── Calumet City, Illinois
Mrs. Julia Lukitis (Gedman) ── ── ── ── ── ── Springfield, Illinois
Mrs. Bertha Adams (Yates) ── ── ── ── ── Springfield, Illinois

*Family photos courtesy of Betty Gedman.*

*Post-script: Anna (Gedman) Pinkes had 5 daughters, and possibly one son, according to Betty Gedman. The daughters were Lena, Ann, Julia, Matilda, and Eleanor (the last two were twins). All were born in Coalton, Okla., and moved to Springfield before Joseph married Helen Beneky and moved here.*

# Chapter 55
# The Bernotas Family in Photos

Peter (Petras) Bernotas, the son of Casimir (Kazimieras) Bernotas and Agatha Tisckos, was born in 1878 in Vilnius, Lithuania. He first immigrated to Chicago, where he became a naturalized U.S. citizen in 1905. As you will read, there is a bit of mystery, perhaps sentimental in nature, as to why Peter didn't receive his citizenship certificate for 41 years.

At age 38 in 1916, Peter married 16-year-old Anna Klimaitis, daughter of Vincent (Vincas) and Anna (Ona Matuliczuite) Klimaitis of Naumiestis, Lithuania.

Klimaitis daughters Anna (born 1900), Adella (born 1902), and Mary had all immigrated to Springfield from the coalfield county of Lanark, Scotland, where their miner father and mother had immigrated after marrying in 1898 in Władysławowo, Poland.

Coal miner Vincent Klimaitis preceded his family to central Illinois, and wife Anna and their three daughters followed him to the U.S. on the Anchor Line ship SS California out of Greenwich, Scotland, in 1913. Given the 22-year difference between the ages of Peter Bernotas and his young bride Anna, I wonder if maybe Anna's father Vincent was a coal-field acquaintance of Peter and made the introduction.

## The Toll of Time

Two things are notable about this series of photos: first, the aging effects of coal mining and perhaps, related illnesses. You can see Peter Bernotas (at right) in his early 40s as the seated fiddler, at age 63 (below) in his 25th wedding anniversary news clipping, and finally, at 68, and likely seriously ill, in his naturalization certificate photo.

Anna (Klimaitis) Bernotas (center) with her mother, Anna (left) and her sister Adella (right). Sitting man in front with fiddle is probably young Anna's husband Peter Bernotas. Circa 1925.

From her 25th anniversary photo (left) at age 41, one can also tell that being a miner's wife was not easy on Anna (Klimaitis) Bernotas.

Peter's naturalization certificate, itself, is interesting in that it appears to have been secured in his last days, 41 years after U.S. citizenship was legally granted. Maybe he wanted to have this precious document before he died, to pass down to his children and grandchildren? One can also tell from his signature that either illness affected his handwriting, or that he learned to read and write after he was an adult, as was the case with so many Lithuanian immigrants of his time.

Photo of Peter Bernotas at age 68 in 1946.

MARRIED TWENTY-FIVE YEARS—Mr. and Mrs. Peter Bernotas, above, of 1705 East Reynolds street, were honored yesterday at a family dinner at their home on the occasion of their twenty-fifth wedding anniversary. The couple was married Sept. 30, 1916, at St. Vincent de Paul church. They are parents of three children, Anthony, Vetout and Bernice Bernotas, all at home.

Bernotas-Klimaitis wedding anniversary, 1941.

## The Second Generation in Photos

After Peter Bernotas and Anna Klimaitis married in 1916 and went to live at 1705 E. Reynolds St., they had three children: Anthony Peter, born in 1917, Vetout (Vytautas), born in 1923, and Bernice (Stevens). The family attended St. Vincent de Paul Lithuanian Catholic Church, where Bernice appears in several photos.

All three of the Klimaitis-Bernotas offspring appear to have served in World War II: Anthony Peter as a U.S. Army corporal, Vetout in the U.S. Air Force, and Bernice as a Navy "Wave." (Bernice later moved to California.)

Anthony married Dorothy Jane Hall and the couple had children Terrence Michael, Susan Marie, Denise Anne, and Stephen Anthony, who affectionately called their Grandma Anna "Nano." After living at Nano's on East Reynolds for a time, Anthony and his wife Dorothy built their own home at 2437 E. Keys, in Grandview. He worked as a machinist at Allis-Chalmers, later FiatAllis. The family attended St. Cabrini Church.

Anthony Peter and Vetout Bernotas, circa 1940.

**NEW OFFICERS FETED AT SODALITY PARTY—**
New officers of the Queen of the Rosary sodality, St. Vincent De Paul's church, were honored Monday night at a party in the church. Pictured are, left to right, seated, Virginia Shadis, assistant prefect; Genevieve Bugveski, prefect; Rev. S. O. Yunker, director; Bernice Rautis, assistant prefect, and Veronica Witkins, program chairman; second row, Eleanor Pinkes, instructor; Mathilda Pinkes, secretary; Florence Miller, publicity; Anastasia Zintelis, instructor, and Bernice Bernotas, treasurer.

Bernice Bernotas, back row, right edge. St. Vincent de Paul Church sodality officers, circa 1940, *Illinois State Register*.

Bottom left: Bernice Stevens and Tony Tamoszaitis as godparents to newborn Susan Bernotas, early 1950s. Bottom right, from left: Klimaitis sisters Adella, Mary, and Anna, 1968.

Front little guy: Stephen Bernotas. Middle row, from left: Anna ("Nano") Bernotas, Denise (Bernotas) Fox, Susan (Bernotas) Potter. Back row, from left: Terry Bernotas, Dorothy (Hall) Bernotas, Anthony Peter Bernotas. Easter Sunday, April 10, 1966.

## Food Traditions

Susan (Bernotas) Potter, the main informant for this piece, fondly remembers "Nano's" Lithuanian cooking. Susan continues to make grated potato and bacon *kugelis* (kugeli), "little ears" (*asuki or asukes*), and a dumpling dish she calls kalasky (*koldūnai?*). She and her brothers also make the warm, honey-citrus, spiced whiskey drink *viritos*, especially for Christmas.

*Family photos courtesy of Susan (Bernotas) Potter.*

*Post-script: In 1933 Adella, the sister of Anna (Klimaitis) Bernotas, married Michael Makarauskas, older brother of Springfield McDonald's restaurant founder John Makarauskas (Mack). Michael left Smilga, Lithuania, and sailed from the Latvian port of Liepāja in 1922 with his mother and younger brother, John, on the vessel Estonia. That was the year they were finally reunited in the U.S. with their father Stanley, who had immigrated to Springfield just before the outbreak of World War I, which ended up dividing the family for almost a decade.*

On left: Michael and Adella (Klimaitis) Makarauskas.
On right, John and Mary (Gidus) Mack. 1933.

However, Adella and Michael Makarauskas's 1933 marriage was ill-fated, according to Dorothy, widow of Michael's younger brother Frank Makarauskas. Michael was killed in a car-train wreck on Springfield's west side while returning from work with a group of miners in 1936.

Records show Adella married again in 1938 to William J. Laukaitis (parents Joseph and Valeria Galinis Laukaitis) of Cherry, Ill. (William was a veteran of World War II and Korea.) Adella and William divorced in 1943, and Adella was subsequently married for a third time, to Marshall Dirksen.

# Chapter 56
# A Miner and His Museum

Will Stone (seated) and Ted Fleming in the Christian
County Coal Miners' Museum, November 2014.

The Christian County Coal Miners' Museum, formerly on the east side of the square in Taylorville, was founded in 2003 by retired Lithuanian-American miners William Stone and Ron Verbiski. Although the museum is in transition, I had the good fortune to be given a private showing of its collections by Will Stone, 81, and his retired miner son-in-law, Ted Fleming, the day after Thanksgiving 2014. (Will died not long afterwards on Jan. 3, 2015.)

Anna (Dabulski) Stone (Stankus).

Born in 1933, Will was the son of Lithuanian immigrants Enoch and Anna (Dabulski) Stone (Lith. Stankus) of Bulpitt, a small Lithuanian-American enclave just outside Kincaid in Christian County, south of Springfield. Enoch came to the United States from Lithuania around 1926 at the age of 38 and was employed at Peabody Coal Co. No. 7 in the South Fork area near Kincaid. He married Anna five years later, in 1931. The couple had two sons.

William Stone, early 1950s.

## Star Athlete to Coal Miner

Enoch's son Will also grew up to become a Christian County coal miner. But first, he was a star Kincaid High School athlete known throughout area sport conferences for his agility and versatility in football, basketball, and track. He made all-state teams in both football and basketball and was a longtime holder of the state's shot put record.

Upon graduating high school in 1953, Will was awarded a full scholarship to play football at the University of Arkansas. However, family needs led him back to Bulpitt to support his widowed mother. After working several factory jobs, Will started mining at Peabody No. 10 (Pawnee) in 1960, from which he retired in 1991.

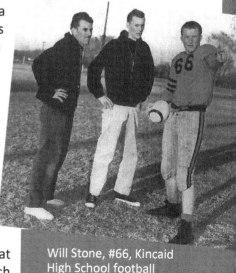

Will Stone, #66, Kincaid High School football player, circa 1952.

After retiring, Will began collecting memorabilia from the area's dying coal industry and decided to exhibit it publicly for younger generations. He said he personally invested about $10,000 in the museum that he operated, in later years, with the help of his step-daughter Linda (Mann) Fleming and her husband. (At about the same time he opened the coal miner's museum, Will placed a granite monument to himself and his fellow miners on the north lawn of the Christian County courthouse.)

# OMMUNITY

BREEZE-COURIER
TAYLORVILLE, ILLINOIS

### RIBBON-CUTTING CEREMONY AT CHRISTIAN COUNTY COAL MINERS MUSEUM

TAYLORVILLE — A ribbon-cutting ceremony was held Saturday as a part of the official opening of the Christian County Coal Miners Museum, located at 115 N. Washington in Taylorville. Many people visited the museum which houses memorabilia related to coal mining and its importance in Christian County. A non-profit venture started by retired coal miners Will Stone and Ron Verbiski, the museum will be open from 9:00 a.m. until 4:00 p.m. Monday through Friday. Saturday hours will be 9:00 a.m. until noon. Shown here are (from left): Taylorville Mayor Jim Montgomery, Jr.; Carol Alexander, President of Taylorville Council; Ron Verbiski and Will Stone, organizers of the Christian County Coal Miners Museum; A. J. McKinney, owner of the N. Washington building and Perfection Paint & Body Works; and John Curtin, Chairman of the Christian County Board.

Taylorville *Breeze-Courier* newspaper article announcing the museum's opening, 2003.

## Artifacts from the 'Mine Wars'

When I saw them, the museum's three tightly-packed rooms and one long hallway stored a wide variety of items related to coal mining and its importance to Christian County (which was, not by coincidence, ground zero for the infamous 1932-36 Central Illinois "Mine Wars.")

Several articles on display that caught my attention were about "Mine War" martyrs for the Progressive Miners of America (PMA), the new union formed by former United Mine Workers of America members in 1932 to strike Peabody Coal.

During the "Wars," dozens of deaths resulted from gunfights and other violent clashes, most of them in the so-called "Midland Tract" around Taylorville where many Peabody mines were located. The county jail in Taylorville was often full of arrested miners, and the city's newspaper was bombed.

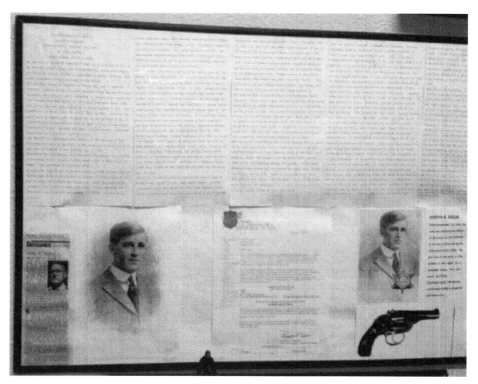

Framed articles about "Mine Wars" martyrs.

Three of the PMA martyrs mentioned in the museum were Andy Gyenes of Tovey, who was shot and killed in 1932, and Mrs. Emma Cumerlato, who was killed by a stray bullet on the porch of her Kincaid home in 1933 (that originated from a gunfight at the entrance of Peabody No. 7 in which PMA miner Vincent Rodems was also killed.) Joseph Sigler was described as the "only law man shot and killed in Taylorville" during the violence, in 1934.

Miners' uniforms and equipment, including hats with carbide headlamps, lunch pails, gas detectors and emergency oxygen generators, were also on display.

Hallway, Christian County Coal Miners' Museum, 2014.

# A Miner's Pride

Will made a point of mentioning to me with great pride that Peabody No. 7 in Kincaid had the highest production numbers (tonnage) in the world at the peak of its operation. Despite mining's difficult conditions, which improved after the 1930s, Will clearly showed the pride in hard work and production—and his miners' union (it was the UMWA that won the "Mine Wars")—that characterize the profession. I am very happy I got the chance to meet him, even briefly, and visit the museum he loved.

Will leaves behind his wife JoAnn (Tonks) Stone, two step-children and numerous step-grandchildren. When I last checked, his museum was in transition to different management.

Advertisement for "colored" miners from the southern states to mine coal in Virden, plus Mother Jones images. Christian County Coal Miners' Museum, 2014.

*Family photos and newspaper clipping courtesy of Linda (Mann) Fleming.*

# Do you know any Lithuanian-Americans in (or from) Springfield?

The following are the family names of men and women who came to the Springfield area during the first, second, and third waves of twentieth-century Lithuanian immigration to the U.S. (Not all lived the rest of their lives here.)

This listing is provided as a resource for family genealogists. All the names were culled either from personal interviews, obituaries, grave stones, the Golden Jubilee Book of St. Vincent de Paul parish (1956), or newspaper articles. Although I tried to be as inclusive and accurate as possible, there may an occasional error of omission or inclusion.

Readers should be aware that the illiteracy of first-wave immigrants and attempts by both Lithuanians and Americans to phonetically translate Lithuanian surnames into English produced a wide variety of spellings, with successive generations of the same family, and even siblings, often adopting different versions of the same name.

**A:** Abraitis, Abramikas, Abroms (Abromas), Adeikis, Adomaitis (Adams and Adamsky) Ajustus, Akulaitis, Alane (Alaunis), Aleksis, Aleveckis, Ambrose, Andruskevitch, Anskis, Antanazitch, Armas, Arnish (Arnasis), Augustitis, Ausrinis.

**B:** Babeckis, Backovitch, Baksys, Bakunas, Baladas, Balciunas, Balisky, Baliunas, Balkauskas, Ballon, Balsis, Baltrusis, Banaitis, Banich, Banzin, Barnick, Baronowsky (Baranauskas) Bartashies, Bartkus, Bastis, Baublis, Bazar (Bazaras), Begaila, Begowy, Belsky, Bender, Bendeskus, Bendick, Benneky (Beneky), Benikas (Benikati), Benya, Bernotas, Bestudik, Beveridge, Biernoski, Blasius, Blaskie (Blaskavicius, Blaskavich), Blazavich, Blazis, Bogdens (Boggens), Bokainis, Bozis, Bracius, Bratizas, Brazaitis, Brazas, Brazinsky, Bruozis, Bubbels (Bubelis), Bubblis, Bubnis, Buckewitch, Buckus, Budulis, Budwitis, Buguveski, Bukovsky, Bukus, Bumpkus, Buragas (Buracas), Burcikas, Burezik, Buskis (Buskus), Busnick, Butkauskas, Burchik.

**C:** Cachmiscus, Casper (Kasparas), Chekas, Chenski, Chepulis (Cepulis), Chernis, Chesnut (Chestnut), Chunes, Chunis, Cikas, Cizauskas (Cizsuckas), Cooper (Kuperis).

**D:** Damkus, Danelevich, Daniusis, Darran, Dedinas, Delunas, Denkevicius (Denkevice), Denushis, Denosky, Deresker, Detrubis, Diczban, Diksonas, Dombroski (Dombrowki), Donner (Donnor), Dowaitt, Draugelis, Dumbris, Dunkus, Dunnetski.

**E:** Egnot (Ignotas), Embrolitus, Endzelis, Evinsky.

**F:** Fraieras (Fraier).

**G:** Galman, Garulis, Gedaminski, Gedman, Gedudis, Genewitch, Genis, Gerchey, Gerke, Gerula, Gestautas (Gestaut), Gidus, Giedrys, Gillette (Gilletties), Giogas, Goodlich, Grinn, Godinas, Grabski, Grabuski (Grabauskas), Grenowage (Green), Gridznis, Gridzuis, Grigalunas, Grigas, Grigiskis (Grigiski), Grigsby, Grinius (Grinn), Grustas, Gudauskas (Gudausky, Gudesky), Gudinas, Guoga, Gurgens (Jurgelionas, Jurgelimos), Gurski, Guzouskis, Gvazdinskas.

**I:** Ignotas (Egnot).

**J:** Jakaitis, Janarauskas, Janeskas (Janesky), Jankauskas, Jasukenas, Jedrosky (Jedrowsky), Jogminas (Jogominis), Jonaitis, Jonikis, Jozaitis, Jugkanis, Juris (Yuris), Jurkins.

**K:** Kacevicius, Kalvaitis (Kalvatis), Kamicitis, Kandrackis, Kantenis, Kapusta, Karalitis, Karciauskas (Karchauskas, Kerchowski), Karecka, Karinausky, Karvelis, Kasauskis, Kasawich (Kosavich), Kasiulynas, Kasmer, Kasparas (Kasper & Casper), Kaston, Kasulis, Kavalauski, Kavirt, Kavish, Kazakaitis, Kaziusis (Kazusis), Kazlauskas, Kazlavsky, Kedis, Kelert, Kellus, Kensman, Kersulis, Kervinus, Keturaki, Klickna, Klim, Kloga, Klutnick, Koskey (Koski), Kowlowski, Krasauskas, Kriscunas, Kristute, Krizonoski, Krodok, Kromelis, Kudirka, Kuizin (Kuizinas), Kukowich, Kulberkis, Kulbokas, Kulys, Kulberskis, Kunski, Kuperis, Kuprenas, Kuprevicius, Kupris, Kurila, Kurlytis, Kutkin, Kutselas, Kutskill, Kuzas, Kuzmitski, Kwedar (Kvedaras).

**L:** Lagunas, Lamsargis (Lumsargis), Lanauskas, Lapinski, Laskaudis, Lasky, Latonis (Laton), Lauduskie, Laugzem (Lang), Laukaitis, Launikonis, Laurenaitis (Lawrence), Lavaitis, Lazdauskas, Lelesius, Lelys, Leschinsky, Lingas, Liutkis, Loda, Lokaitis, Lokavich, Lookis, Lornaitis, Loukis, Luishes, Lukitis.

**M:** Machulis, Macius, Mack, Maculevicius, Makarauskas, Makauskas, Malinisky, Malisky, Malkowski, Malsky, Mankus, Mantowich, Marciulionis (Marchulonis, Marchulones), Markunas, Markus, Marshellitus, Martinkus, Maslouski (Maslauski), Masus, Matalones, Matevius, Matula, Matulaitis, Matulis, Matulizius, Mauragis, Mazika, Mazrim (Mazrum), McCaskey (MeCaskey), Meiron, Meizelis, Meszeikis, Micklus, Mickalites (Mykolaitis), Mielkaitis, Miernikas, Miglin, Mikalauskis (McCluskey), Mikelonis, Milleris (Miller), Milouskas, Missavich, Mitskus, Mitkus, Mockus (Moskers), Modiovsky, Molatis, Morris, Moskers, Mosteika (Mostaka), Mouske, Mozeris, Mucinskas, Muckakitis.

**N:** Nargelenas, Narmont, Naumovich, Nevada (Nevardoskus or Nevidauski) Nevitt, Norus, Novick (Novickas or Navickas).

**O:** Oleseskis, Olshevsky, Olzewski, Orback.

**P:** Pachules, Pakutinsky (Pakey or Pakutinskas), Paldwich, Palauskas, Palusinskas (Palusinski), Papavis, Papir, Patkes (Patkus), Patrilla, Paukstaitis, Paulanski, Paulionis, Pauliski, Paulovich, Paustates, Pavlak, Pavletich, Payauys (Pajaujis), Pazemetsky (Pazmetsis, Pazinsius, or Pazinskas), Peciokas, Peckeris, Peleckis, Pelton, Peterite, Petkus, Petraits, Petrakus, Petreikis, Petrokas, Petrouch, Petrovitch (Petrowich), Petrushunas, Pickeritis, Pikcilingis, Pinkes, Pittcavich, Plaskas, Poderis, Pokora, Poliskie, Poska, Potsus, Pranskevicius, Punibajas (sp?) Pupkis.

**R:** Rachkus, Rackauskas, Raczaitis (Rassas), Radavich, Ragoznice, Raguskis, Ramanauskas (Romanowski), Randarchick, Raskuskas, Rautis, Razuskinas, Rekesius, Relzda, Repaitis, Repske, Rester, Rigalonis, Rimbutis, (Rumbutis), Rimkus, Rinkavich, Rieskevicius, Rizutis, Rodems, Rodutskey, Rokinh, Romanduski, Rudis, Rulinaitis, Rukai, Rukis, Rulberskis, Rumsas, Rupslaukas (Ruplauskas), Rutoski, Ružinauskas (Rusinaukus).

**S:** Sabeckis, Sacadelskis (Sucodelskis), Samosky, Senalik, Senkus, Setatavich, Shadis (Shedis), Shadwich, Shalamskas, Shalunas, Shaudis (Shoudis), Sheraika (Sheraka) Shereikis, Shidlauski, Shimanskis (Shimanckas), Shimkus, Shodwit, Shupenas, Shuris, Shvagzdis, Sidlauskas (Sidlau, Sidlauski), Simonavich, Sinkus, Sirtout, Sitki, Sketchus, Skimutis, Skrelevicius, Sleveski, Slezevich, Sluzalis, Skritski, Sneckus, Sockel (Sockol), Soltis, Sonwaites, Sotek, Spendzninas (Springjunas), Spudis, Staken, Stanisauskas, Stankavich (Stankvich or Stankevicius), Stanks, Stankus, Stanslovas, Stanslow, Stantuslauskas, Stanulis, Starkewich (Stark), Stasukynas (Stasukinas), Steskal, Stimburis, Stirbis, Stockus, Stonicus, Stonys, Strauckas, Stravinski, Strunk, Stuches, Stulzinski (Stulginski), Stuches, Sugentas (Sugent), Surgis, Susinskas, Swaja, Swerplus, Swieguski, Swinkunas, Szedis, Szerletich.

**T:** Tacilauskas, Tamoszaitis, Tamoliunas, Tater, Tekoris (Tekeris, Tekors), Terlis, Thomas, Timko(?), Timmis, Tiskus (Tisckos), Tonelis, Tonila, Totoraitis (Tutorites), Treinis, Tribicius (Tribich), Trijonis (Triyonis Tyrones, Trienas), Trumbit, Turasky, Tureskis, Tverjonas, Tweryon.

**U:** Ulak, Ulaski, Ulinski, Urban, Urbanckas, Urba, Urbas, Urbik, Urbis, Usalas (Usalis), Usas, Usman, Usus, Utinsky, Uzgiris.

**V:** Vadakus, Valatkas, Valansky, Valentinas, Valentonovich (Valentinavich, Valontinis), Valiukenas, Vaskas, Vinoskas, Vinson, Vonagus, Vosylius, Vysniauskas (Wisnosky).

**W:** Waitkunas (Witkins), Waitkus, Waiwaris, Wallentukonis, Walons, Wecksnis, Weidikas, Weiklas, Widowski, Wiesnauckas, Wilcauskas (Welch), Wilitis, Wishnosky, Wisnosky, Witcuskie, Witkins, Wunkus.

**Y:** Yacktis, Yacubauskas (Yacubasky, Yates), Yakas (Yakus), Yakst (Yakastis), Yamont and Yarmont (Jomantas), Yanak, Yaniski, Yanarauskas (Yanor), Yanushitis (Janusitis), Yaris, Yasinski, Yezdauski (Yezdauskas), Yoggerst, Yogminas, Yonic (Yonikas), Yotus, Younik, Yuhas, Yukus (Yukas, Yucas), Yurgil, Yuris (Juris), Yuronis, Yuscius (Juscius), Yuskanich, Yuskavich, Yuskus, Yuris. (All the "Y" names originally began with a "J.")

**Z:** Zacarosky, Zakar, Zavickas, Zapkus, Zebrawskie, Zeldonis, Zelowski, Zelvis, Zemaitis, Zibitus (Zibutis), Zikatis, Zilinski, Zilkes, Zinkevicz, Zintelis, Zipsnis, Zolden, Zubkus, Zubles, Zwinak, Zwingles (Zvingilas), Zylins.


Names that were obviously Americanized are: Adams, Alane, Ambrose, Bender, Beveridge, Casper, Kasper, Chesnut and Chestnut, Cooper, Darran, Donner and Donnor, Galman, Gedman, Gillette, Grinn, Kaston, Kensman, Klim, Lang, Lawrence, Miller, Morris, Nevada, Pelton, Stark, Strunk, Tater, Thomas, Welch, Witkins, Yates and Yanor. Other American names reported in various *State Journal-Register* articles to belong to first-wave Lithuanian men were: Kerns, Linc, Savage, Skeets, Gabriel and Soto.

Professional page design for this book would not have been possible without the generosity of the following donors:

## Platinum
Ben & Grazina Zemaitis

## Gold
William Cellini, Jr.
Kathleen Farney
Betty Gedman
Maria Race
John (Steve) White
Terri White
August Wisnosky, Jr.

## Silver
Cindy Baksys
Terry Baksys and Bill Byrd
Regina (Abramikas) Buedel
The Chepulis Family
Linda Gladu
Amy Green
The Lithuanian-American Club
Tom & Mary Mann
Kent & Susan Massie
Irena Ivoskute Sorrells

## Bronze
Elaine Alane
Diana Barbour
Nancy Chapin
Joyce Downey
Draugas Publishing
David Grimm
Careen Jennings
Mike Kienzler

Elaine Kuhn
Georgeann Madison
Glenn Manning
Dan Naumovich
Barbara Pelan
Patty Shillington
Patricia (Chepulis) Wade
Samuel Wheeler

## About the Author

Springfield native Sandy Baksys has been a newspaper reporter, medical trade journalist, and for the last 19 years, a public relations pro and writer. She holds a bachelor's degree in journalism from Northwestern University, as well as a B.A. in Italian and an M.A. in English literature from the University of Kentucky.

From 1989 through 1991, Sandy participated, state-side, in the Lithuanian "Singing Revolution" as Kentucky coordinator for the Lithuanian Information Center. In 2012, she spearheaded the erection of a historical marker titled, "Lithuanians in Springfield," and launched a blog that can be found at *lithspringfield.com*.

Sandy has lived in four states and traveled widely, including trips to Lithuania in 1995 and 2005. For the past 15 years, she has lived in Springfield with her husband Ted and their beloved Maltese dogs Poco and Ricky-Bobby. This is her first book.